Dugald Stewart

Selected Philosophical Writings

Edited and Introduced
by Emanuele Levi Mortera

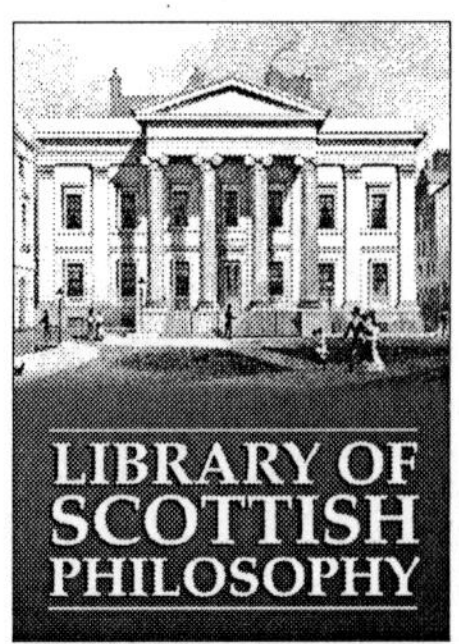

ia

IMPRINT ACADEMIC

Published in the UK by Imprint Academic
PO Box 200, Exeter EX5 5YX, UK

Published in the USA by Imprint Academic
Philosophy Documentation Center
PO Box 7147, Charlottesville, VA 22906-7147, USA

ISBN 9781845400620

A CIP catalogue record for this book is available from the British Library and US Library of Congress

Contents

Series Editor's Note

The principal purpose of volumes in this series is not to provide scholars with accurate editions, but to make the writings of Scottish philosophers accessible to a new generation of modern readers. In accordance with this purpose, certain changes have been made to the original texts:

- Spelling and punctuation have been modernized.
- In some cases, the selected passages have been given new titles.
- Some original footnotes and references have not been included.
- Some extracts have been shortened from their original length.
- Quotations from Greek have been transliterated, and passages in foreign languages translated, or omitted altogether.

Care has been taken to ensure that in no instance do these amendments truncate the argument or alter the meaning intended by the original author. For readers who want to consult the original texts, bibliographical details are provided for each extract.

The Library of Scottish Philosophy was launched at the Third International Reid Symposium on Scottish Philosophy in July 2004 with an initial six volumes. Attractively produced and competitively priced, these appeared just fifteen months after the original suggestion of such a series. This remarkable achievement owes a great deal to the work and commitment of the editors of the individual volumes, but it was only possible because of the energy and enthusiasm of the publisher, Keith Sutherland, and the outstanding work of Jon Cameron, Editorial and Administrative Assistant to the Centre for the Study of Scottish Philosophy.

Acknowledgements

Grateful acknowledgement is made to the Carnegie Trust for the Universities of Scotland for generous financial support for the Library of Scottish Philosophy in general, and to George Stevenson for a subvention for this volume in particular. Acknowledgement is also made to the University of Aberdeen Special Libraries and Collections for the engravings for the cover of this volume of the Edinburgh Faculty of Advocates and of Leith Harbour from *Modern Athens* (1829).

Gordon Graham,
Aberdeen, July 2004

Introduction

When in 1772, at only 19, Dugald Stewart was appointed assistant professor to his father Matthew in the chair of Mathematics in the University of Edinburgh, he began a career which would confirm him, in subsequent years, as one of the most influential academics in the eighteenth and nineteenth-century European 'Republic of Letters.' Both Stewart's contemporaries and modern scholars have recognised the impact his influential figure had over many young minds. Indeed, in accordance with the broad educational perspective that characterised the intellectual context of his age, Stewart was persuaded that only through an intellectual and liberal education could one become 'happy as an individual, and an agreeable, a respectable, and a useful member of society.'[1] Stewart spent the majority of his life between the walls of a college: he was professor of mathematics from 1772 to 1785 and then, as successor to Adam Ferguson, professor of moral philosophy until 1810 when he retired from University. The last twenty years of his life, until his death in 1828, he dedicated to writing the greater part of his published works. But Stewart was also a restless man who moved houses many times, travelled incessantly throughout Great Britain, visited France four times, and encountered the same difficulties that any family man would. He was a loyal Whig in politics and, for this reason, was accused of sympathising with the French Revolution, an accusation which caused him trouble both in his professional and private life.[2] His actual life, therefore, does not correspond to the traditional and rather limited image of a "good professor" which has often been handed down.

Stewart was one of the leading figures of the Scottish Common Sense school, a name by which we are used to identifying the philosophical tradition headed by Thomas Reid and comprising philosophers such as James Beattie, Thomas Brown, William Hamilton and James Ferrier. The

---

[1] *Elements of the Philosophy of the Human Mind*, 1, in *Coll. W.*, II, p. 61.

[2] For Stewart's life see Gordon Macintyre's beautiful sketch *Dugald Stewart. The Pride and Ornament of Scotland*, Brighton-Portland, Sussex Academic Press, 2003. The classical source remains J. Veitch, *Memoir of Dugald Stewart*, in *The Collected Works of Dugald Stewart* (*Coll. W.*), ed W. Hamilton, Edinburgh, 1854-60, X, pp. vii-clxxvii.

philosophy of common sense represents the first systematic answer to scepticism arising from the 'way of ideas'; an answer that appeals to universal and intuitive principles of knowledge independent of experience. In the nineteenth century John Stuart Mill referred to this philosophical tradition as the 'intuitionist school,' particularly in order to launch his attack on its religious and moral implications, but also including under this title thinkers such as William Whewell. Yet, while the common sense philosophers shared a common commitment to the solution of certain crucial philosophical problems in the development of the philosophical debate, each furnished different and unique answers to those problems. Because of this differentiation the philosophy of common sense cannot be considered a monolithic phenomenon in the history of ideas.

A useful exposition of Stewart's thought can be found in his *Outlines of Moral Philosophy*, written as a textbook for his students and published in 1793. Here, he offers a synthetic description of the method and purposes of what he calls philosophy of the human mind. According to Stewart, this is the new metaphysics, designed to replace the old metaphysics of causes and occult qualities and to investigate, instead, the general laws of human nature according to the inductive criteria of experimental philosophy. Moreover, Stewart singles out the proper subjects of moral philosophy, distinguishing between the study of man's intellectual and moral powers, and the study of man as a member of a political body. The first of this three-part system is dedicated to the analysis of the faculties of the human mind, to the principles of knowledge and types of evidence, to themes connected with language, taste, and the differences between humans and animals. The second and longest part is dedicated to ethics, and the third, though only hinted at, to the principles of politics. Stewart wrote extensively on the first part in the three volumes of his *Elements of the Philosophy of the Human Mind* (1792, 1814, 1827), and on the second in the two volumes of his *Philosophy of the Active and Moral Powers of Man* (1828). The third part appeared posthumously in two volumes of *Lectures on Political Economy* (1856), collected by Sir William Hamilton and based on Stewart's University lectures given between 1800 and 1809. His *Philosophical Essays* (1810) may be considered an independent but fundamental work concerning metaphysics and aesthetics. His biographical sketches of Adam Smith (1793), William Robertson (1796) and Thomas Reid (1803), the three parts of his *Dissertation: exhibiting the Progress of Metaphysical, Ethical and Political Philosophy since the Revival of Letters in Europe* (1815, 1821 and, posthumously, 1854,) and a few other less known works are not to be properly considered a part of his philosophical 'system', notwithstanding their influence on the subsequent European circulation of ideas.

However, it is the philosophy of mind, as the science of first principles, that must precede all the other sciences, included Moral philosophy. Many of the topics Stewart himself singles out as the proper objects of moral philosophy, really should belong to the philosophy of mind in general, notwithstanding the traditional wide range of subjects which moral philosophy covered at the time in which Stewart wrote. It is thus necessary to distinguish between moral philosophy – the counterpart of natural philosophy and one of the core disciplines of the university curriculum of the time – and the philosophy of mind as a kind of 'meta-science' to which all the other branches of philosophy should refer.

The selection here presented departs in some ways from Stewart's own division of the subject, which would have been the most reasonable choice to follow. Instead, this sequence aims to reflect the logical priority of each discipline, a priority which Stewart himself seems to give in the internal development of his 'system'.

I

The great object of the philosophers of the Scottish Enlightenment was the construction of a science of man, aimed at tracing the general principles or laws of human nature according to the criteria of experimental philosophy. The most renowned attempt of this kind is to be found in Hume's *Treatise of Human Nature*, where the study of human nature is considered preliminary to that of other sciences, and is compared to a citadel to be conquered in order to attain a general and clearer view of them[3]. Neither Thomas Reid, the most profound of Hume's opponents, nor Reid's most brilliant pupil, Stewart, had ever thought to call Hume's claim into question. Rather, Stewart significantly elaborates this claim through an eloquent geographical metaphor:

> When our views are limited to one particular science...the course of our studies resembles the progress of a traveller through an unexplored country...whose opportunities of information must necessarily be limited to the objects which accidentally present themselves to his notice. It is the philosophy of the mind alone which, by furnishing us with a general map of the field of human knowledge, can enable us to proceed with steadiness, and in a useful direction; and...can conduct us to those eminences from whence the eye may wander over the vast and unexplored regions of science.[4]

According to Stewart, the development of the philosophy of mind depends chiefly on a proper method of inquiry which, laying aside the analogy of matter, should be grounded in reflection on and introspection of the operations of mind. Stewart does not deny a relation between mind and matter, but the task of the philosopher is not to discover the mechanisms of this connection so much as to establish the laws by which the mind is regulated. Therefore, the physical and the moral worlds, though separate, must be studied by the same method of inquiry, based on the criteria of inductive logic (selection 1). From the methodological

[3] D. Hume, *Treatise of Human Nature*, ed. L.A. Selby-Bigge & P.H. Nidditch, Oxford, Clarendon, 1978, p. xvi.

[4] *Elements*, 1, in *Coll. W.*, II, p. 79.

point of view, Stewart was a follower more of Newton than of Bacon; he praised the first for his great synthesis and blamed the latter—though sincerely respecting his venerated name—for the insufficiency of the heuristic power of his logic. Moreover, he was aware of the necessity of a new systematisation of the criteria of inductive logic in order to make them applicable beyond the compass of Natural philosophy (selections 2 and 3). Indeed, his work on logic furnished more than a hint to later nineteenth-century authors on this subject, such as Richard Whately, William Whewell and John Stuart Mill.

As already noted, the philosophers of common sense aimed at the construction of an alternative theory of knowledge to that of the 'way of ideas.' It can be said that Stewart's position on this problem stems basically from a reinterpretation of Locke through the inevitable—but not uncritical—influence of Reid: He sought a mediation between Locke's empiricist heritage and the tradition of moral sense, reinterpreted in the light of Reid and Newton. Stewart was less worried by Locke's own doctrine on the origin of knowledge than by the materialistic interpretations which other philosophers, especially the French *philosophes*, had given. His strategy consists in restoring the balance between ideas of sensation and ideas of reflection, so as to render the former the *occasions* which 'awaken the mind to a consciousness of its own existence, [giving] rise to the exercise of its various faculties.' The qualities of matter are the unknown causes of sensations, which are the known effects that lead to consciousness in a sentient being endowed with operating faculties. It is the exercise of these faculties that produces simple ideas or notions, such as number, duration, cause and effect, personal identity. This re-interpretation allowed Stewart to combine the independence of Lockean ideas of reflection, the Reidian distinction between qualities and sensations, and the metaphysical distinction between mind and matter (selection 5).

Similarly, Stewart agrees with Hume's analysis of causation, while insisting on the fundamental distinction to be made between physical and efficient causes (selection 6). Only the former, as constant conjunctions, may be admitted in physical inquiries, while the latter, as necessary connections, naturally lead the mind to think of, and believe in an efficient power. This power is, according to Stewart, the efficient and intelligent cause whose continuous intervention in the physical world ensures the continuity of general laws of nature, thus allowing the philosopher to infer the benevolent design by which the universe is governed from the evidence of its physical effects (selection 10). Stewart's apparent Newtonian bent, is accompanied by a significant re-evaluation of the heuristic role of final causes in philosophical inquiry at the level both of natural and of moral philosophy; this latter is a relevant and influential aspect of his thought, but is not reflected in this selection.

II

Stewart's theory of the origins of knowledge is directly connected with the problem of its conditions and the intellectual 'tools' by which it is acquired. It concerns, on the one hand, a re-assessment of the metaphysical status of the so-called 'principles of common sense' (an expression which Stewart rejected in its entirety) as well as an analysis of the intellectual faculties. The investigation of the conditions of knowledge takes as its starting point a clarification concerning the distinction between mathematical axioms and mathematical definition. According to Stewart, mathematical definition bears an analogy to the first principles of other sciences, from which a chain of deductive reasoning may be derived. Definitions or principles have to be accurately distinguished from *axioms* or elementary truths, from which no deductive reasoning may proceed but which form 'the *vincula* which give coherence to all the particular links of the chain'. In geometry these 'vincula' correspond to the first nine of the mathematical axioms prefixed to Euclid's *Elements*, while, in the philosophy of the human mind, Stewart lists as examples the belief in personal identity, the belief in the existence of an external world, and the belief in the continuance of the laws of nature. These are the *Fundamental laws of human belief*, the pre-conditions of every act of belief and reasoning which are endowed with a '*metaphysical* or *transcendental*' nature. The necessity of rendering the first principles of knowledge universal and a priori stemmed also from a terminological confusion which Stewart found in the works of Newton and Reid. In calling his laws of motion 'axioms', Newton had indeed neglected their original nature as experimental-inductive truths, while Reid, following Newton in this conflation of language, endowed the first principles of truth with the same nature as the Newtonian laws of motion. It is precisely in order to avoid this confusion that Stewart underlined the metaphysical import of the 'laws of belief', reinforcing their intuitive and *a priori* nature. And he thought that the term 'common sense', employed in a technical and philosophical meaning, had relinquished its original and proper signification of 'mother-wit', thereby giving rise to conflicting opinions on its real import (selections 4 and 7).

In his *Philosophical Essays* (1810) Stewart had already faced the problem of the 'laws of belief', though without the mathematical premises which appear in the second volume of his *Elements* (1814). In the former work he resorts to his theory of 'occasions' in order to show the connexion between the sensible impression and the 'awakened' simple notion; thus, for example, personal identity is always accompanied by the subject's consciousness, and yet personal identity presupposes a prior exercise of memory and the idea of time (selection 8). Stewart then 'refines' Reid's theory of original principles, resolving the belief in the independent and permanent existence of external objects in another 'original law': the belief in the continuity of the laws of nature. Finally, he puts forward an original theory concerning the qualities of matter. He introduces the notion of 'mathematical affections of matter,' peculiar kinds of primary qualities, such as extension and figure, which are endowed with universal certainty; Stewart maintains that it is these affections that suggest the very notions of space and time, and that is why they appear to be universal and formal conditions of knowledge. In treating these subjects, Stewart had in mind not only Locke and Reid but also Kant, whom he explicitly quotes. Although he did not read Kant's works directly, there is no doubt that he took Kant's philosophy into consideration more than might appear at first glance (selection 9).[5]

Regarding the second issue formerly mentioned, the analysis of the intellectual faculties attempts to mediate empiricist and intuitionist elements. Stewart aimed to construct a 'rational logic' understood not only as a 'map' of the intellectual and active powers of the mind, but one that would make explicit the cognitive processes that produce knowledge and at the same time reveal the conditions or fundamental laws by which this knowledge is constructed. This kind of logic represents a re-assessment of Reid's doctrines while drawing on other authors—particularly Locke, Hume, Smith—traditionally considered far from, if not antithetical to the philosophical perspective of common sense. In this sense, the distinction Stewart makes between operations of the mind which are intuitive, and those which are seemingly intuitive but are in fact the effect of extremely rapid cognitive processes is crucial. The latter, though at first glance appearing to be natural 'automatisms,' are actually determined by the combined action of elementary faculties such as attention, memory and the association of ideas, all of which contribute to the 'construction' of the perceived object (selections 11 and 13.) The association of ideas, in particular, is the leading faculty to which the attention of the educator must be addressed. Stewart here shows a great awareness of the power of association in moulding character and habit. According to him 'association...furnishes the chief instrument of education; insomuch that whoever has the regulation of the associations of another from early infancy, is, to a great degree, the arbiter of his happiness or misery.'[6] The same sentence could have well been written by a philosopher of the associationist school, but for Stewart, the reduction of the complex phenomena of the human mind to a single explanatory principle would have been an unpardonable methodological error. Consequently, in Stewart the plasticity of the mind as that envisaged by the associationist philosophers, is seriously limited, notwithstanding his

---

[5] A rather Kantian interpretation of Stewart's thought on these arguments is given in Jonathan Friday's excellent article *Dugald Stewart on Reid, Kant and the Refutation of Idealism*, in 'British Journal for the History of Philosophy,' 13 (2), 2005, pp. 263-86. Even in its comment on the term 'common sense' Stewart probably wished indirectly to answer to Kant's criticism of Scottish philosophers, stated in his *Prolegomena*.

[6] *Elements*, 1, in *Coll. W.*, II, note R, p. 499.

faith in the idea of a general improvement of mankind. Stewart's rather non-orthodox tendency emerges finally in the long analysis of the faculty of abstraction. Here, he maintains a decidedly nominalistic position according to which the functions of abstraction and generalization, operating upon artificial signs, ground the possibility of formulating logical processes of reasoning, and consequently of establishing general principles that can guide the *praxis* of each discipline. In Stewart's view, the idea of artificial language as an instrument of thought, though it has its limitations, satisfies two main goals: providing one of the highest *desiderata* in every science, a universal, philosophical and 'technical' language (as for example that of algebra); and explaining that the improvement of mind and the progress of society would be impossible without artificial language (selection 12).

III

Stewart's most interesting contribution, as far as concerns both the internal development of the Common Sense tradition and the broader history of thought concerns the analysis of the human mind. Specifically, it entails inquiry into the limits and conditions of knowledge, and investigates the application of the experimental method to the philosophy of the human mind. His works on ethics reveals a more traditional and 'conservative' treatment of the major themes of morals, in which the 'method' of common sense finds its best application. The four books of the *Philosophy of the Active and Moral Powers of Man* published in 1828 reproduce 'nearly in the same words' what Stewart had already succinctly put forth in the second part of his *Outlines*. In this latter work, published during the most turbulent years of the French Revolution, he had adopted a very prudent line of thought, since he was responsible for the education of students from all over Europe and America. Of his concern for his students, he writes,

> the danger with which I conceived the youth of this country to be threatened, by that inundation of sceptical or rather atheistical publications which were then imported from the Continent, was immensely increased by the enthusiasm which, at the dawn of the French Revolution, was naturally excited in young and generous minds.[7]

It is significant that, if a prudent and well-balanced exposition of the principles of morals and natural religion was justified during the years of the Revolution, more than thirty years later Stewart did not find it necessary to change his view on the subject. He remained mindful of that potentially dangerous connection between 'an enlightened zeal for political liberty and the reckless boldness of the uncompromised free-thinkers.' However, it must be said that the spirit of religious belief which permeates the whole of Stewart's work on Morals is not a mere

[7] *The Philosophy of the Active and Moral Powers of Man*, Preface, in *Coll. W.*, VI, p. 111.

effect of political prudence, but was inspired by sincere devotion to those fundamental principles which, enjoined directly by the Deity, must inform conduct. Hence—and notwithstanding an actual departure from Reid in some core points and in the arrangement of the material—Stewart's primary commitment is to demonstrating the universality of the moral faculty and the reality and immutability of moral distinctions (selection 15) He also aims to preserve the relation between motive and action in favour of man's free agency and against necessity (selection 16) and to show that respecting one's duty is the most direct way to happiness. In this sense, the study of natural religion has to be considered a branch of our 'duty which respect[s] the Deity'. Stewart's *a posteriori* demonstration of benevolent design in the universe deserves particular attention. It touches on significant issues concerning power and efficient causes, the problems raised in Hume's *Dialogues* on the legitimacy of design, and the essential agreement between the study of natural religion and the procedures of scientific inquiry (selection 10.)[8] The words of Lord Henry Broughman, one of his former pupils, epitomize Stewart's view of natural religion:

> The highest of all our gratifications in the contemplation of science remains: we are raised by it to an understanding of the infinite wisdom of goodness which the Creator has displayed in all his works. Not a step can we take in any direction without perceiving the most extraordinary traces of design; and the skill everywhere conspicuous, is calculated in so vast a proportion of instances to promote the happiness of living creatures, and especially of ourselves, that we can feel no hesitation in concluding, that, if we knew the whole scheme of Providence, every part would be in harmony with a plan of absolute benevolence.[9]

A similar intellectual and religious bent characterised the Oxbridge scientists and philosophers of the same period, most of whom were not alien to Stewart's teaching. And it was precisely this speculation about design which definitively came to crisis once the implications of Darwin's theory of evolution became clear.

IV

Among the faculties of the mind, Stewart devoted great attention to the powers of language and taste. We already hinted to the importance Stewart assigned to language, a subject developed throughout his work. The themes concerning natural signs and the power of sympathetic imitation appear in the third volume of his *Elements*, published in 1827. Here, Stewart recovers Reid's account of natural signs, though with less

[8] Stewart's relevance in the history of natural religion is briefly commented by M.A. Stewart, *The Scottish Enlightenment: Religion and Rational Theology*, in *The Cambridge Companion to the Scottish Enlightenment*, ed. by A. Broadie, Cambridge, Cambridge University Press, 2003, pp. 31-59.

[9] Quoted in *Active Powers*, pp. 113-14.

emphasis on the Reidian metaphor concerning the grammar of nature, according to which there would be a natural correspondence between outward and inward signs and our capacity for interpreting them. Even though Stewart recognises an instinctive faculty which allows us to connect the most basic natural and artificial signs with what they signify, he also recognizes the role of experience in the interpretation of more complex and articulated signs, for example those related to the manifestation of character (selection 17.) At the same time, he is well aware of the danger of pushing experience too far: the analysis of the power of sympathetic imitation is an occasion to criticise authors such as Joseph Priestley and Erasmus Darwin, who tended to reduce instinct and morals to physiological devices and intellectual mechanisms regulated by the association of ideas. According to Stewart, such a simplification of the complexity of the human mind would reduce man to the level of animals, neglecting that '*physico-moral* sympathy which, through the medium of the body, harmonises different minds with each other' (selection 18.) Rather, the distinction between humans and animals is marked by human use of artificial language, a natural gift (not a divine one), which shows that humankind is the only species capable of improvement.

The ghost of materialism was what finally prompted Stewart to write a long confutation of the etymological theory of the English philologer and radical John Horne-Tooke. Tooke's 'etymological metaphysics' aimed to show that the human mind could be analysed or deconstructed through an etymological approach to language based on the 'atomic' correspondence between words, things and sensations/ideas. Stewart counters Tooke's linguistic reductionism and his alleged 'science' of etymology, putting great emphasis instead on the contextualisation of words and their slow interpretation by inductive procedures. In pointing out the importance of a synchronic analysis of language, Stewart wanted to reaffirm the activity of the mind in every intellectual process, an activity essentially denied by Tooke's genetic or diachronic analysis. Such an analysis was, in Stewart's view, a further move towards an untenable simplification of the complex laws and mechanisms of mental phenomena (selection 19.)[10]

Stewart's aesthetic theory is less interspersed throughout his work than that of language. Aside from an early chapter dedicated to taste in the first volume of his *Elements*, the greater part of his aesthetic theory is to be found in his *Philosophical Essays*, which offer long and in-depth analysis of beauty, sublime and taste. Taste was one of Stewart's favourite subjects: in the selection presented here, it is remarkable that Stewart appeals to experience in order to account for the origin of the 'compounded power' of the mind, what he calls 'intellectual' taste as distinct

[10] I have discussed these themes in my *Dugald Stewart's Theory of Language and Philosophy of Mind*, in 'Journal of Scottish Philosophy', 1, (1), 2003, pp. 35-56.

from 'moral' taste. This appeal refers to experience understood not as mere sensibility, but as the *occasion* which puts the mind in motion. Thus, on the one hand, Stewart's definition of taste as a '*distinguishing* or *discriminating* perception' shows the psychological and terminological balance between the operations of the senses and those of the intellect (selection 20). On the other hand, although he emphasised the role of the association of ideas as the leading principle in critical theory (as did many of his contemporaries), he clearly limited this faculty just in compliance of that balance. Thus association can explain 'how a thing indifferent in itself may become a source of pleasure, by being connected in the mind with something else which is naturally agreeable,' but 'it presupposes, in every instance, the existence of those notions and those feelings which it is its province to combine.' Notwithstanding that association may produce some changes in our judgments in matters of taste, 'it does so by co-operating with some natural principle of the mind, and implies the existence of certain original sources of pleasure and uneasiness.'[11] Stewart's analysis of the power of imagination and his literary digressions are further elements which make his æsthetic theory one of the most rich and interesting subjects within his philosophical speculation.

V

In his university course on political economy, Stewart gave priority to the exposition of the general principles of political economy, and only secondarily to those concerning the theory of government or *politics proper*. He pointed out that the theory of government traditionally addressed the formation of constitutional and legislative contrivances, and attempted to determine the rules of the legislative intervention through a few select examples comparing particular forms of government. Because of their merely empirical nature, these rules should be distinguished from those 'universal principles of justice and expediency which ought, under *every* form of government, to regulate the social order.'[12] Such principles, obtained from the 'examination of human constitution' are the result of 'a more extensive induction than any inference which can be obtained from the history of positive institutions.' Just as the science of rational mechanics starts from first principles established by inductive processes, so the science of politics ought to start from the first principles of the human mind in order to determine the laws which regulate political and social phenomena. Aside from these methodological assumptions, Stewart's science of politics is based on the belief in the existence of a spontaneous natural order which, left to develop freely, gradually achieves the perfection of the social order. On the level of political *praxis*, this very Smithian and Physiocratic idea means that a

[11] *Elements*, 1, in *Coll. W.*, II, p. 323.
[12] *Account of the Life and Writings of Adam Smith*, in *Coll. W.*, X, p. 54.

legislator should comply with the 'order of nature,' removing any hindrances that thwart its free course and should adapt, gradually and prudently, institutional reforms according to the multifarious opinions, habits and circumstances of humankind. Stewart justifies this 'gradualism' in political reform by citing those 'sudden and rush innovations' which had characterised the events of the French Revolution, and which had revealed the danger of any reckless application of unproved general principles to the political context (selection 21.)

Even in defining it as a branch of the science of legislation, Stewart considered political economy to be the main science with the purpose of enlightening the task of the legislator. Political economy need not be confined to the study of wealth and population. Rather, it must inquire into 'the motives which stimulate human industry,' and formulate predictions on the future course of a nation according to them. In Stewart's view, the close connection between political economy and the philosophy of the human mind was immediately evident: if political wisdom is founded on a knowledge of 'the prevailing springs of human action,' this knowledge can be obtained only by a previous determination of 'those moral powers which give motion to the whole,' and which are derived from a proper inquiry into human nature. It is in this framework that Stewart discusses the conditions and limits of the application of the experimental-inductive method to 'human affairs,' though he never systematically addressed the possibility of the construction of a social science. His conviction that political economy cannot be reduced to methods of political arithmetic or economic statistics represents two caveats: an epistemological criticism of the abuse of the role of experience as the sole instrument in social inquiries, and a warning about the difficulties of tracing general and uniform laws from the infinity and variety of human phenomena. To the 'practitioners' of politics Stewart thus opposed a eulogy of Adam Smith, from whom he derives the 'natural facts' based on individual motivation, and the common desire of modern *homo œconomicus* to improve his own material condition. These facts, no doubt, were warranted by a more secure and wider induction than those set out by the alleged science of the political 'practitioners' (selection 22.)

Stewart's view of politics and society is characterised by a kind of teleological optimism accompanied by a strong idea of progress.[13] The late eighteenth-century ideal of humankind's indefinite perfectibility is connected, in Stewart, with a providential optimism in so far as people are considered to be 'fellow-workers with God in forwarding the gracious

---

[13] See for example D. Winch, 'The System of the North: Dugald Stewart and his Pupils', in D. Winch, S. Collini, J. Burrow (eds.), *That Noble Science of Politics: A Study in Nineteenth Century Intellectual History*, Cambridge: Cambridge University Press, 1983, pp. 23-61, and K. Haakonssen, *Natural Law and Moral Philosophy. From Grotius to the Scottish Enlightenment*, Cambridge: Cambridge University Press, 1996.

purposes of his government.' Stewart insists on scientific and technical progress – and on progress in moral and political science – as well as the achievements that characterised the passage to modern civilisation: the invention of printing and the freedom of the press, new geographical discoveries and the consequent creation of a commercial society. Recalling the Baconian theme of intellectual cooperation and planning, he emphasises the similarity between free trade and the division of labour, along with the free trade of ideas and a division of intellectual labour. According to Stewart, all these facts represent an answer to those pessimistic views that tend to deny the real progress of society. They confirm that people must trust in the improvement of the human condition, since people themselves are the chief actors, even if unconscious ones, in a moral and political order which tends to perfection (selection 23.) According to this view, every historical reconstruction, as conjectural as it might be (selection 24), has the function of re-confirming the 'march of the mind', the metaphor which epitomizes Stewart's whole philosophy.

Chronology

1753 Born in Edinburgh, 22 November, third son of Matthew Stewart, Professor of Mathematics in the University of Edinburgh and Marjory Stewart of Catrine.

1761-65 Attended the Edinburgh High School.

1765-69 Entered Edinburgh University. Attended courses of Greek, Logic, Natural Philosophy and probably Moral Philosophy with Adam Ferguson.

1769-71 Decided to move to India and to the ecclesiastical career in the Church of England. In 1771 moved to Glasgow to attend Thomas Reid's Moral Philosophy course.

1772 Read some early essays before the 'Literary' and 'Speculative' Societies: *Essay on Dreaming; The Causes and Effects of Scepticism; Taste; The Conduct of Literary Institutions, with a View to Philosophical Improvement.* Appointed assistant professor of mathematics in the University of Edinburgh.

1775 Appointed associate professor of mathematics until 1785. In 1778-79 replaced Ferguson for a whole session.

1783 First journey to France. Married Helen Bannatyne (died in 1787). Birth of his first son Matthew, in 1784.

1785 Appointed professor of Moral Philosophy, succeeding Adam Ferguson.

1788 Second Journey to France.

1789 Third Journey to France. Witnessed some sessions of the General States in Paris (described in some letters to Archibald Alison) and probably the disorders of the Bastille.

1790 Married Helen D'Arcy Cranstoun. Birth of George in 1791 and Maria in 1793.

1792 Published the first volume of the *Elements of the Philosophy of the Human Mind.*

1793 Published the *Outlines of Moral Philosophy.*

1794 Published the *Account of the Life and Writings of Adam Smith* in the Transactions of the R.S.E. Suspected of sympathising with the French Revolution.

1796 Published the *Account of the Life and Writings of William Robertson.*

1799-1800 First separated course of Political Economy.

1801-02 Second edition of the first volume of the *Elements* with some clarifications on his political ideas. Read before the R.S.E. the *Account of the Life and Writings of Thomas Reid*, published in 1803.

1805 Published *A Short Statement of Some Important Facts Relative to the Late Election of a Mathematical Professor in the University of Edinburgh*, where he took sides in favour of his friend and colleague John Leslie.

1806 Fourth journey to France accompanying Lord Lauderdale in a diplomatic mission. Named honorary director of the "Edinburgh Gazette"; granted a pension of £300 per annum.

1809 Death of son, George.

1810 Retired from teaching and succeeded by Thomas Brown. Published the *Philosophical Essays* dedicated to Pierre Prévost. Moved to Kinneil House

1811 Edited and published the *Works of Adam Smith.*

1812 Published in the Transactions of the R.S.E. *Some Account of James Mitchell, a Boy Born Deaf and Blind.*

1814 Published the second volume of the *Elements.*

1815 Published the first part of the *Dissertation: Exhibiting the Progress of Metaphisical, Ethical and Political Philosophy since the Revival of Letters in Europe*, as a supplement to the fourth edition of the *Encyclopaedia Britannica.*

1820 At the death of Thomas Brown, refused to occupy again the chair of Moral Philosophy pointing out first Macvey Napier and then William Hamilton as successors. The chair will be taken by John Wilson.

1821 Published the second part of the *Dissertation* as a supplement to the fifth edition of the *Encyclopaedia Britannica.* Partially paralysed by a stroke.

1827 Published the third volume of the *Elements.*

1828 Published the *Philosophy of the Active and Moral Powers of Man* in four books. In consequence of a new ictus died 11 June in Edinburgh at n.5 of Ainslie Place. He is buried in Canongate near Adam Smith. A small monument is erected in his honour in Calton Hill.

1836 Death of Helen D'Arcy.

1846 Death of daughter, Maria.

1851 Death of son, Matthew Stewart. He published in 1828 a biography of his father, but unfortunately, in consequence of a mental disorder, burned many other documents related to him.

1854 William Hamilton began the publication of *The Collected Works of Dugald Stewart* (11 vols.) continued by John Veitch. Publication of the third part of the *Dissertation*.

1856 Publication of the *Lectures on Political Economy*.

One

Philosophy of the Human Mind

SELECTION 1

Nature and Object of the Philosophy of the Human Mind

The prejudice which is commonly entertained against metaphysical speculations, seems to arise chiefly from two causes: First, from an apprehension that the subjects about which they are employed are placed beyond the reach of the human faculties; and, secondly, from a belief that these subjects have no relation to the business of life.

The frivolous and absurd discussions which abound in the writings of most metaphysical authors, afford but too many arguments in justification of these opinions; and if such discussions were to be admitted as a fair specimen of what the human mind is able to accomplish in this department of science, the contempt into which it has fallen of late, might with justice be regarded as no inconsiderable evidence of the progress which true philosophy has made in the present age. Among the various subjects of inquiry, however, which, in consequence of the vague use of language, are comprehended under the general title of Metaphysics, there are some which are essentially distinguished from the rest, both by the degree of evidence which accompanies their principles, and by the relation which they bear to the useful sciences and arts: and it has unfortunately happened, that these have shared in that general discredit into which the other branches of metaphysics have justly fallen. To this circumstance is probably to be ascribed the little progress which has hitherto been made in the PHILOSOPHY OF THE HUMAN MIND; a science so interesting in its nature, and so important in its applications, that it could scarcely have failed, in these inquisitive and enlightened times, to have excited a very general attention, if it had not accidentally been classed, in the public opinion, with the vain and unprofitable disquisitions of the schoolmen.

In order to obviate these misapprehensions with respect to the subject of the following work, I have thought it proper, in this preliminary chapter, first, to explain the Nature of the truths which I propose to investigate; and, secondly, to point out some of the more important Applications of which they are susceptible. In stating these preliminary observations, I may perhaps appear to some to be minute and tedious; but this fault, I am confident, will be readily pardoned by those who have studied with care the principles of that science of which I am to treat; and who are anxious to remove the prejudices which have, in a great measure, excluded it from the modern systems of education. In the progress of my work, I flatter myself that I shall not often have occasion to solicit the indulgence of my readers for an unnecessary diffuseness.

The notions we annex to the words Matter and Mind as is well remarked by Dr. Reid are merely relative. If I am asked, what I mean by Matter? I can only explain myself by saying, it is that which is extended, figured, coloured, moveable, hard or soft, rough or smooth, hot or cold; that is, I can define it in no other way than by enumerating its sensible qualities. It is not matter, or body, which I perceive by my senses; but only extension, figure, colour, and certain other qualities which the constitution of my nature leads me to refer to something which is extended, figured, and coloured. The case is precisely similar with respect to Mind. We are not immediately conscious of its existence, but we are conscious of sensation, thought, and volition; operations which imply the existence of something which feels, thinks, and wills. Every man, too, is impressed with an irresistible conviction that all these sensations, thoughts, and volitions belong to one and the same being; to that being which he calls *himself*: a being which he is led, by the constitution of his nature, to consider as something distinct from his body, and as not liable to be impaired by the loss or mutilation of any of his organs.

From these considerations it appears that we have the same evidence for the existence of mind that we have for the existence of body; nay, if there be any difference between the two cases that we have stronger evidence for it; inasmuch as the one is suggested to us by the subjects of our own consciousness, and the other merely by the objects of our perceptions: and in this light, undoubtedly, the fact would appear to every person, were it not that from our earliest years, the attention is engrossed with the qualities and laws of matter, an acquaintance with which is absolutely necessary for the preservation of our animal existence. Hence it is, that these phenomena occupy our thoughts more than those of mind; that we are perpetually tempted to explain the latter by the analogy of the former, and even to endeavour to refer them to the same general laws; and that we acquire habits of inattention to the subjects of our consciousness, too strong to be afterwards surmounted without the most persevering industry.

If the foregoing observations be well founded, they establish the distinction between mind and matter without any long process of metaphysical reasoning: for if our notions of both are merely relative; if we know the one only by such sensible qualities as extension, figure, and solidity; and the other by such operations as sensation, thought, and volition, we are certainly entitled to say, that matter and mind, considered as objects of human study are essentially different; the science of the former resting ultimately on the phenomena exhibited to our senses; that of the latter, on the phenomena of which we are conscious. Instead, therefore, of objecting to the scheme of materialism, that its conclusions are false, it would be more accurate to say, that its aim is unphilosophical. It proceeds on a misapprehension of the proper object of science; the difficulty which it professes to remove being manifestly placed beyond the reach of our faculties. Surely, when we attempt to explain the nature of that principle which feels and thinks and wills by saying that it is a material substance, or that it is the result of material organization, we impose on ourselves by words; forgetting, that matter as well as mind is known to us by its qualities and attributes alone, and that we are totally ignorant of the essence of either.

As all our knowledge of the material world is derived from the information of our senses, natural philosophers have, in modern times, wisely abandoned to metaphysicians all speculations concerning the nature of that substance of which it is composed; concerning the possibility or impossibility of its being created; concerning the efficient causes of the changes which take place in it; and even concerning the reality of its existence, independent of that of percipient beings: and have confined themselves to the humbler province of observing the phenomena it exhibits, and of ascertaining their general laws. By pursuing this plan steadily, they have, in the course of the two last centuries, formed a body of science, which not only does honour to the human understanding, but has had a most important influence on the practical arts of life. -This experimental philosophy no one now is in danger of confounding with the metaphysical speculations already mentioned. Of the importance of these, as a separate branch of study, it is possible that some may think more favourably than others; but they are obviously different in their nature, from the investigations of physics, and it is of the utmost consequence to the evidence of this last science, that its principles should not be blended with those of the former.

A similar distinction takes place among the questions which may be stated relative to the human mind. Whether it be extended or unextended; whether or not it has any relation to place; and (if it has) whether it resides in the brain, or be spread over the body by diffusion, are questions perfectly analogous to those which Metaphysicians have started on the subject of matter. It is unnecessary to inquire at present, whether or not they admit of answer. It is sufficient for my purpose to remark, that they are as widely and obviously different from the view which I propose to take of the human mind in the following work, as the reveries of Berkeley concerning the non-existence of the material world, are from the conclusions of Newton and his followers. It is farther evident that the metaphysical opinions which we may happen to have formed concerning the nature either of body or of mind, and the efficient causes by which their phenomena are produced, have no necessary connexion with our inquiries concerning the laws, according to which these phenomena take place. Whether (for example) the cause of gravitation be material or immaterial, is a point about which two Newtonians may differ, while they agree perfectly in their physical opinions. It is sufficient, if both admit the general fact that bodies tend to approach each other, with a force varying with their mutual distance, according to a certain law. In like manner, in the study of the human mind, the conclusions to which we are led, by a careful examination of the phenomena it exhibits, have no necessary connexion with our opinions concerning its nature and essence. That when two subjects of thought, for instance, have been repeatedly presented to the mind in conjunction, the one has a tendency to suggest the other, is a fact of which I can no more doubt, than of anything for which I have the evidence of my senses; and it is plainly a fact totally unconnected with any hypothesis concerning the nature of the soul, and which will be as readily admitted by the materialist as by the Berkeleian.

Notwithstanding, however, the reality and importance of this distinction, it has not hitherto been sufficiently attended to by the philosophers who have treated of the human mind. Dr. Reid is perhaps the only one who has perceived it clearly, or at least who has kept it steadily in view in all his inquiries. In the writings, indeed, of several other modern metaphysicians, we meet with a variety of important and well-ascertained facts; but, in general, these facts are blended with speculations upon subjects which are placed beyond the reach of the human faculties. It is this mixture of fact and of hypothesis, which has brought the philosophy of mind into some degree of discredit; nor will ever its real value be generally acknowledged, till the distinction I have endeavoured to illustrate be understood and attended to, by those who speculate on the subject. By confining their attention to the sensible qualities of body and to the sensible phenomena it exhibits, we know what discoveries natural philosophers have made; and if the labours of metaphysicians shall ever be rewarded with similar success it can only be by attentive and patient reflection on the subjects of their own consciousness.

I cannot help taking this opportunity of remarking, on the other hand, that if physical inquirers should think of again employing themselves in speculations about the nature of matter, instead of attempting to ascertain its sensible properties and laws, (and of late there seems to be such a tendency among some of the followers of Boscovich,[1]) they will soon involve themselves in an inextricable labyrinth, and the first principles of physics will be rendered as mysterious and chimerical, as the pneumatology of the schoolmen.

---

[1] [Roger Joseph Boscovich (1711–1787), Serbian Jesuit. He was mathematician, natural philosopher and astronomer.]

The little progress which has hitherto been made in the philosophy of mind, will not appear surprising to those who have attended to the history of natural knowledge. It is only since the time of Lord Bacon, that the study of it has been prosecuted with any degree of success, or that the proper method of conducting it has been generally understood. There is even some reason for doubting, from the crude speculations on medical and chemical subjects which are daily offered to the public, whether it be yet understood so completely as is commonly imagined; and whether a fuller illustration of the rules of philosophizing, than Bacon or his followers have given, might not be useful, even to physical inquirers.

When we reflect, in this manner, on the shortness of the period during which natural philosophy has been successfully cultivated; and, at the same time, consider how open to our examination the laws of matter are, in comparison of those which regulate the phenomena of thought, we shall neither be disposed to wonder, that the philosophy of mind should still remain in its infancy, nor be discouraged in our hopes concerning its future progress. The excellent models of this species of investigation, which the writings of Dr. Reid exhibit, give us ground to expect that the time is not far distant, when it shall assume that rank which it is entitled to hold among the sciences.

It would probably contribute much to accelerate the progress of the philosophy of mind, if a distinct explanation were given of its nature and object; and if some general rules were laid down with respect to the proper method of conducting the study of it. To this subject, however, which is of sufficient extent to furnish matter for a separate work, I cannot attempt to do justice at present; and shall therefore confine myself to the illustration of a few fundamental principles, which it will be of essential importance for us to keep in view in the following inquiries.

Upon a slight attention to the operations of our own minds, they appear to be so complicated, and so infinitely diversified, that it seems to be impossible to reduce them to any general laws. In consequence, however, of a more accurate examination, the prospect clears up; and the phenomena, which appeared at first to be too various for our comprehension, are found to be the result of a comparatively small number of simple and uncompounded faculties, or of simple and uncompounded principles of action. These faculties and principles are the general laws of our constitution, and hold the same place in the philosophy of mind, that the general laws we investigate in physics, hold in that branch of science. In both cases, the laws which nature has established, are to be investigated only by an examination of facts; and in both cases, a knowledge of these laws leads to an explanation of an infinite number of phenomena.

In the investigation of physical laws, it is well known, that our inquiries must always terminate in some general fact of which no account can be given, but that such is the constitution of nature. After we have established for example, from the astronomical phenomena, the universality of the law of gravitation, it may still be asked, whether this law implies the constant agency of mind; and (upon the supposition that it does) whether it be probable that the Deity always operates immediately, or by means of subordinate instruments? But these questions, however curious, do not fall under the province of the natural philosopher. It is sufficient for his purpose, if the universality of the fact be admitted.

The case is exactly the same in the philosophy of mind. When we have once ascertained a general fact, such as the various laws which regulate the association of ideas, or the dependence of memory on that effort of the mind which we call Attention; it is all we ought to aim at, in this branch of science. If we proceed no farther than facts for which we have the evidence of our own consciousness, our conclusions will be no less certain than those in physics: but if our curiosity leads us to attempt an explanation of the association of ideas, by certain supposed vibrations, or other changes, in the state of the brain; or to explain memory, by means of supposed impressions and traces in the sensorium; we evidently blend a collection of important and well-ascertained truths, with principles which rest wholly on conjecture.[2]

The observations which have been now stated, with respect to the proper limits of philosophical curiosity, have too frequently escaped the attention of speculative men, in all the different departments of science. In none of these, however, has this inattention produced such a variety of errors and absurdities, as in the science of mind; a subject to which, till of late, it does not seem to have been suspected, that the general rules of philosophising are applicable. The strange mixture of fact and hypothesis, which the greater part of metaphysical inquiries exhibit, had led almost universally to a belief, that it is only a very faint and doubtful light which human reason can ever expect to throw on this dark, but interesting, field of speculation.

Beside this inattention to the proper limits of philosophical inquiry, other sources of error, from which the science of physics is entirely exempted, have contributed to retard the progress of the philosophy of mind. Of these, the most important proceed from that disposition which is so natural to every person at the commencement of his philosophical pursuits, to explain intellectual and moral phenomena by the analogy of the material world.

I before took notice of those habits of inattention to the subjects of our consciousness, which take their rise in that period of our lives when we are necessarily employed in acquiring a knowledge of the properties and laws of matter. In consequence of this early familiarity with the phenomena of the material world, they appear to us less mysterious than

---

[2] There is indeed one view of the connexion between Mind and Matter, which is perfectly agreeable to the just rules of philosophy. The object of this is, to ascertain the laws which regulate their union, without attempting to explain in what manner they are united.

those of mind; and we are apt to think that we have advanced one step in explaining the latter, when we can point out some analogy between them and the former. It is owing to the same circumstance, that we have scarcely any appropriated language with respect to mind, and that the words which express its different operations, are almost all borrowed from the objects of our senses. It must, however, appear manifest, upon a very little reflection, that as the two subjects are essentially distinct, and as each of them has its peculiar laws, the analogies we are pleased to fancy between them, can be of no use in illustrating either; and that it is no less unphilosophical to attempt an explanation of perception, or of the association of ideas, upon mechanical principles, than it would be to explain the phenomena of gravitation, by supposing, as some of the ancients did, the particles of matter to be animated with principles of motion; or to explain the chemical phenomena of elective attractions, by supposing the substances among which they are observed, to be endowed with thought and volition. The analogy of matter, therefore, can be of no use in the inquiries which form the object of the following work; but, on the contrary, is to be guarded against, as one of the principal sources of the errors to which we are liable.

Among the different philosophers who have speculated concerning the human mind, very few indeed can be mentioned, who have at all times been able to guard against analogical theories. At the same time, it must be acknowledged, that since the publication of Descartes' writings, there has been a gradual and on the whole a very remarkable improvement in this branch of science. One striking proof of this is the contrast between the metaphysical speculations of some of the most eminent philosophers in England at the end of the last century, and those which we find in the systems, however imperfect, of the present age. Would any writer now offer to the world, such conclusions with respect to the mind as are contained in the two following passages from Locke and Newton? "Habits", says Locke, "seem to be but trains of motion in the animal spirits, which, once set a-going, continue in the same steps they had been used to, which, by often treading, are worn into a smooth path". And Newton himself has proposed the following query, concerning the manner in which the mind perceives external objects. "Is not", says he, "the sensorium of animals the place where the sentient substance is present and to which the sensible species of things are brought through the nerves and brain, that they may be perceived by the mind present in that place?": In the course of the following Essays, I shall have occasion to quote various other passages from later writers, in which an attempt is made to explain the other phenomena of mind upon similar principles.

It is however much to be regretted, that even since the period when philosophers began to adopt a more rational plan of inquiry with respect to such subjects, they have been obliged to spend so much of their time in clearing away the rubbish collected by their predecessors. This, indeed, was a preliminary step, which the state of the science, and the conclusions to which it had led, rendered absolutely necessary; for however important the positive advantages may be, which are to be expected from its future progress, they are by no means so essential to human improvement and happiness, as a satisfactory refutation of that sceptical philosophy, which had struck at the root of all knowledge and all belief. Such a refutation seems to have been the principal object which Dr. Reid proposed to himself in his metaphysical inquiries; and to this object his labours have been directed with so much ability, candour, and perseverance, that unless future sceptics should occupy a ground very different from that of their predecessors, it is not likely that the controversy will ever be renewed. The rubbish being now removed, and the foundations laid, it is time to begin the superstructure.

Two

Logic

SELECTION 2

Inductive Logic

I have had occasion to observe more than once, in the course of the foregoing speculations,[1] that the object of physical science is *not* to trace necessary connexions, but to ascertain constant conjunctions; *not* to investigate the nature of those efficient causes on which the phenomena of the universe ultimately depend, but to examine with accuracy what the phenomena are, and what the general laws by which they are regulated.

...

This idea of the *object* of physical science (which may be justly regarded as the ground-work of Bacon's *Novum Organon*) differs essentially from that which was entertained by the ancients; according to whom, "Philosophy is the science of *causes*". If, indeed, by *causes* they had meant merely the constant forerunners or antecedents of events, the definition would have coincided nearly with the statement which I have given. But it is evident, that by *causes* they meant such antecedents as were *necessarily* connected with the effects, and from a knowledge of which the effects might be foreseen and demonstrated; and it was owing to this confusion between the proper objects of physics and of metaphysics, that, neglecting the observation of facts exposed to the examination of their senses, they vainly attempted, by synthetical reasoning, to deduce, as necessary consequences from their supposed causes, the phenomena and laws of nature. ...

From this disposition to confound efficient with physical causes, may be traced the greater part of the theories recorded in the history of philosophy. It is this which has given rise to the attempts, both in ancient and modern times, to account for all the phenomena of moving bodies by means of *impulse*, and it is this also which has suggested the simpler expedient of explaining them by the agency of *minds* united with the particles of matter. As the communication of motion by apparent impulse,

---

[1] [See selection 6.]

and our own power to produce motion by a volition of the mind, are two facts of which, from our earliest infancy, we have every moment had experience; we are apt to fancy that we understand perfectly the *nexus* by which cause and effect are here necessarily conjoined; and it requires a good deal of reflection to satisfy us that, in both cases, we are as completely in the dark, as in our guesses concerning the ultimate causes of magnetism or of gravitation.

...

In contrasting, as I have now done, the spirit of Bacon's mode of philosophizing with that of the ancients, I do not mean to extol his own notions concerning the relation of Cause and Effect in physics, as peculiarly correct and consistent. On the contrary, it seems to me evident that he was led to his logical conclusions, not by any metaphysical analysis of his ideas, but by a conviction founded on a review of the labours of his predecessors, that the plan of inquiry by which they had been guided must have been erroneous. If he had perceived as clearly as Barrow, Berkeley, Hume, and many others have done since his time, that there is not a single instance in which we are able to trace a necessary connexion between two successive events, or to explain in what manner the one follows from the other as an infallible consequence, he would have been naturally led to state his principles in a form far more concise and methodical, and to lay aside much of that scholastic jargon by which his meaning is occasionally obscured. Notwithstanding, however, this vagueness and indistinctness in his language, his comprehensive and penetrating understanding, enlightened by a discriminating survey of the fruitless inquiries of former ages, enabled him to describe, in the strongest and happiest terms, the nature, the object, and the limits of philosophical investigation. The most valuable part of his works, at the same time, consists perhaps in his reflections on the errors of his predecessors, and on the various causes which have retarded the progress of the sciences and the improvement of the human mind. That he should have executed, with complete success, a system of logical precepts for the prosecution of experimental inquiries, at a period when these were, for the first time, beginning to engage the attention of the curious, was altogether impossible; and yet in his *attempt* towards this undertaking, he has displayed a reach of thought and a justness of anticipation, which, when compared with the discoveries of the two succeeding centuries, seem frequently to partake of the nature of prophecy. ... Had he foreseen all the researches of the Newtonian school, his language could not have been more precise or more decided. [2]

---

[2] By the word *Axiom,* Bacon means a general principle obtained by induction, from which we may safely proceed to reason synthetically. It is to be regretted, that he did not make choice of a less equivocal term, as Newton has plainly been misled by his example, in the very illogical application of this name to the laws of motion,

"Bacon", it has been observed by Mr. Hume, "was ignorant of geometry, and only pointed out at a distance the road to true philosophy".-"As an author and philosopher", therefore, this historian pronounces him, "*though very estimable*, yet inferior to his contemporary Galileo, perhaps even to Kepler". The parallel is by no means happily imagined, inasmuch as the individuals whom it brings into contrast directed their attention to pursuits essentially different, and were characterized by mental powers unsusceptible of comparison. As a geometer or astronomer, Bacon has certainly no claim whatever to distinction; nor can it even be said, that as an experimentalist, he has enriched science by one important discovery; but, in just and enlarged conceptions of the proper aim of philosophical researches, and of the means of conducting them, how far does he rise above the level of his age! Nothing, indeed, can place this in so strong a light as the history of Kepler himself, unquestionably one of the most extraordinary persons who adorned that memorable period, but deeply infected, as his writings, with prejudices borrowed from the most remote antiquity.

...

In calling man the *interpreter* of Nature, Bacon had plainly the same idea of the object of physics, which I attempted to convey, when I said, that what are commonly called the *causes* of phenomena, are only their established antecedents or *signs;* and the same analogy which this expression suggests to the fancy, has been enlarged upon, at considerable length, by the inventive and philosophical Bishop of Cloyne, as the best illustration which he could give of the doctrine in question.

...

According to the doctrine now stated, the highest, or rather the only proper object of Physics, is to ascertain those established conjunctions of successive events, which constitute the order of the universe; to record the phenomena which it exhibits to our observations, or which it discloses to our experiments, and to refer these phenomena to their general laws. While we are apt to fancy, therefore, (agreeably to popular conceptions and language,) that we are investigating efficient causes, we are, in reality, only generalizing effects; and when we advance from discovery to discovery, we do nothing more than resolve our former conclusions into others still more comprehensive. It was thus that Galileo and Torricelli proceeded in proving that all terrestrial bodies gravitate towards the earth; and that the apparent levity of some of them is merely owing to the greater gravity of the atmosphere. In establishing this

---

and to those general *facts* which serve as the basis of our reasonings in catoptrics and dioptrics.

I shall take this opportunity to remark, that Newton had evidently studied Bacon's writings with care, and has followed them (sometimes too implicitly) in his logical phraseology.

important conclusion, they only generalized the law of gravity, by reconciling with it a variety of seeming exceptions; but they threw no light whatever on that mysterious power, in consequence of which all these phenomena take place. In like manner, when Newton showed that the same law of gravity extends to the celestial spaces, and that the power by which the moon and planets are retained in their orbits, is precisely similar in its effects to that which is manifested in the fall of a stone, he left the efficient cause of gravity as much in the dark as ever, and only generalized still farther the conclusions of his predecessors. It was, indeed, the most astonishing and sublime discovery which occurs in the history of science; a discovery not of less consequence in Natural Religion than in Natural Philosophy, and which at once demonstrated (in direct contradiction to all the ancient systems) that the phenomena exhibited by the heavenly bodies, are regulated by the same laws which fall under our observation on the surface of this globe. Still, however, it was not the discovery of an efficient cause, but only the generalization of a fact.

...

For acquiring a knowledge of facts more recondite, *observation* and *experiment* must be employed; and, accordingly, the use of these *media* forms one of the characteristical circumstances by which the studies of the philosopher are distinguished from the experience of the multitude. How much the stock of his information must thereby be enlarged is sufficiently manifest. By habits of scientific attention, his accuracy as an observer is improved, and a precision is given to his judgment, essentially different from the vagueness of ordinary perception; by a combination of his own observations with those made by others, he arrives at many conclusions unknown to those who are prevented, by the necessary avocations of human life, from indulging the impulse of a speculative curiosity, while the experiments which his ingenuity devises, enable him to place nature in situations in which she never presents herself spontaneously to view, and to extort from her secrets over which she draws a veil to the eyes of others.

But the observations and experiments of the philosopher are commonly only a step towards a farther end. This end is, *first,* to resolve particular facts into other facts more simple and comprehensive; and, *secondly,* to apply these general facts (or, as they are usually called, these *laws of nature)* to a synthetical explanation of particular phenomena. These two processes of the mind, together with that judicious employment of observation and experiment which they presuppose, exhaust the whole business of philosophical investigation; and the great object of the rules of philosophizing is to show in what manner they ought to be conducted.

I. For the more complete illustration of this fundamental doctrine, it is necessary for me to recur to what has been already stated with respect to our ignorance of *efficient causes.* As we can, in no instance, perceive the link by which two successive events are connected, so as to deduce, by any reasoning *a priori,* the one from the other as a consequence or effect, it follows that when we see an event take place which has been preceded by a combination of different circumstances, it is impossible for human sagacity to ascertain whether the effect is connected with *all* the circumstances, or only with a *part* of them; and (on the latter supposition) which of the circumstances is essential to the result, and which are merely accidental accessories or concomitants. The only way, in such a case, of coming at the truth, is to repeat over the experiment again and again, leaving out all the different circumstances successively, and observing with what particular combinations of them the effect is conjoined. If there be no possibility of making this separation, and if, at the same time, we wish to obtain the same result, the only method of *insuring* success is to combine together *all* the various circumstances which were united in our former trials. It is on this principle that I have attempted, in a former chapter of this work,[3] to account for the superstitious observances which always accompany the practice of medicine among rude nations. These are commonly ascribed to the influence of imagination, and the low state of reason in the earlier periods of society; but the truth is, that they are the necessary and unavoidable consequences of a limited experience, and are to be corrected, not by mere force of intellect, but by a more enlarged acquaintance with the established order of nature.

Observations perfectly similar to those which I made with respect to medicine are applicable to all the other branches of philosophy. Wherever an interesting *change* is preceded by a combination of different circumstances, it is of importance to vary our experiments in such a manner as to distinguish what is essential from what is accessory; and when we have carried the decomposition as far as we can, we are entitled to consider this simplest combination of indispensable conditions, as the *physical cause* of the event.

When, by thus comparing a number of cases, agreeing in some circumstances, but differing in others, and all attended with the same result, a philosopher connects, as a general law of nature, the event with its *physical cause,* he is said to proceed according to the method of *induction.* This, at least, appears to me to be the idea which, in general, Bacon himself annexes to the phrase; although I will not venture to affirm that he has always employed it with uniform precision. I acknowledge, also, that it is often used by very accurate writers, to denote the whole of that system of rules, of which the process just mentioned forms the most essential and characteristical part.

. . .

II. There is another circumstance which frequently adds to the difficulty of tracing the laws of nature; and which imposes on the philosopher,

[3] [*Elements,* 1, V, pt. ii, 1.]

while carrying on the process of induction, the necessity of following a still more refined logic than has been hitherto described. When a uniformity is observed in a number of different events, the curiosity is roused by the coincidence, and is sometimes led insensibly to a general conclusion. In a few other cases, a multiplicity of events, which appear to common observers to be altogether anomalous, are found, upon a more accurate and continued examination of them, to be subjected to a regular law. The cycles by which the ancients predicted eclipses of the sun and moon; the three laws inferred by Kepler from the observations of Tycho Brahe; the law of refraction inferred by Snellius from the tables of Kircher and Scheiner, are instances of very comprehensive and most important rules obtained by the mere examination and comparison of particulars. Such purely *empirical discoveries*, however, are confined almost entirely to optics and astronomy, in which the physical laws combined together are comparatively few, and are insulated from the influence of those incalculable accidents which, in general, disturb the regularity of terrestrial phenomena. In by far the greater number of instances, the appearances of nature depend on a variety of different laws, all of which are often combined together in producing one single event: And, wherever such a combination happens, although each law may take place with the most complete uniformity, it is likely that nothing but confusion will strike the mere observer. A collection of such results, therefore, would not advance us one step in the knowledge of nature; nor would it enable us to anticipate the issue of one new experiment. In cases of this description, before we can avail ourselves of our past experience, we must employ our reasoning powers in comparing a variety of instances together, in order to discover, by a sort of *analysis* or decomposition, the simple laws which are concerned in the phenomenon under consideration; after which we may proceed safely, in determining *a priori* what the result will be of any hypothetical combination of them, whether total or partial.[4]

These observations have led us to the same conclusion with that which forms the great outline of Bacon's plan of philosophizing; and which Newton has so successfully exemplified in his inquiries concerning gravitation and the properties of light. While they point out, too, the

---

[4] "Itaque naturæ facienda est prorsus solutio et separatio; non per ignem certe, sed per mentem, tanquam ignem divinum". (Nov. *Organ*. lib. ii. aphor. xvi.)

The remainder of the aphorism is equally worthy of attention; in reading which, however, as well as the rest of Bacon's philosophical works, I must request, for a reason afterwards to be mentioned, that the word *Law* may be substituted for *Form*, wherever it may occur. An attention to this circumstance will be found of much use in studying the *Novum Organon*.

A similar idea, under other metaphorical disguises, often occurs in Bacon. Considering the circumstances in which he wrote, logical precision was altogether impossible; yet it is astonishing with what force he conveys the *spirit* of the soundest philosophy of the eighteenth century.

respective provinces and uses of the *analytic* and the *synthetic* methods, they illustrate the etymological propriety of the names by which, in the Newtonian School, they are contradistinguished from each other.

In fact, the meaning of the words *analysis* and *synthesis*, when applied to the two opposite modes of investigation in physics, is extremely analogous to their use in the practice of chemistry. The chief difference lies in this, that, in the former case, they refer to the logical processes of the understanding in the study of *physical laws*; in the latter, to the operative processes of the laboratory in the examination of material substances.

...

If the view which I have given of Lord Bacon's plan of investigation be just, it will follow that the Newtonian theory of gravitation can, in no respect whatever, admit of a comparison with those systems which are, in the slightest degree, the offspring of imagination;[5] inasmuch as the principle employed to explain the phenomena is not a hypothesis, but a *general fact* established by induction; for which fact we have the very same evidence as for the various particulars comprehended under it. The Newtonian theory of gravitation, therefore, and every other theory which rests on a similar basis, is as little liable to be supplanted by the labours of future ages, as the mathematical conclusions of Euclid and Archimedes. The doctrines which it involves may be delivered in different, and perhaps less exceptionable forms; but till the order of the universe shall be regulated by new physical laws, their substance must for ever remain essentially the same. On the *chains, indeed, which nature makes use of to bind together her several operations*, Newton has thrown no light whatever; nor was it the aim of his researches to do so. The subjects of his reasonings were not occult connexions, but particular phenomena and general laws; both of them possessing all the evidence which can belong to *facts* ascertained by observation and experiment. From the one or the other of these all his inferences, whether analytical or synthetical, are deduced. Nor is a single hypothesis involved in his *data*, excepting the authority of that Law of Belief, which is tacitly and necessarily assumed in all our physical conclusions: The stability of the order of nature.

SELECTION 3

Use and Abuse of Hypotheses

The indiscriminate zeal against hypotheses, so generally avowed at present by the professed followers of Bacon, has been much encouraged by the strong and decided terms in which, on various occasions, they are reprobated by Newton. But the language of this great man, when he happens to touch upon logical questions, must not always

[5] [Stewart refers to Adam Smith's *History of Astronomy*.]

be too literally interpreted. It must be qualified and limited, so as to accord with the exemplifications which he himself has given of his general rules. Of the truth of this remark, the passages now alluded to afford a satisfactory proof; for, while they are expressed in the most unconditional and absolute terms, so many exceptions to them occur in his own writings, as to authorize the conclusion, that he expected his readers would of themselves be able to supply the obvious and necessary comments. It is probable that, in these passages, he had more particularly in his eye the Vortices of Descartes.

"The votaries of hypotheses", says Dr. Reid, "have often been challenged to shew one useful discovery in the works of nature that was ever made in that way". In reply to this challenge, it is sufficient, on the present occasion, to mention the theory of Gravitation and the Copernican system. Of the former we have the testimony of Dr. Pemberton, that it took its first rise from a conjecture or hypothesis suggested by *analogy*; nor, indeed, could it be considered in any other light, till that period in Newton's life, when, by a calculation founded on the accurate measurement of the earth by Picard, he evinced the coincidence between the law which regulates the fall of heavy bodies, and the power which retains the moon in her orbit. The Copernican system, however, furnishes a case still stronger, and still more directly applicable to our purpose, inasmuch as the only evidence which the author was able to offer in its favour, was the advantage which it possessed over every other hypothesis, in explaining with simplicity and beauty all the phenomena of the heavens. In the mind of Copernicus, therefore, this system was nothing more than a hypothesis; but it was a hypothesis conformable to the universal *analogy* of nature, always accomplishing her ends by the simplest means.

According to this view of the subject, the confidence which we repose in Analogy rests ultimately on the Evidence of Experience, and hence an additional argument in favour of the former method of investigation, when cautiously followed, as well as an additional proof of the imperceptible shades by which Experience and Analogy run into each other.

Nor is the utility of hypothetical theories confined to those cases in which they have been confirmed by subsequent researches; it may be equally great where they have completely disappointed the expectations of their authors. Nothing, I think, can be juster than Hartley's remark, that "any hypothesis which possesses a sufficient degree of plausibility to account for a number of facts, helps us to digest these facts in proper order, to bring new ones to light, and to make *experimenta crucis* for the sake of future inquirers".[6] Indeed it has probably been in this way that most discoveries have been made; for although a knowledge of facts must be prior to the formation of a legitimate theory, yet a

[6] [David Hartley (1705-57). English philosopher and physician. His *Observations on Man, His Frame, His Duty and His Expectations* (1749) is the first complete account of the human mind based on the theory of the association of ideas.]

hypothetical theory is generally the best guide to the knowledge of connected and of useful facts.

The first conception of a hypothetical theory, it must always be remembered, (if the theory possesses any plausibility whatever,) presupposes a general acquaintance with the phenomena which it aims to account for; and it is by reasoning synthetically from the hypothesis, and comparing the deductions with observation and experiment, that the cautious inquirer is gradually led, either to correct it in such a manner as to reconcile it with facts, or finally to abandon it as an unfounded conjecture. Even in this latter case, an approach is made to the truth in the way of *exclusion*; while, at the same time, an accession is gained to that class of associated and kindred phenomena, which it is his object to trace to their parent stock.

In thus apologizing for the use of hypotheses, I only repeat in a different form the precepts of Bacon, and the comments of some of his most enlightened followers. "The prejudice against hypotheses which many people entertain", says the late Dr. Gregory, "is founded on the equivocal signification of a word. It is commonly confounded with theory; but a hypothesis properly means the supposition of a principle of whose existence there is no proof from experience, but which may be rendered more or less probable by facts which are neither numerous enough, nor adequate to infer its existence. When such hypotheses are proposed in the modest and diffident manner that becomes mere suppositions or conjectures, they are not only harmless, but even necessary for establishing a just theory. *They are the first rudiments or anticipations of Principles.* Without these there could not be useful observation, nor experiment, nor arrangement, because there could be no motive or principle in the mind to form them. Hypotheses then only become dangerous and censurable, when they are imposed on us for just principles; because, in that case they put a stop to further inquiry, by leading the mind to acquiesce in principles which may as probably be ill as well founded".

Another eminent writer has apologized very ingeniously, and I think very philosophically, for the hypotheses and conjectures which are occasionally to be found in his own works. The author I mean is Dr. Stephen Hales, who, in the preface to the second volume of his *Vegetable Statics*, has expressed himself thus:

"In natural philosophy we cannot depend on any mere speculations of the mind; we can only reason with any tolerable certainty from proper data, such as arise from the united testimony of many good and credible experiments.

"Yet it seems not unreasonable, on the other hand, though not far to indulge, to carry our reasonings a little farther than the plain evidence of experiments will warrant; for since at the utmost boundaries of those things, which we clearly know, a kind of twilight is cast on the adjoining borders of *Terra Incognita*, it seems reasonable, in some degree, to indulge conjecture *there*; otherwise we should make but very slow advances, either by experiments or reasoning. For new experiments and discoveries usually owe their first rise only to lucky guesses and probable conjectures; and even disappointments in these conjectures often lead to the thing sought for".

...

The argument in favour of Hypotheses might he pushed much farther, by considering the tentative or *hypothetical* steps by which the most cautious philosophers are often under the necessity of proceeding, in conducting inquiries strictly experimental. These cannot be better described than in the words of Boscovich, the slightest of whose logical hints are entitled to peculiar attention. "In some instances, observations and experiments at once reveal to us all that we wish to know. In other cases, we avail ourselves of the aid of *hypotheses; -by which word, however, is to be understood, not fictions altogether arbitrary, but suppositions conformable to experience or to analogy.* By means of these, we are enabled to supply the defects of our *data,* and to conjecture or divine the path to truth; always ready to abandon our hypothesis, when found to involve consequences inconsistent with fact. And, indeed, in most cases, I conceive this to be the method best adapted to physics; a science in which the procedure of the inquirer may be compared to that of a person attempting to decypher a letter written in a secret character; and in which legitimate theories are generally the slow result of disappointed essays, and of errors which have led the way to their own detection".

Nor is it solely by the erroneous results of his *own* hypotheses, that the philosopher is assisted in the investigation of truth. Similar lights are often to be collected from the errors of his predecessors; and hence it is that accurate histories of the different sciences may justly be ranked among the most effectual means of accelerating their future advancement. It was from a review of the endless and hopeless wanderings of preceding inquirers, that Bacon inferred the necessity of avoiding every beaten track; and it was this which encouraged him—with a confidence in his own powers amply justified by the event—to explore and to open a new path to the mysteries of nature: *Inveniam viam, aut faciam.* In this respect, the maturity of reason in the *species* is analogous to that in the *individual;* not the consequence of any sudden or accidental cause, but the fruit of reiterated disappointments correcting the mistakes of youth and inexperience. "There is no subject", says Fontenelle, "on which men ever come to form a reasonable opinion, till they have once exhausted all the absurd views which it is possible to take of it. "What follies", he adds, "should we not be repeating at this day, if we had not been anticipated in so many of them by the ancient philosophers!" Those systems, therefore, which are false, are by no means to be regarded as altogether useless. That of Ptolemy, (for example,) as Bailly has well observed, is founded on a prejudice so natural and so unavoidable, that it may be considered as a necessary step in the progress of astronomical science; and if it had not been proposed in ancient times, it would infallibly have preceded, among the moderns, the system of Copernicus, and retarded the period of its discovery.

In what I have hitherto said in defence of the method of hypothesis, I have confined myself entirely to its utility as an organ of investigation; taking all along for granted, that, till the principle assumed has been fairly inferred as a law of nature, from undoubted facts, none of the explanations which it affords are to be admitted as legitimate theories. Some of the advocates for this method have, however, gone much farther, asserting that if a hypothesis be sufficient to account for all the phenomena in question, no other proof of its conformity to truth is necessary. "Supposing", says Dr. Hartley, "the existence of *the æther* to be destitute of all direct evidence, still, if it serves to explain and account for a great variety of phenomena, it will, by this means, have an indirect argument in its favour. Thus, we admit the key of a cypher to be a true one, when it explains the cypher completely; and the decypherer judges himself to approach to the true key, in proportion as he advances in the explanation of the cypher; and *this* without any direct evidence at all". On another occasion he observes, that "Philosophy is the art of *decyphering* the mysteries of nature; and that every theory which can explain all the phenomena, has the same evidence in its favour, that it is possible the key of a cypher can have from its explaining that cypher".

The same very ingenious and plausible reasoning is urged by Le Sage in one of his posthumous fragments; and long before the publication of Hartley's work, it had struck Gravesande so strongly, that, in his *Introductio ad Philosophiam,* he has subjoined to his chapter on the Use of Hypotheses, another on the Art of Decyphering. Of the merit of the latter it is no slight proof, that D'Alembert has inserted the substance of it in one of the articles of the *Encyclopédie.*

In reply to Hartley's comparison between the business of the philosopher and that of the decypherer, Dr. Reid observes, that "to find the key requires an understanding equal or superior to that which made the cypher. This instance, therefore", he adds", will *then* be in point, when he who attempts to decypher the works of nature by a hypothesis, has an understanding equal or superior to that which made them".

This argument is not stated with the author's usual correctness in point of logic; inasmuch as the first proposition contrasts the sagacity of the decypherer with that of the contriver of the *cypher;* and the second, with that of the author of the *composition* decyphered. Nor is this all. The argument proceeds on the supposition that, if the task of the scientific inquirer be compared to that of the decypherer, the views of the Author of Nature may, with equal propriety, be compared to those of the inventor of the cypher. It is impossible to imagine that this was Hartley's idea. The object of true philosophy is, in no case presumptuously to divine an alphabet of *secret* characters or cyphers, purposely employed by infinite Wisdom to *conceal* its operations; but, by the diligent study of facts and analogies legible to all, to discover the key which infinite Wisdom has itself prepared for the interpretation of its own laws. In other words, its object is to concentrate and to cast on the unknown parts of the universe, the lights which are reflected from those which are known.

In this instance, as well as in others where Reid reprobates hypotheses, his reasoning uniformly takes for granted, that they are wholly arbitrary and gratuitous. "If a thousand of the greatest wits", says he, "that ever the world produced, were, *without any previous knowledge in anatomy*, to sit down and contrive how, and by what internal organs, the various functions of the human body are carried on - how the blood is made to circulate, and the limbs to move - they would not, in a thousand years, hit upon anything like the truth". Nothing can be juster than this remark; but does it authorize the conclusion, that, to an experienced and skilful anatomist, conjectures founded on analogy, and on the consideration of *uses*, are of no avail as media of discovery? The logical inference, indeed, from Dr. Reid's own statement, is not against anatomical conjectures in general, but against the anatomical conjectures of those who are ignorant of anatomy.

...

But although I do not think that Reid has been successful in his attempt to refute Hartley's argument, I am far from considering that argument as sound or conclusive. My chief objections to it are the two following:

1. The cases compared are by no means parallel. In that of the *cypher* we have *all* the facts before us, and if the key explains them, we may be certain that nothing can directly contradict the justness of our interpretation. In *our physical researches*, on the other hand, we are admitted to see only a few detached sentences extracted from a volume, of the size of which we are entirely ignorant. No hypothesis, therefore, how numerous soever the facts may be with which it tallies, can completely exclude the possibility of exceptions or limitations hitherto undiscovered.

It must, at the same time, be granted that the probability of a hypothesis increases in proportion to the number of phenomena for which it accounts, *and to the simplicity of the theory by which it explains them*; and that, in some instances, this probability may amount to a moral certainty. The most remarkable example of this which occurs in the history of science is, undoubtedly, the Copernican system. I before observed, that at the period when it was first proposed, it was nothing more than a hypothesis, and that its only proof rested on its conformity in point of simplicity, to the general economy of the Universe.

...

Of the truth of this hypothesis, the discoveries of the last century have afforded many new proofs of a direct and even demonstrative nature; and yet, it may be fairly questioned, whether to Copernicus and Galileo, the analogical reasoning, did not of itself appear so conclusive as to supersede the necessity of any farther evidence. The ecclesiastical persecutions which the latter encountered in defence of his supposed heresy, sufficiently evinces the faith which he reposed in his astronomical creed.

It is, however, extremely worthy of remark, with respect to the Copernican system, that it affords no illustration whatever of the justness of Hartley's logical maxim. The Ptolemaic system was not demonstrably *inconsistent* with any phenomena known in the sixteenth century; and consequently, the presumption for the new hypothesis did not arise from its exclusive coincidence with the facts, but from the simplicity and beauty which it possessed as a theory. The inference to be deduced from it is, therefore, *not* in favour of hypothesis in general, but of hypothesis sanctioned by analogy.

The fortunate hypothesis of a Ring encircling the body of Saturn, by which Huygens accounted, in a manner equally simple and satisfactory, for a set of appearances which for forty years had puzzled all the astronomers of Europe, bears in all its circumstances a closer resemblance than any other instance I know of to the key of a cypher. Of its *truth* it is impossible for the most sceptical mind to entertain any doubt, when it is considered that it not only enabled Huygens to explain all the *known* phenomena, but to predict those which were afterwards to be observed. This instance, accordingly, has had much stress laid upon it by different writers, particularly by Gravesande and Le Sage. I must own, I am somewhat doubtful if the discovery of a key to so limited and insulated a class of optical facts, authorizes any valid argument for the employment of mere hypotheses, to decypher the complicated phenomena resulting from the general laws of nature. It is, indeed, an example most ingeniously and happily selected, but would not perhaps have been so often resorted to, if it had been easy to find others of a similar description.

2. The chief objection, however, to Hartley's comparison of the theorist to the decypherer is, that there are few if any physical hypotheses, which afford the *only* way of explaining the phenomena to which they are applied; and therefore, admitting them to be perfectly consistent with all the known facts; they leave us in the same state of uncertainty, in which the decypherer would find himself, if he should discover a variety of keys to the same cypher. Descartes acknowledges that the same effect might, upon the principles of his philosophy, admit of manifold explanations, and that nothing perplexed him more than to know which he ought to adopt in preference to the others. "The powers of nature", says he, "I must confess are so ample, that no sooner do I observe any particular effect, than I immediately perceive that it may be deduced from *my* principles in a variety of different ways; and nothing in general appears to me more difficult, than to ascertain by which of these processes it is really produced". The same remark may (with a very few exceptions) be extended to every hypothetical theory which is unsupported by any collateral probabilities arising from experience or analogy; and it sufficiently shows how infinitely inferior such theories are, in

point of evidence, to the conclusions obtained by the art of the decypherer. The principles, indeed, on which this last art proceeds, may be safely pronounced to be nearly infallible.

In these strictures upon Hartley, I have endeavoured to do as much justice as possible to his general argument, by keeping entirely out of sight the particular purpose which it was intended to serve. By confining too much his attention to this, Dr. Reid has been led to carry, farther than was necessary or reasonable, an indiscriminate zeal against every speculation to which the epithet *hypothetical* can in any degree be applied. He has been also led to overlook the essential distinction between hypothetical inferences from one department of the Material World to another, and hypothetical inferences from the Material World to the Intellectual. It was with the view of apologizing for inferences of the latter description, that Hartley advanced the logical principle which gave occasion to the foregoing discussion; and therefore, I apprehend, the proper answer to his argument is this: Granting your principle to be true in all its extent, it furnishes no apology whatever for the Theory of Vibrations. If the science of mind admit of any illustration from the aid of hypotheses, it must be from such hypotheses alone as are consonant to *the analogy of its own phenomena.* To assume, as a fact, the existence of analogies between these phenomena and those of matter, is to sanction that very prejudice which it is the great object of the inductive science of mind to eradicate.

SELECTION 4

Mathematical Axioms

On the evidence of mathematical axioms it is unnecessary to enlarge, as the controversies to which they have given occasion are entirely of a speculative or rather scholastic description, and have no tendency to affect the certainty of that branch of science to which they are supposed to be subservient.

It must, at the same time, be confessed, with respect to this class of propositions (and the same remark may be extended to axioms in general), that some of the logical questions connected with them continue still to be involved in much obscurity. In proportion to their extreme simplicity is the difficulty of illustrating or of describing their nature in unexceptionable language; or even of ascertaining a precise criterion by which they may be distinguished from other truths which approach to them nearly. It is chiefly owing to this, that in geometry there are no theorems of which it is so difficult to give a rigorous demonstration, as those of which persons unacquainted with the nature of mathematical evidence are apt to say, that they require no proof whatever. But the inconveniences arising from these circumstances are of trifling moment; occasioning at the worst some embarrassment to those mathematical writers, who are studious of the most finished elegance in their exposition of elementary principles, or to metaphysicians anxious to display their subtlety upon points which cannot possibly lead to any practical conclusion.

It was long ago remarked by Locke, of the axioms of geometry, as stated by Euclid, that although the proposition be at first enunciated in *general* terms, and afterwards appealed to, in its *particular* applications, as a principle *previously* examined and admitted, yet that the truth is not less evident in the latter case than in the former. He observes farther, that it is in some of its particular applications that the truth of every axiom is originally perceived by the mind; and, therefore, that the general proposition, so far from being the *ground* of our assent to the truths which it comprehends, is only a verbal generalization of what, in particular instances, has been already acknowledged as true.

...

Another observation of this profound writer deserves our attention while examining the nature of axioms; "that they are not the foundations on which any of the sciences is built, nor at all useful in helping men forward to the discovery of unknown truths". ... At present I shall only add, to what Mr. Locke has so well stated, that even in *mathematics* it cannot with any propriety be said, that the axioms are the foundation on which the science rests, or the first principles from which its more recondite truths are deduced. Of this I have little doubt that Locke was perfectly aware; but the mistakes which some of the most acute and enlightened of his disciples have committed in treating of the same subject, convince me that a further elucidation of it is not altogether superfluous. With this view I shall here introduce a few remarks on a passage in Dr. Campbell's *Philosophy of Rhetoric,* in which he has betrayed some misapprehensions on this very point, which a little more attention to the hints already quoted from the *Essay on Human Understanding* might have prevented. These remarks will, I hope, contribute to place the nature of axioms, more particularly of mathematical axioms, in a different and clearer light than that in which they have been commonly considered.

"Of intuitive evidence", says Dr. Campbell, "that of the following propositions may serve as an illustration:- 'One and four make five'. 'Things equal to the same thing are equal to one another'. 'The whole is greater than a part;' and, in brief, all *axioms* in arithmetic and geometry. These are, in effect, but so many different expositions of our own general notions taken in different views. Some of them are no more than definitions, or equivalent to definitions. To say 'One and four make *five*', is precisely the same thing as to say, 'We give the name of *five* to one added to four'. In fact, they are all in some respects reducible to this axiom, 'Whatever is, is'. ...

"But in order to prevent mistakes, it will be necessary further to illustrate this subject. It might be thought that, if axioms were propositions perfectly identical, it would be impossible to advance a step, by their means, beyond the simple ideas first perceived by the mind. And it must be owned, if the predicate of the proposition were nothing but a repetition of the subject, under the same aspect, and in the same or synonymous terms, no conceivable advantage could be made of it for the furtherance of knowledge. Of such propositions, for instance, as these - 'Seven are seven', 'Eight are eight', and 'Ten added to eleven are equal to ten added to eleven', it is manifest that we could never avail ourselves for the improvement of science. Nor does the change of the term make any alteration in point of utility. The propositions, 'Twelve are a dozen', 'Twenty are a score', unless considered as explications of the words *dozen* and *score*, are equally insignificant with the former. But when the thing, though in effect coinciding, is considered under a different aspect; when what is single in the subject is divided in the predicate, and conversely; or when what is a whole in the one, is regarded as a part of something else in the other; such propositions lead to the discovery of innumerable and apparently remote relations. One added to four may be accounted no other than a definition of the word *five*, as was remarked above. But when I say, 'Two added to three are equal to five', I advance a truth which, though equally clear, is quite distinct from the preceding. ...

> Now, it is by the aid of such simple and elementary principles, that the arithmetician and algebraist proceed to the most astonishing discoveries. Nor are the operations of the geometrician essentially different. . . .

I have little to object to these observations of Dr. Campbell, as far as they relate to arithmetic and to algebra; for in these sciences, all our investigations amount to nothing more than to a comparison of different expressions of the same thing. Our common language, indeed, frequently supposes the case to be otherwise; as when an equation is defined to be, "A proposition asserting the equality of two quantities". It would, however, be much more correct to define it, "A proposition asserting the equivalence of two expressions of the same quantity"; for algebra is merely a *universal arithmetic*; and the names of numbers are nothing else than collectives, by which we are enabled to express ourselves more concisely than could be done by enumerating all the units that they contain. Of this doctrine, the passage now quoted from Dr. Campbell shows that he entertained a sufficiently just and precise idea.

But if Dr. Campbell perceived that arithmetical equations, such as "one and four make five", are no other than definitions, why should he have classed them with the axioms he quotes from Euclid, "That the whole is greater than a part", and that "things equal to the same thing are equal to one another"; propositions which, however clearly their truth be implied in the meaning of the terms of which they consist, cannot certainly, by any interpretation, be considered in the light of definitions at all analogous to the former? The former, indeed, are only explanations of the relative import of particular names; the latter are universal propositions, applicable alike to an infinite variety of instances.

Another very obvious consideration might have satisfied Dr. Campbell, that the simple arithmetical equations which he mentions do not hold the same place in that science which Euclid's axioms hold in geometry. What I allude to is, that the greater part of these axioms are equally essential to all the different branches of mathematics. That "the whole is greater than a part", and that "things equal to the same thing are equal to one another", are propositions as essentially connected with our arithmetical computations as with our geometrical reasonings; and therefore, to explain in what manner the mind makes a transition, in the case of numbers, from the more simple to the more complicated equations, throws no light whatever on the question *how* the transition is made, either in arithmetic or in geometry, from what are properly called axioms, to the more remote conclusions in these sciences.

The very fruitless attempt thus made by this acute writer to illustrate the importance of axioms as the basis of mathematical truth, was probably suggested to him by a doctrine which has been repeatedly inculcated of late, concerning the grounds of that peculiar evidence which is allowed to accompany mathematical demonstration. "All the sciences (it has been said) rest ultimately on first principles, which we must take for granted without proof; and whose evidence determines, both in kind and degree, the evidence which it is possible to attain in our conclusions. In some of the sciences, our first principles are intuitively certain, in others they are intuitively probable; and such as the evidence of these principles is, such must that of our conclusions be. If our first principles are intuitively certain, and if we reason from them consequentially, our conclusions will be demonstratively certain; but if our principles be only intuitively probable, our conclusions will be only demonstratively probable. In mathematics, the first principles from which we reason are a set of axioms which are not only intuitively certain, but of which we find it impossible to conceive the contraries to be true: and hence the peculiar evidence which belongs to all the conclusions that follow from these principles as necessary consequences".

To this view of the subject Dr. Reid has repeatedly given his sanction, at least in the most essential points; more particularly, in controverting an assertion of Locke's, that "no science is, or hath been, built on *maxims*". "Surely", says Dr. Reid, "Mr. Locke was not ignorant of geometry, which hath been built upon maxims prefixed to the *Elements*, as far back as we are able to trace it. But though they had not been prefixed, which was a matter of utility rather than necessity, yet it must be granted, that every demonstration in geometry is grounded either upon propositions formerly demonstrated, or upon self-evident principles".

On another occasion he expresses himself thus: "I take it to be certain, that whatever can, by just reasoning, be inferred from a principle that is necessary, must be a necessary truth. Thus, as the axioms in mathematics are all necessary truths, so are all the conclusions drawn from them; that is, the whole body of that science".

That there is something fundamentally erroneous in these very strong statements with respect to the relation which Euclid's axioms bear to the geometrical theorems which follow, appears sufficiently from a consideration which was long ago mentioned by Locke - that from these axioms it is not possible for human ingenuity to deduce a single inference. ... But surely, if this be granted, and if, at the same time, by the first principles of a science be meant those fundamental propositions from which its remoter truths are derived, the axioms cannot, with any consistency, be called the First Principles of Mathematics. They have not (it will be admitted) the most distant analogy to what are called the First Principles of Natural Philosophy; to those general facts, for example, of the gravity and elasticity of the air, from which may be deduced, as consequences, the suspension of the mercury in the Torricellian tube, and its fall when carried up to an eminence. According to this meaning of the word, the principles of mathematical science are, *not* the axioms, but the *definitions*; which definitions hold, in mathematics, precisely the same place that is held in natural philosophy by such general facts as have now been referred to.

From what principle are the various properties of the circle derived, but from the definition of a circle? From what principle the properties of the parabola or ellipse, but from the definitions of these curves? A similar observation may be extended to all the other theorems which the mathematician demonstrates: And it is this observation, (which, obvious as it may seem, does not appear to have occurred in all its force, either to Locke, to Reid, or to Campbell,) that furnishes, if I mistake not, the true explanation of the peculiarity already remarked in mathematical evidence.

...

After what has been just stated, it is scarcely necessary for me again to repeat, with regard to mathematical axioms, that although they are not the *principles* of our reasoning, either in arithmetic or in geometry, their truth is supposed or implied in all our reasonings in both; and, if it were called in question, our further progress would be impossible. In both of these respects, we shall find them analogous to the other classes of primary or elemental truths which remain to be considered.

Nor let it be imagined, from this concession, that the dispute turns merely on the meaning annexed to the word *principle.* It turns upon an important question of fact, - Whether the theorems of geometry rest on the *axioms*, in the same sense in which they rest on the *definitions*? Or, (to state the question in a manner still more obvious,) — Whether axioms hold a place in geometry at all analogous to what is occupied in natural philosophy, by those sensible phenomena which form the basis of that science? Dr. Reid compares them sometimes to the one set of propositions, and sometimes to the other. If the foregoing observations be just, they bear no analogy to either.

Into this indistinctness of language Dr. Reid was probably led in part by Sir Isaac Newton, who, with a very illogical latitude in the use of words, gave the name of *axioms* to the *laws of motion*, and also to those general experimental truths which form the ground-work of our reasonings in catoptrics and dioptrics. For such a misapplication of the technical terms of mathematics some apology might perhaps be made, if the author had been treating on any subject connected with moral science; but surely in a work entitled *Mathematical Principles of Natural Philosophy*, the word *axiom* might reasonably have been expected to be used in a sense somewhat analogous to that which every person liberally educated is accustomed to annex to it, when he is first initiated into the elements of geometry.

...

The difference of opinion between Locke and Reid, of which I took notice in the foregoing part of this Section, appears greater than it really is, in consequence of an ambiguity in the word *principle*, as employed by the latter. In its proper acceptation, it seems to me to denote an assumption, (whether resting on fact or on hypothesis,) upon which, as a *datum*, a train of reasoning proceeds; and for the falsity or incorrectness of which no logical rigour in the subsequent process can compensate. Thus the gravity and the elasticity of the air are *principles of reasoning* in our speculations about the barometer. The equality of the angles of incidence and reflexion; the proportionality of the sines of incidence and refraction, are *principles of reasoning* in catoptrics and in dioptrics. In a sense perfectly analogous to this, the *definitions* of geometry (all of which are merely *hypothetical)* are the *first principles* of reasoning in the subsequent demonstrations, and the basis on which the whole fabric of the science rests.

I have called this the *proper* acceptation of the word, because it is that in which it is most frequently used by the best writers. It is also most agreeable to the literal meaning which its etymology suggests, expressing the original point from which our reasoning sets out or commences.

Dr. Reid often uses the word in this sense, as, for example, in the following sentence already quoted: "From three or four axioms, which he calls *regulæ philosophandi*, together with *the phenomena observed by the senses, which he likewise lays down as first principles*, Newton deduces, by strict reasoning, the propositions contained in the third book of his *Principia*, and in his *Optics*".

On other occasions, he uses the same word to denote those *elemental* truths (if I may use the expression) which are virtually taken for granted or assumed in every step of our reasoning, and without which, although no *consequences* can be directly inferred from them, a train of reasoning would be impossible. Of this kind, in mathematics are the *axioms*, or (as

Mr. Locke and others frequently call them) the *maxims;* in physics, a belief of *the continuance of the Laws of Nature;* in all our reasonings, without exception, a belief in *our own identity,* and in *the evidence of memory.* Such truths are the *last elements* into which reasoning resolves itself when subjected to a metaphysical analysis, and which no person but a metaphysician or a logician ever thinks of stating in the form of propositions, or even of expressing verbally to himself. It is to truths of this description that Locke seems in general to apply the name of *maxims;* and, in this sense, it is unquestionably true, that no science (not even geometry) is founded on maxims as its first principles.

In one sense of the word *principle,* indeed, maxims may be called principles of reasoning; for the words *principles* and *elements* are sometimes used as synonymous. Nor do I take upon me to say that this mode of speaking is exceptionable. All that I assert is, that they cannot be called *principles of reasoning,* in the sense which has just now been defined; and that accuracy requires that the word on which the whole question hinges, should not be used in both senses in the course of the same argument. It is for this reason that I have employed the phrase *principles of reasoning* on the one occasion, and *elements of reasoning* on the other.

It is difficult to find unexceptionable language to mark distinctions so completely foreign to the ordinary purposes of speech; but, in the present instance, the line of separation is strongly and clearly drawn by this criterion—that from *principles of reasoning* consequences may be deduced; from what I have called *elements of reasoning,* none ever can.

A process of logical reasoning has been often likened to a chain supporting a weight. If this similitude be adopted, the *axioms* or *elemental truths* now mentioned may be compared to the successive concatenations which connect the different links immediately with each other; the *principles* of our reasoning resemble the hook, or rather the beam, from which the whole is suspended. ...

...

Before dismissing this subject, I must once more repeat, that the doctrine which I have been attempting to establish, so far from degrading *axioms* from that rank which Dr. Reid would assign them, tends to identify them still more than he has done with the exercise of our reasoning powers; inasmuch as, instead of comparing them with the *data,* on the accuracy of which that of our conclusion necessarily depends, it considers them as the *vincula* which give coherence to all the particular links of the chain; or (to vary the metaphor) as *component elements,* without which the faculty of reasoning is inconceivable and impossible.

Three

Knowledge and Belief

SELECTION 5

Origin of Knowledge

The philosophers who endeavoured to explain the operations of the human mind by the theory of ideas, and who took for granted, that in every exertion of thought there exists in the mind some object distinct from the thinking substance, were naturally led to inquire whence these ideas derive their origin; in particular, whether they are conveyed to the mind from without by means of the senses, or form part of its original furniture?

With respect to this question, the opinions of the ancients were various; but as the influence of these opinions on the prevailing systems of the present age is not very considerable, it is not necessary, for any of the purposes I have in view in this work, to consider them particularly. The moderns, too, have been much divided on the subject; some holding, with Descartes, that the mind is furnished with certain innate ideas; others, with Mr. Locke, that all our ideas may be traced from sensation and reflection; and many, (especially among the later metaphysicians in France,) that they may be all traced from sensation alone.

Of these theories, that of Mr. Locke deserves more particularly our attention; as it has served as the basis of most of the metaphysical systems which have appeared since his time, and as the difference between it and the theory which derives all our ideas from sensation alone, is rather apparent than real.

In order to convey a just notion of Mr. Locke's doctrine concerning the origin of our ideas, it is necessary to remark, that he refers to sensation all the ideas which we are supposed to receive by the external senses; our ideas, for example, of colours, of sounds, of hardness, of extension, of motion, and, in short, of all the qualities and modes of matter: to reflection, the ideas of our own mental operations which we derive from consciousness; our ideas, for example, of memory, of imagination, of volition, of pleasure, and of pain. These two sources, according to him, furnish us with all our simple ideas, and the only power which the mind possesses over them, is to perform certain operations, in the way of composition, abstraction, generalization, &c., on the materials which it thus collects in the course of its experience. The laudable desire of Mr. Locke to introduce precision and perspicuity into metaphysical speculations, and his anxiety to guard the mind against error in general, naturally prepossessed him in favour of a doctrine which, when compared with those of his predecessors, was intelligible and simple; and which, by suggesting a method, apparently easy and palpable, of analyzing our knowledge into its elementary principles, seemed to furnish an antidote against those prejudices which had been favoured by the hypothesis of innate ideas. It is now a considerable time since this fundamental principle of Mr. Locke's system began to lose its authority in England; and the sceptical conclusions which it had been employed to support by some later writers, furnished its opponents with very plausible arguments against it. The late learned Mr. Harris, in particular, frequently mentions this doctrine of Mr. Locke, and always in terms of high indignation. "Mark", says he, in one passage, "the order of things, according to the account of our later metaphysicians. First comes that huge body, the sensible world. Then this, and its attributes, beget sensible ideas. Then, out of sensible ideas, by a kind of lopping and pruning, are made ideas intelligible, whether specific or general. Thus, should they admit that mind was coeval with body, yet till the body gave it ideas, and awakened its dormant powers, it could at best have been nothing more than a sort of dead capacity, for innate ideas it could not possibly have any". And, in another passage: "For my own part, when I read the detail about sensation and reflection, and am taught the process at large how my ideas are all generated, I seem to view the human soul in the light of a crucible, where truths are produced by a kind of logical chemistry".

If Dr. Reid's reasonings on the subject of ideas be admitted, all these speculations with respect to their origin fall to the ground; and the question to which they relate is reduced merely to a question of fact, concerning the occasions on which the mind is first led to form those simple notions into which our thoughts may be analyzed, and which may be considered as the principles or elements of human knowledge. With respect to many of these notions, this inquiry involves no difficulty. No one, for example, can be at a loss to ascertain the occasions on which the notions of colours and sounds are first formed by the mind; for these notions are confined to individuals who are possessed of particular senses, and cannot, by any combination of words, be conveyed to those who never enjoyed the use of them. The history of our notions of extension and figure, (which may be suggested to the mind by the exercise either of sight or of touch,) is not altogether so obvious; and accordingly, it has been the subject of various controversies. To trace the origin of these, and of our other simple notions with respect to the qualities of matter; or, in other words, to describe the occasions on which, by the laws of our nature, they are suggested to the mind, is one of the leading objects of Dr. Reid's inquiry, in his analysis of our external senses; in which he carefully avoids every hypothesis with respect to the inexplicable phenomena of perception and of thought, and confines himself scrupulously to a literal statement of facts. Similar inquiries to these may be proposed, concerning the occasions on which we form the notions of *time*, of *motion*, of *number*, of *causation*, and an infinite variety of others. Thus, it has been observed by different authors, that every perception of change suggests to the mind the notion of a *cause*, without which that change could not have happened. Dr. Reid remarks that, without the faculty of memory, our perceptive powers could never have led us to form the idea of *motion*. I shall afterwards show, in the sequel of this work, that without the same faculty of memory we never could have formed the notion of *time* and that without the faculty of abstraction, we could not have formed the notion of *number*. Such inquiries with respect to the origin of our knowledge are curious and important; and if conducted with judgment, they may lead to the most certain conclusions, as they aim at nothing more than to ascertain facts, which, although not obvious to superficial observers, may yet be discovered by patient investigation.

From the remarks which have been just made on our notions of time, of motion, and of number, it is evident that the inquiry concerning the origin of human knowledge cannot possibly be discussed at the commencement of such a work as this; but that it must be resumed in different parts of it, as those faculties of the mind come under our view, with which the formation of our different simple notions is connected.

With respect to the general question, Whether all our knowledge may be ultimately traced from our sensations? I shall only observe at present, that the opinion we form concerning it is of much less consequence than is commonly supposed. That the mind cannot, without the grossest absurdity, be considered in the light of a receptacle which is gradually furnished from without, by materials introduced by the channel of the senses; nor in that of a *tabula rasa,* upon which copies or resemblances of things external are imprinted, I have already shown at sufficient length. Although, therefore, we should acquiesce in the conclusion, that without our organs of sense, the mind must have remained destitute of knowledge, this concession could have no tendency whatever to favour the principles of materialism; as it implies nothing more than that the impressions made on our senses by external objects, furnish the occasions on which the mind, by the laws of its constitution, is led to perceive the qualities of the material world, and to exert all the different modifications of thought of which it is capable.

From the very slight view of the subject, however, which has been already given, it is sufficiently evident, that this doctrine which refers the origin of all our knowledge to the occasions furnished by sense, must be received with many limitations. That those ideas, which Mr. Locke calls ideas of reflection, (or, in other words, the notions which we form of the subjects of our own consciousness,) are not suggested to the mind immediately by the sensations arising from the use of our organs of perception, is granted on all hands; and, therefore, the amount of the doctrine now mentioned is nothing more than this: that the first occasions on which our various intellectual faculties are exercised, are furnished by the impressions made on our organs of sense; and consequently, that without these impressions, it would have been impossible for us to arrive at the knowledge of our faculties. Agreeably to this explanation of the doctrine, it may undoubtedly be said with plausibility, (and, I am inclined to believe, with truth,) that the occasions on which all our notions are formed, are furnished either immediately or ultimately by sense; but, if I am not much mistaken, this is not the meaning which is commonly annexed to the doctrine, either by its advocates or their opponents. One thing at least is obvious, that in this sense it does not lead to those consequences which have interested one party of philosophers in its defence, and another in its refutation.

There is another very important consideration which deserves our attention in this argument: that, even on the supposition that certain impressions on our organs of sense are necessary to awaken the mind to a consciousness of its own existence, and to give rise to the exercise of its various faculties; yet all this might have happened, without our having any knowledge of the qualities, or even of the existence, of the material world. To facilitate the admission of this proposition, let us suppose a being formed in every other respect like man, but possessed of no senses, excepting those of hearing and smelling. I make choice of these two senses, because it is obvious that by means of them alone we never could have arrived at the knowledge of the primary qualities of matter, or even of the existence of things external. All that we could possibly have inferred from our occasional sensations of smell and sound, would have been, that there existed some unknown cause by which they were produced.

Let us suppose then, a particular sensation to be excited in the mind of such a being. The moment this happens, he must necessarily acquire the knowledge of two facts at once: that of the existence of *the sensation*, and that of *his own existence*, as a sentient being. After the sensation is at an end, he can *remember* he felt it; he can *conceive* that he feels it again. If he has felt a variety of different sensations, he can compare them together in respect of the pleasure or the pain they have afforded him, and will naturally *desire* the return of the agreeable sensations, and be *afraid* of the return of those which were painful. If the sensations of smell and sound are both excited in his mind at the same time, he can *attend* to either of them he chooses, and withdraw his attention from the other; or he can withdraw his *attention* from both, and fix it on some sensation he has felt formerly. In this manner he might be led, merely by sensations existing in his mind, and conveying to him no information concerning matter, to exercise many of his most important faculties; and amidst all these different modifications and operations of his mind, he would feel, with irresistible conviction, that they all belong to one and the same sentient and intelligent being; or, in other words, that they are all modifications and operations of himself. I say nothing at present of the various simple notions (or simple ideas, as they are commonly called) which would arise in his mind; for example, the ideas of *number*, of *duration*, of *cause* and *effect*, of *personal identity*, all of which, though perfectly unlike his sensations, could not fail to be suggested by means of them. Such a being, then, might know all that we know of mind at present; and as his language would be appropriated to mind solely, and not borrowed by analogy from material phenomena, he would even possess important advantages over us in conducting the study of pneumatology.

From these observations it sufficiently appears what is the real amount of the celebrated doctrine, which refers the origin of all our knowledge to our sensations; and that, even granting it to be true, (which for my own part I am disposed to do, in the sense in which I have now explained it,) it would by no means follow from it, that our notions of the operations of mind, nor even many of those notions which are commonly suggested to us, *in the first instance*, by the perception of external objects, are *necessarily subsequent* to our knowledge of the qualities, or even of the existence of matter.

The remarks which I have offered on this doctrine will not appear superfluous to those who recollect that, although it has for many years past been a subject of controversy in England, it continues still to be implicitly adopted by the best philosophical writers in France; and that it has been employed by some of them to support the system of materialism, and by others to show that the intellectual distinctions between man and brutes arise entirely from the differences in their animal organization, and in their powers of external perception.[1]

SELECTION 6

Causation

It seems now to be pretty generally agreed among philosophers, that there is no instance in which we are able to perceive a necessary connexion between two successive events, or to comprehend in what manner the one proceeds from the other as its cause. From experience, indeed, we learn that there are many events which are constantly conjoined, so that the one invariably follows the other: but it is possible, for any thing we know to the contrary, that this connexion, though a constant one as far as our observation has reached, may not be a necessary

[1] [Stewart means respectively the French philosophers Denis Diderot (1713–84) and Claude Adrienne Helevétius (1715–71).]

connexion; nay, it is possible that there may be no necessary connexions among any of the phenomena we see: and, if there are any such connexions existing, we may rest assured that we shall never be able to discover them.

I shall endeavour to show, in another part of this work, that the doctrine I have now stated does not lead to these sceptical conclusions, concerning the existence of a First Cause, which an author of great ingenuity has attempted to deduce from it. At present, it is sufficient for my purpose to remark, that the word *cause* is used, both by philosophers and the vulgar, in two senses, which are widely different. When it is said, that every change in nature indicates the operation of a cause, the word *cause* expresses something which is supposed to be necessarily connected with the change; and without which it could not have happened. This may be called the *metaphysical* meaning of the word; and such causes may be called *metaphysical* or *efficient causes*. In natural philosophy, however, when we speak of one thing being the cause of another, all that we mean is that the two are constantly conjoined; so that when we see the one we may expect the other. These conjunctions we learn from experience alone; and without an acquaintance with them we could not accommodate our conduct to the established course of nature. The causes which are the objects of our investigation in natural philosophy, may, for the sake of distinction, be called *physical causes*.

I am very ready to acknowledge, that this doctrine, concerning the object of natural philosophy, is not altogether agreeable to popular prejudices. When a man, unaccustomed to metaphysical speculations, is told, for the first time, that the science of physics gives us no information concerning the efficient causes of the phenomena about which it is employed, he feels some degree of surprise and mortification. The natural bias of the mind is surely to conceive physical events as somehow linked together; and material substances, as possessed of certain powers and virtues, which fit them to produce particular effects. That we have no reason to believe this to be the case, has been shown in a very particular manner by Mr. Hume, and by other writers; and must, indeed, appear evident to every person, on a moment's reflection. It is a curious question, what gives rise to the prejudice?

In stating the argument for the existence of the Deity, several modern philosophers have been at pains to illustrate that law of our nature which leads us to refer every change we perceive in the universe, to the operation of an efficient cause. This reference is not the result of reasoning, but necessarily accompanies the perception, so as to render it impossible for us to see the change, without feeling a conviction of the operation of some cause by which it was produced; much in the same manner in which we find it to be impossible to conceive a sensation, without being impressed with a belief of the existence of a sentient being. Hence it is, I apprehend, that when we see two events constantly conjoined, we are led to associate the idea of causation, or efficiency, with the former, and to refer to it that power or energy by which the change was produced; in consequence of which association, we come to consider philosophy as the knowledge of efficient causes, and lose sight of the operation of mind, in producing the phenomena of nature. It is by an association somewhat similar, that we connect our sensations of colour with the primary qualities of body. A moment's reflection must satisfy anyone, that the sensation of colour can only reside in a mind; and yet our natural bias is surely to connect colour with extension and figure, and to conceive *white, blue,* and *yellow,* as something spread over the surfaces of bodies. In the same way we are led to associate with inanimate matter, the ideas of *power, force, energy,* and *causation,* which are all attributes of mind, and can exist in a mind only.

The bias of our nature is strengthened by another association. Our language, with respect to cause and effect, is borrowed by analogy from material objects. Some of these we see scattered about us, without any connexion between them; so that one of them may be removed from its place without disturbing the rest. We can, however, by means of some material *vinculum,* connect two or more objects together; so that whenever the one is moved, the others shall follow. In like manner, we see some events, which occasionally follow one another, and which are occasionally disjoined: we see others, where the succession is constant and invariable. The former we conceive to be analogous to objects which are loose, and unconnected with each other, and whose contiguity in place is owing merely to accidental position; the others to objects which are tied together by a material vinculum. Hence we transfer to such events, the same language which we apply to connected objects. We speak of a connexion between two events, and of a chain of causes and effects.

That this language is merely analogical, and that we know nothing of physical events but the laws which regulate their succession, must, I think, appear very obvious to every person who takes the trouble to reflect on the subject; and yet it is certain, that it has misled the greater part of philosophers, and has had a surprising influence on the systems which they have formed in very different departments of science.

A few remarks, on some of the mistaken conclusions to which the vulgar notions concerning the connexions among physical events have given rise, in natural philosophy, will illustrate clearly the origin of the common theories of perception; and will, at the same time, satisfy the reader with respect to the train of thought which suggested the foregoing observations.

The maxim, that nothing can act but where it is, and when it is, has always been admitted, with respect to metaphysical or efficient causes. "Whatever objects", says Mr. Hume, "are considered as causes or effects, are contiguous; and nothing can operate in a time or place, which is ever so little removed from those of its existence". "We may therefore (he adds) consider the relation of contiguity as essential to that of causation". But although this maxim should be admitted, with respect to causes which are efficient, and which, as such, are necessarily connected with their effects, there is surely no good reason for extending it to physical causes, of which we know nothing, but that they are the constant forerunners and signs of certain natural events. It may, indeed, be improper, according to this doctrine, to retain the expressions *cause* and *effect* in natural philosophy; but as long as the present language upon the subject continues in use, the propriety of its application, in any particular instance, does not depend on the contiguity of the two events in place or time, but solely on this question, whether the one event be the constant and invariable forerunner of the other, so that it may be considered as its infallible sign? Notwithstanding, however, the evidence of this conclusion, philosophers have in general proceeded upon a contrary supposition; and have discovered an unwillingness, even in physics, to call one event the cause of another, if the smallest interval of space or time existed between them. In the case of motion communicated by impulse, they have no scruple to call the impulse the cause of the motion; but they will not admit that one body can be the cause of motion in another, placed at a distance from it, unless a connexion is carried on between them, by means of some intervening medium.

...

Although, however, it be obvious on a moment's consideration, that we are as ignorant of the connexion between impulse and motion, as of the connexion between fire and any of the effects we see it produce, philosophers in every age seem to have considered the production of motion by impulse as almost the only physical fact which stood in need of no explanation. When we see one body attract another at a distance, our curiosity is roused, and we inquire how the connexion is carried on between them. But when we see a body begin to move in consequence of an impulse which another has given it, we inquire no farther; on the contrary, we think a fact sufficiently accounted for, if it can be shown to be a case of impulse. This distinction, between motion produced by impulse, and the other phenomena of nature, we are led in a great measure to make, by confounding together efficient and physical causes; and by applying to the latter, maxims which have properly a reference only to the former. Another circumstance, likewise, has probably considerable influence; that, as it is by means of impulse alone that we ourselves have a power of moving external objects, this fact is more familiar to us from our infancy than any other, and strikes us as a fact which is necessary, and which could not have happened otherwise. Some writers have even gone so far as to pretend that, although the experiment had never been made, the communication of motion by impulse might have been predicted by reasoning *a priori*.

From the following passage, in one of Sir Isaac Newton's letters to Dr. Bentley, it appears that he supposed the communication of motion by impulse to be a phenomenon much more explicable, than that a connexion should subsist between two bodies placed at a distance from each other without any intervening medium. "It is inconceivable", says he, "that inanimate brute matter should, without the mediation of something else which is not material, operate upon, and affect other matter without mutual contact, as it must do, if gravitation, in the sense of Epicurus, be essential and inherent in it. And this is one reason why I desired that you would not ascribe innate gravity to me. That gravity should be innate, inherent, and essential to matter, so that one body may act on another, through a vacuum, without the mediation of anything else, by and through which their action and force may be conveyed from one to another, is to me so great an absurdity, that I believe no man who has, in philosophical matters, a competent faculty of thinking, can ever fall into it."

With this passage I so far agree, as to allow that it is impossible to conceive in what manner one body acts on another at a distance, through a vacuum. But I cannot admit that it removes the difficulty to suppose that the two bodies are in actual contact. That one body may be the efficient cause of the motion of another body, placed at a distance from it, I do by no means assert; but only, that we have as good reason to believe that this may be possible, as to believe that any one natural event is the efficient cause of another.

I have been led into this very long disquisition, concerning efficient and physical causes, in order to point out the origin of the common theories of perception; all of which appear to me to have taken rise from the same prejudice, which I have already remarked to have had so extensive an influence upon the speculations of natural philosophers.

That, in the case of the perception of distant objects, we are naturally inclined to suspect either something to be emitted from the object to the organ of sense, or some medium to intervene between the object and organ, by means of which the former may communicate an impulse to the latter, appears from the common modes of expression on the subject, which are to be found in all languages. ... I think, however, it is evident that the existence of such a medium does not in any case appear *a priori*; and yet the natural prejudices of men have given rise to a universal belief of it, long before they were able to produce any good arguments in support of their opinion.

Nor is it only to account for the connexion between the object and the organ of sense, that philosophers have had recourse to the theory of impulse. They have imagined that the impression on the organ of sense is communicated to the mind in a similar manner. As one body produces a change in the state of another by impulse, so it has been supposed that the external object produces perception, (which is a change in the state of the mind,) first, by some material impression made on the organ of sense; and, secondly, by some material impression communicated from the organ to the mind, along the nerves and brain. These suppositions, indeed, as I had occasion already to hint, were, in the ancient theories of perception, rather implied than expressed; but by modern philosophers they have been stated in the form of explicit propositions.

...

All these theories appear to me to have taken their rise, first, from an inattention to the proper object of philosophy, and an application of the same general maxims to physical and to efficient causes; and, secondly, from an apprehension that we understand the connexion between impulse and motion better than any other physical fact. From the detail which I have given, it appears how extensive an influence this prejudice has had on the inquiries both of natural philosophers and of metaphysicians.

In the foregoing reasonings, I have taken for granted that motion may be produced by impulse; and have contented myself with asserting, that this fact is not more explicable than the motions which the Newtonians refer to gravitation; or than the intercourse which is carried on between the mind and external objects in the case of perception. The truth, however, is that some of the ablest philosophers in Europe are now satisfied, not only that there is no evidence of motion being in any case produced by the actual contact of two bodies, but that very strong proofs may be given of the absolute impossibility of such a supposition; and hence they have been led to conclude, that all the effects which are commonly referred to impulse, arise from a power of repulsion, extending to a small and imperceptible distance round every element of matter. If this doctrine shall be confirmed by future speculations in physics, it must appear to be a curious circumstance in the history of science, that philosophers have been so long occupied in attempting to trace all the phenomena of matter, and even some of the phenomena of mind, to a general fact, which, upon an accurate examination, is found to have no existence. I do not make this observation with a view to depreciate the labours of these philosophers; for although the system of Boscovich were completely established, it would not diminish, in the smallest degree, the value of those physical inquiries which have proceeded on the common hypothesis with respect to impulse. The laws which regulate the communication of motion in the case of apparent contact, are the most general facts we observe among the terrestrial phenomena; and they are, of all physical events, those which are the most familiar to us from our earliest infancy. It was therefore not only natural, but proper, that philosophers should begin their physical inquiries with attempting to refer to these, (which are the most general laws of nature, exposed to the examination of our senses,) the particular appearances they wished to explain. And if ever the theory of Boscovich should be completely established, it will have no other effect than to resolve these laws into some principle still more general, without affecting the solidity of the common doctrine so far as it goes.

SELECTION 7

Laws of Belief [and the Word 'Common Sense']

It is by the immediate evidence of consciousness that we are assured of the *present existence* of our various sensations, whether pleasant or painful; of all our affections, passions, hopes, fears, desires, and volitions. It is thus, too, we are assured of the *present existence* of those thoughts which, during our waking hours, are continually passing through the mind, and of all the different effects which they produce in furnishing employment to our intellectual faculties.

According to the common doctrine of our best philosophers, it is by the evidence of *consciousness* we are assured that we ourselves exist. The proposition, however, when thus stated, is not accurately true; for our own existence (as I have elsewhere observed[2]) is not a direct or immediate object of consciousness, in the strict and logical meaning of that term. We are conscious of sensation, thought, desire, volition; but we are not conscious of the existence of Mind itself; nor would it be possible for us to arrive at the knowledge of it, (supposing us to be created in the full possession of all the intellectual *capacities* which belong to human nature,) if no impression were ever to be made on our external senses. The moment that, in consequence of such an impression, a sensation is excited, we learn two facts at once: the existence of the sensation; and our own existence as sentient beings. In other words, the very first exercise of consciousness necessarily implies a belief, not only of the present existence of what is felt, but of the present existence of *that* which feels and thinks: or (to employ plainer language) the present existence of that being which I denote by the words *I* and *myself.* Of these facts, however, it is the former alone of which we can properly be said to be conscious, agreeably to the rigorous interpretation of the expression. A conviction of the latter, although it seems to be so inseparable from the exercise of consciousness, that it can scarcely be considered as posterior to it in the order of *time,* is yet (if I may be allowed to make use of a scholastic distinction) posterior to it in the order of *nature;* not only as it supposes consciousness to be already awakened by some sensation, or some other mental affection; but as it is evidently rather a judgment accompanying the exercise of that power, than one of its immediate intimations concerning its appropriate class of internal phenomena. It appears to me, therefore, more correct to call the belief of our own existence a concomitant or accessory of the exercise of consciousness, than to say that our existence is a fact falling under the immediate cognizance of consciousness, like the existence of the various agreeable or painful sensations which external objects excite in our minds.

2. That we cannot, without a very blameable latitude in the use of words, be said to be *conscious* of our personal identity, is a proposition

[2] *Philosophical Essays* [See selection 8.]

still more indisputable; inasmuch as the very idea of personal identity involves the idea of *time*, and consequently presupposes the exercise not only of *consciousness*, but of *memory*. The belief connected with this idea is implied in every thought and every action of the mind, and may be justly regarded as one of the simplest and most essential elements of the understanding. Indeed, it is impossible to conceive either an intellectual or an active being to exist without it. It is, however, extremely worthy of remark, with respect to this belief, that, universal as it is among our species, nobody but a metaphysician ever thinks of expressing it in words, or of reducing into the shape of a proposition the truth to which it relates. To the rest of mankind, it forms not an object of knowledge, but a condition or supposition, necessarily and unconsciously involved in the exercise of all their faculties. On a part of our constitution, which is obviously one of the last or primordial elements at which it is possible to arrive in analyzing our intellectual operations, it is plainly unphilosophical to suppose that any new light can be thrown by metaphysical discussion. All that can be done with propriety, in such cases, is to state the fact.

And here, I cannot help taking notice of the absurd and inconsistent attempts which some ingenious men have made, to explain the gradual process by which they suppose the mind to be led to the knowledge of its own existence, and of that continued identity which our constitution leads us to ascribe to it. How (it has been asked) does a child come to form the very abstract and metaphysical idea expressed by the pronoun *I* or *moi*? In answer to this question, I have only to observe, that when we set about the explanation of a phenomenon, we must proceed on the supposition that it is possible to resolve it into some more general law or laws with which we are already acquainted. But, in the case before us, how can this be expected, by those who consider that all our knowledge of mind is derived from the exercise of reflection; and that every act of this power implies a conviction of our own existence as reflecting and intelligent beings? Every theory, therefore, which pretends to account for this conviction, must necessarily involve that sort of paralogism which logicians call a *petitio principii*; inasmuch as it must resolve the thing to be explained into some law or laws, the evidence of which rests ultimately on the assumption in question. From this assumption, which is necessarily implied in the joint exercise of consciousness and memory, the philosophy of the human mind, if we mean to study it analytically, must of necessity set out; and the very attempt to dig deeper for its foundation, betrays a total ignorance of the logical rules, according to which alone it can ever be prosecuted with any hopes of success.

...

3. The belief which all men entertain of the existence of the material world, (I mean their belief of its existence independently of that of percipient beings,) and their expectation of the continued uniformity of the laws of nature, belong to the same class of ultimate or elemental laws of

thought, with those which have been just mentioned. The truths which form their objects are of an order so radically different from what are commonly called *truths*, in the popular acceptation of that word, that it might perhaps be useful for logicians to distinguish them by some appropriate appellation, such, for example, as that of *metaphysical* or *transcendental* truths. They are not *principles* or *data* (as will afterwards appear) from which any consequence can be deduced; but form a part of those original *stamina* of human reason, which are equally essential to all the pursuits of science, and to all the active concerns of life.

4. I shall only take notice farther, under this head, of the confidence which we must necessarily repose in the evidence of memory, (and, I may add, in the continuance of our personal identity,) when we are employed in carrying on any process of deduction or argumentation, in following out, for instance, the steps of a long mathematical demonstration. In yielding our assent to the conclusion to which such a demonstration leads, we evidently trust to the fidelity with which our memory has connected the different links of the chain together. The reference which is often made, in the course of a demonstration, to propositions formerly proved, places the same remark in a light still stronger; and shows plainly that, in this branch of knowledge, which is justly considered as the most certain of any, the authority of the same laws of belief which are recognised in the ordinary pursuits of life, is tacitly acknowledged. Deny the evidence of memory as a ground of certain knowledge, and you destroy the foundations of mathematical science as completely as if you were to deny the truth of the axioms assumed by Euclid.

The foregoing examples sufficiently illustrate the nature of that class of truths which I have called *Fundamental Laws of Human Belief*, or *Primary Elements of Human Reason*. A variety of others, not less important, might be added to the list[3]; but these I shall not at present stop to enumerate, as my chief object, in introducing the subject here, was to explain the common relation in which they all stand to deductive evidence. In this point of view, two analogies, or rather coincidences, between the truths which we have been last considering, and the mathematical axioms which were treated of formerly, immediately present themselves to our notice.

1. From neither of these classes of truths can any direct inference be drawn for the farther enlargement of our knowledge. This remark has been already shown to hold universally with respect to the axioms of geometry; and it applies equally to what I have called Fundamental Laws of Human Belief. From such propositions as these—*I exist; I am the same person to-day that I was yesterday; the material world has an existence independent of my mind; the general laws of nature will continue, in future, to operate uniformly as in time past*—no inference can be deduced, any more

---

[3] Such, for example, as our belief of the existence of *efficient* causes; our belief of the existence of other intelligent beings besides ourselves, &c. &c.

than from the intuitive truths prefixed to the *Elements* of Euclid. Abstracted from other *data,* they are perfectly barren in themselves; nor can any possible combination of them help the mind forward one single step in its progress. It is for this reason that, instead of calling them, with some other writers, *first principles,* I have distinguished them by the title of *fundamental laws of belief;* the former word seeming to me to denote, according to common usage, some *fact,* or some *supposition,* from which a series of consequences may be deduced.

If the account now given of these *laws of belief* be just, the great argument which has been commonly urged in support of their authority, and which manifestly confounds them with what are properly called *principles of reasoning,* is not at all applicable to the subject; or at least does not rest the point in dispute upon its right foundation. If there were no first principles, (it has been said,) or in other words, if a reason could be given for everything, no process of deduction could possibly be brought to a conclusion. The remark is indisputably true; but it only proves (what no logician of the present times will venture to deny) that the mathematician could not demonstrate a single theorem, unless he were first allowed to lay down his definitions; nor the natural philosopher explain or account for a single phenomenon, unless he were allowed to assume, as acknowledged facts, certain general laws of nature. What inference does this afford in favour of that particular class of truths to which the preceding observations relate, and against which the ingenuity of modern sceptics has been more particularly directed? If I be not deceived, these truths are still more intimately connected with the operations of the reasoning faculty than has been generally imagined; not as the *principles* from which our reasonings set out, and on which they ultimately depend, but as the necessary *conditions* on which every step of the deduction tacitly proceeds; or rather (if I may use the expression) as essential elements which enter into the composition of reason itself.

2. In this last remark I have anticipated, in some measure, what I had to state with respect to the *second* coincidence alluded to, between mathematical axioms, and the other propositions which I have comprehended under the general title of *fundamental laws of human belief.* As the truth of axioms is virtually presupposed or implied in the successive steps of every demonstration, so, in every step of our reasonings concerning the order of Nature, we proceed on the supposition, that the laws by which it is regulated will continue uniform as in time past; and that the material universe has an existence independent of our perceptions. I need scarcely add that, in all our reasonings whatever, whether they relate to necessary or to contingent truths, our own personal identity, and the evidence of memory, are virtually taken for granted. These different truths all agree in this, that they are essentially involved in the exercise of our rational powers; although, in themselves, they furnish no *principles* or *data* by which the sphere of our knowledge can, by any ingenuity, be enlarged. They agree farther in being tacitly acknowledged by

all men, learned or ignorant, without any formal enunciation in words, or even any conscious exercise of reflection. It is only at that period of our intellectual progress when scientific arrangements and metaphysical refinements begin to be introduced, that they become objects of attention to the mind, and assume the form of propositions.

...

Corresponding to the extension which some late writers have given to *axioms*, is that of the province which they have assigned to *intuition*; a term which has been applied, by Dr. Beattie and others, not only to the power by which we perceive the truth of the axioms of geometry, but to that by which we recognise the authority of the fundamental laws of belief, when we hear them enunciated in language. My only objection to this use of the word is that it is a departure from common practice; according to which, if I be not mistaken, the proper objects of intuition are propositions analogous to the axioms prefixed to Euclid's *Elements*. In some other respects, this innovation might perhaps be regarded as an improvement on the very limited and imperfect vocabulary of which we are able to avail ourselves in our present discussions.

To the class of truths which I have here called *laws of belief*, or *elements of reason*, the title of *principles of common sense* was long ago given by Father Buffier,[4] whose language and doctrine concerning them bears a very striking resemblance to those of some of our later Scottish logicians. This, at least, strikes me as the meaning which these writers *in general* annex to the phrase, although all of them have frequently employed it with a far greater degree of latitude. When thus limited in its acceptation, it is obviously liable, in point of scientific accuracy, to two very strong objections, both of which have been already sufficiently illustrated. The first is, that it applies the appellation of *principles* to laws of belief from which no inference can be deduced; the second, that it refers the origin of these laws to Common Sense. Nor is this phraseology more agreeable to popular use than to logical precision. If we were to suppose an individual, whose conduct betrayed a disbelief of his own existence, or of his own identity, or of the reality of surrounding objects, it would by no means amount to an adequate description of his condition to say, that he was destitute of *common sense*. We should at once pronounce him to be destitute of *reason*, and would no longer consider him as a fit subject of discipline or of punishment. The former expression, indeed, would only imply that he was apt to fall into absurdities and improprieties in the common concerns of life. To denominate, therefore, such laws of belief as we have now been considering, *constituent elements of human reason*, while it seems quite unexceptionable in point of technical distinct-

[4] [Claude Buffier (1661-1737) French Jesuit author of *Traité de première vérités et de la source des nos jugements*, (1724) (*Treatise on First Truths and the Origins of our Judgements*).]

ness, cannot be justly censured as the slightest deviation from our habitual forms of speech. On the same grounds, it may be fairly questioned, whether the word *reason* would not, on some occasions, be the best substitute which our language affords for *intuition*, in that enlarged acceptation which has been given to it of late. If not quite so definite and precise as might be wished, it would be at least employed in one of those significations in which it is already familiar to every ear; whereas the meaning of *intuition*, when used for the same purpose, is stretched very far beyond its ordinary limits. And in cases of this sort, where we have to choose between two terms, neither of which is altogether unexceptionable, it will be found much safer to trust to the context for restricting in the reader's mind what is too general, than for enlarging what use has accustomed us to interpret in a sense too narrow.

***

The criticisms which have been made on what Dr. Reid has written concerning the intuitive truths which he distinguishes by the title of *Principles of Common Sense*, would require a more ample discussion than I can now bestow on them; not that the importance of these criticisms (of such of them, at least, as I have happened to meet with) demands a long or elaborate refutation; but because the subject, according to the view I wish to take of it, involves some other questions of great moment and difficulty, relative to the foundations of human knowledge. ...

That the doctrine in question has been, in some publications, presented in a very exceptionable form, I most readily allow; nor would I be understood to subscribe to it implicitly, even as it appears in the works of Dr. Reid. It is but an act of justice to him, however, to request that his opinions may be judged of from his own works alone, not from those of others who may have happened to coincide with him in certain tenets, or in certain modes of expression; and that, before any ridicule be attempted on his conclusions concerning the authority of Common Sense, his antagonists would take the trouble to examine in what acceptation he has employed that phrase.

...

One of the first writers who introduced the phrase *Common Sense* into the technical or appropriate language of logic, was Father Buffier, in a book entitled, *Traité des Premières Vérités*. It has since been adopted by several authors of note in this country, particularly by Dr. Reid, Dr. Oswald, and Dr. Beattie; by all of whom, however, I am afraid, it must be confessed, it has been occasionally employed without a due attention to precision. The last of these writers uses it to denote that power by which the mind perceives the truth of any intuitive proposition; whether it be an axiom of abstract science, or a statement of some fact resting on the immediate information of consciousness, of perception, or of memory, or one of those fundamental laws of belief which are implied in the application of our faculties to the ordinary business of life. The same extensive use of the word may, I believe, be found in the other authors just mentioned. But no authority can justify such a laxity in the employment of language in philosophical discussions; for, if mathematical axioms be (as they are manifestly and indisputably) a class of propositions essentially distinct from the other kinds of intuitive truths now described, why refer them all indiscriminately to the same principle in our constitution? If this phrase, therefore, be at all retained, precision requires that it should be employed in a more limited acceptation; and, accordingly, in the works under our consideration, it is appropriated most frequently, though by no means uniformly, to that class of Intuitive Truths which I have already called "Fundamental Laws of Belief". When thus restricted, it conveys a notion, unambiguous at least, and definite; and, consequently, the question about its propriety or impropriety turns entirely on the coincidence of this definition with the meaning of the word as employed in ordinary discourse. Whatever objections, therefore, may be stated to the expression as now defined, will apply to it with additional force when used with the latitude which has been already censured.

I have said, that the question about the propriety of the phrase *Common Sense,* as employed by philosophers, must be decided by an appeal to general practice. For, although it be allowable and even necessary for a philosopher, to limit the acceptation of words which are employed vaguely in common discourse, it is always dangerous to give to a word a scientific meaning essentially distinct from that in which it is usually understood. It has, at least, the effect of misleading those who do not enter deeply into the subject; and of giving a paradoxical appearance to doctrines, which, if expressed in more unexceptionable terms, would be readily admitted.

It appears to me that this has actually happened in the present instance. The phrase *Common Sense,* as it is generally understood, is nearly synonymous with *Mother-wit;* denoting that degree of sagacity (depending partly on original capacity, and partly on personal experience and observation) which qualifies an individual for those simple and essential occupations which all men are called on to exercise habitually by their common nature. In this acceptation, it is opposed to those mental acquirements which are derived from a regular education and from the study of books; and refers, not to the speculative convictions of the understanding, but to that prudence and discretion which are the foundation of successful conduct. ...

To speak, accordingly, of appealing from the conclusions of philosophy to common sense, had the appearance, to title-page readers, of appealing from the verdict of the learned to the voice of the multitude; or of attempting to silence free discussion, by a reference to some arbitrary and undefinable standard, distinct from any of the intellectual powers hitherto enumerated by logicians. Whatever countenance may be supposed to have been given by some writers to such an interpretation of this doctrine, I may venture to assert, that none is afforded by the works of Dr. Reid. The standard to which he appeals is neither the creed of a particular sect, nor the inward light of enthusiastic presumption, but that constitution of human nature without which all the business of the world would immediately cease; and the substance of his argument amounts merely to this, that those essential laws of belief, to which sceptics have objected when considered in connexion with our scientific reasonings, are implied in every step we take as active beings; and if called in question by any man in his practical concerns, would expose him universally to the charge of insanity.

In stating this important doctrine, it were perhaps to be wished, that the subject had been treated with somewhat more of analytical accuracy; and it is certainly to be regretted, that a phrase should have been employed so well calculated by its ambiguity to furnish a convenient handle to misrepresentations; but in the judgment of those who have perused Dr. Reid's writings with an intelligent and candid attention, these misrepresentations must recoil on their authors; while they who are really interested in the progress of useful science, will be disposed rather to lend their aid in supplying what is defective in his views, than to reject hastily a doctrine which aims, by the development of some logical principles, overlooked in the absurd systems which have been bestowed from the schools, to vindicate the authority of truths intimately and extensively connected with human happiness.

SELECTION 8

Personal Identity

In speculating concerning any of the intellectual phenomena, it is of essential importance constantly to recollect, that, as our knowledge of the material world is derived entirely from our External Senses, so all our knowledge of the Human Mind is derived from Consciousness. As to the blind or the deaf, no words can convey the notions of particular colours, or of particular sounds; so to a being who had never been conscious of sensation, memory, imagination, pleasure, pain, hope, fear, love, hatred, no intelligible description could be given of the import of these terms. They all express *simple* ideas or notions, which are perfectly familiar to every person who is able to turn his thoughts inwards, and which we never fail to involve in obscurity when we attempt to define them.

The habits of inattention which all men contract, in their early years, to the operations of their own minds, have been pointed out by various writers, as the most powerful of all obstacles to the progress of our inquiries concerning the theory of human nature. These habits, it has also been remarked, are to be conquered only by the most persevering industry in accustoming the thoughts to turn themselves at pleasure to the phenomena of this internal world; an effort by no means easy to any individual, and to a large proportion of mankind almost impracticable. ...To this power of directing the attention steadily and accurately to the phenomena of thought, Mr. Locke and his followers have very properly given the name of *Reflexion*. It bears precisely the same relation to *Consciousness* which *Observation* does to *Perception*; the former supplying us with the facts which form the only solid basis of the Science of Mind, as we are indebted to the latter for the ground-work of the whole fabric of Natural Philosophy.

With respect to the exercise of Reflection, the following precept of an old-fashioned writer is so judicious, and the caution it suggests of so great moment in the inquiries on which we are about to enter, that I shall make no apology for introducing it here, although not more immediately connected with the subject of the present Essay, than with those of all the others contained in this volume.

"When I speak", says Crousaz, in his *Art of Thinking*, "of desire, contentment, trouble, apprehension, doubt, certainty; of affirming, denying, approving, blaming; I pronounce words, the meaning of which I distinctly understand, and yet I do not represent the things spoken of under any image or corporeal form. While the intellect, however, is thus busy about its own phenomena, the imagination is also at work in presenting its analogical theories; but so far from aiding us, it only misleads our steps, and retards our progress. Would you know what thought is? It is precisely that which passes within you when you think: stop but here, and you are sufficiently informed. But the imagination, eager to proceed farther, would gratify our curiosity by comparing it to fire, to vapour, or to other active and subtile principles in the material world. And to what can all this tend, but to divert our attention from what thought is, and to fix it upon what it is not?"

The belief which accompanies Consciousness, as to the *present existence* of its appropriate phenomena, has been commonly considered as much less obnoxious to cavil, than any of the other principles which philosophers are accustomed to assume as self-evident, in the formation of their metaphysical systems. No doubts on this head have yet been suggested by any philosopher how sceptical soever, even by those who have called in question the existence both of mind and of matter: And yet the fact is, that it rests on no foundation more solid than our belief of the existence of external objects; or our belief, that other men possess intellectual powers and faculties similar to those of which we are conscious in ourselves. In all these cases, the only account that can be given of our belief is, that it forms a necessary part of our constitution; against which metaphysicians may easily argue so as to perplex the judgment, but of which it is impossible to divest ourselves for a moment, when called on to employ our reason, either in the business of life, or in the pursuits of science. While we are under the influence of our appetites, passions, or affections, or even of a strong speculative curiosity, all those difficulties which bewildered us in the solitude of the closet vanish before the essential principles of the human frame.

According to the common doctrine of our best philosophers, it is by the evidence of *consciousness* we are assured that we ourselves exist. The proposition, however, when thus stated, is not accurately true; for our own existence is not a direct or immediate object of consciousness, in the strict and logical meaning of that term. We are conscious of sensation, thought, desire, volition; but we are not conscious of the existence of mind itself; nor would it be possible for us to arrive at the knowledge of it, (supposing us to be created in the full possession of all the intellectual *capacities* that belong to human nature,) if no impression were ever to be made on our external senses. The moment that, in consequence of such an impression, a sensation is excited, we learn two facts at once: the existence of the sensation, and our own existence as sentient beings. In other words, the very first exercise of consciousness necessarily implies a belief, not only of the present existence of what is felt, but of the present existence of *that* which feels and thinks; or (to employ plainer language) the present existence of that being which I denote by the words *I* and *myself*. Of these facts, however, it is the former alone of which we can properly be said to be conscious, agreeably to the rigorous interpretation of the expression. The latter is made known to us by a suggestion of the understanding *consequent* on the sensation, but so intimately *connected* with it, that it is not surprising that our belief of both should be generally referred to the same origin.

If this distinction be just, the celebrated enthymeme of Descartes, *Cogito, ergo sum*, does not deserve *all* the ridicule bestowed on it by those writers who have represented the author as attempting to demonstrate his own existence by a process of reasoning. To me it seems more probable, that he meant chiefly to direct the attention of his readers to a circumstance which must be allowed to be not unworthy of notice in the history of the Human Mind; the impossibility of our ever having learned the fact of our own existence, without some sensation being excited in the mind, to awaken the faculty of thinking.

As the belief of our *present existence* necessarily accompanies every act of consciousness, so, from a comparison of the sensations and thoughts of which we are *now* conscious, with those of which we recollect to have been conscious formerly, we are impressed with an irresistible conviction of our *personal identity*. Notwithstanding the strange difficulties that have been raised upon the subject, I cannot conceive any conviction more complete than this, nor any truth more intelligible to all, whose understandings have not been perplexed by metaphysical speculations. The objections founded on the change of substance in certain material objects to which we continue to apply the same name, are plainly not applicable to the question concerning the identity of the same person, or of the same thinking being; inasmuch as the words *sameness* and *identity* are here used in different senses. Of the meaning of these words, when applied to persons, I confess I am not able to give a logical definition; but neither can I define sensation, memory, volition, nor even existence; and if anyone should bring himself by this and other scholastic subtleties to conclude, that he has no interest in making provision for tomorrow, because *personality is not a permanent, but a transient thing*, I can think of no argument to convince him of his error.

But although it is by Consciousness and Memory that the sameness of our being is ascertained to ourselves, it is by no means correct to say with Locke, that *consciousness constitutes personal identity*; a doctrine which, as Butler justly remarks, "involves, as an obvious consequence, that a person has not existed a single moment, nor done one action but what he can remember; indeed, none but what he reflects upon". "One should really think it self-evident", as the same author further remarks, "that consciousness of personal identity presupposes, and therefore cannot constitute, personal identity, any more than knowledge, in any other case, constitutes those truths which are its own objects". The previous existence of the *truths* is manifestly implied in the very supposition of their being *objects* of knowledge.

While, however, I assent completely to the substance of these acute and important strictures upon Locke's doctrine, I think it necessary to observe that the language of Butler himself is far from being unexceptionable. He speaks of *our consciousness of personal identity*; whereas it must appear evident, upon a moment's reflection, even to those who acquiesce in the common statement which ascribes *immediately* to consciousness our belief of our *present existence*, that our belief of our *personal identity* presupposes, over and above this knowledge, the exercise of *memory*, and the idea of *time*.

The importance of attending carefully to the distinction between the phenomena which are the *immediate objects* of Consciousness, and the concomitant notions and truths which are *suggested* to our thoughts by these phenomena, will appear from the considerations to be stated in the next chapter; in following which, however, I must request my readers to remember, that the distinction becomes important merely from the palpable refutation it affords of the prevailing theory concerning the origin of our knowledge; and not from any difference between the two classes of truths, in point of evidence.

It was already observed, that it is from Consciousness, or rather from Reflection, that we derive all our notions of the faculties and operations of the Mind; and that, in analyzing these, we must lay our account with arriving, sooner or later, at certain simple notions or ideas, which we have no means of conveying to others, but by teaching those to whom our reasonings are addressed, how to direct their attention with accuracy to what passes within them. These mental phenomena form the direct and appropriate subjects of Consciousness; and, indeed, the *only* direct and appropriate subjects of Consciousness, in the strict acceptation of that word.

It must not, however, be concluded from this, that the proper subjects of consciousness (when the phrase is *thus* understood) comprehend all the simple notions or ideas about which the science of mind is conversant; far less (as some philosophers have imagined) that they comprehend all the elements into which human knowledge may, in the last result, be analyzed. Not to mention such notions as those of Extension and Figure, (both of which are inseparable concomitants of some of our external perceptions, and which certainly bear no *resemblance* to anything of which we are conscious within ourselves,) there is a great variety of others so connected with our different intellectual faculties, that the exercise of the faculty may be justly regarded as a condition indispensably necessary to account for the first origin of the notion. Thus, by a mind destitute of the faculty of *memory*, neither the ideas of *time*, nor of *motion*, nor of *personal identity*, could possibly have been formed; ideas which are confessedly among the most familiar of all those we possess, and which cannot be traced immediately to *consciousness*, by any effort of logical subtlety. In like manner, without the faculty of *abstraction*, we never could have formed the idea of *number*, nor of *lines, surfaces, and solids*, as they are considered by the mathematician; nor would it have been possible for us to comprehend the meaning of such words as *classes* or *assortments*, or, indeed, of anyone of the grammatical *parts of speech*, but proper names. Without the power of *reason* or *understanding*, it is no less evident, that no comment could have helped us to unriddle the import of the words, *truth, certainty, probability, theorem, premises, conclusion*; nor of anyone of those which express the various sorts of *relation* which fall under our knowledge. In such cases, all that can be said is, that the exercise of a particular faculty furnishes the *occasion* on which certain simple notions are, by the laws of our constitution, presented to our thoughts; nor does it seem possible for us to trace the origin of a particular notion any farther, than to ascertain what the nature of the *occasion* was, which, in the first instance, introduced it to our acquaintance.

The conclusions we thus form concerning the Origin of our Knowledge, constitute what may be properly called the *First Chapter* of the Natural History of the Human Mind. They constitute, at the same time, the only solid basis of a rational Logic; of that part of logic, more especially, which relates to the theory of Evidence. In the order of investigation, however, they necessarily *presuppose* such analysis of the faculties of the mind as I have attempted in another work;[5] a consideration of which I do not know that any logical writer has been hitherto aware, and to which I must request my readers carefully to attend, before they pass a judgment on the plan I have followed in the arrangement of my philosophical speculations.

---

[5] [*Elements*, especially in vol. 1. See here selections 11, 12, 13.]

SELECTION 9

External World

It is well known to all who have the slightest acquaintance with the history of philosophy, that among the various topics on which the ancient Sceptics exercised their ingenuity, the question concerning the existence of the Material World was always a favourite subject of disputation. Some doubts on the same point occur even in the writings of philosophers, whose general leaning seems to have been to the opposite extreme of dogmatism. Plato himself has given them some countenance, by hinting it as a thing not quite impossible, that human life is a continued sleep, and that all our thoughts are only dreams. This scepticism (which I am inclined to think most persons have occasionally experienced in their early years) proceeds on principles totally different from the doctrine of Berkeley, who asserts, with the most dogmatical confidence, that the existence of matter is *impossible,* and that the very supposition of it is absurd. "The existence of bodies out of a mind perceiving them," he tells us explicitly, "is not only impossible, and a contradiction in terms; but were it possible, and even real, it were impossible we should ever know it."

The attempt of Berkeley to disprove the existence of the Material World, took its rise from the attempt of Descartes to demonstrate the truth of the contrary proposition. Both undertakings were equally unphilosophical; for, to argue in favour of any of the fundamental laws of human belief is not less absurd than to call them in question. In this argument, however, it must be granted, that Berkeley had the advantage; the conclusion which he formed being unavoidable, if the common principles be admitted on which they both proceeded. It was reserved for Dr. Reid to show, that these principles are not only unsupported by proof, but contrary to incontestable facts; nay, that they are utterly inconceivable, from the manifest inconsistencies and absurdities which they involve. All this he has placed in so clear and strong a light, that Dr. Priestley, the most acute of his antagonists, has found nothing to object to his argument, but that it is directed against a phantom of his own creation, and that the opinions which he combats were never seriously maintained by any philosophers, ancient or modern.

With respect to Mr. Hume, who is commonly considered as an advocate for Berkeley's system, the remarks which I have offered on the latter writer must be understood with great limitations. For, although his fundamental principles lead necessarily to Berkeley's conclusion, and although he has frequently drawn from them this conclusion himself, yet, on other occasions, he relapses into the language of doubt, and only speaks of the existence of the Material World as a thing of which we have no satisfactory evidence. The truth is, that whereas Berkeley was sincerely and *bona fide* an idealist, Hume's leading object, in his metaphysical writings, plainly was to inculcate a universal scepticism. In this respect the real scope of his arguments has, I think, been misunderstood by most, if not by all, of his opponents. It evidently was *not,* as they seem to have supposed, to exalt *reasoning* in preference to our instinctive principles of belief; but by illustrating the contradictory conclusions to which our different faculties lead, to involve the whole subject in the same suspicious darkness. In other words, his aim was not to *interrogate* Nature, with a view to the discovery of truth, but by a *cross-examination* of Nature, to involve her in such contradictions as might set aside the whole of her evidence as good for nothing.

With respect to Berkeley, on the other hand, it appears from his writings, not only that he considered his scheme of idealism as resting on demonstrative proof, but as more agreeable to the common apprehensions of mankind, than the prevailing theories of philosophers, concerning the independent existence of the Material World. "If the principles", he observes in the Preface to his *Dialogues,* "which I here endeavour to propagate, are admitted for true, the consequences which I think evidently flow from them are, that atheism and scepticism will be utterly destroyed; many intricate points made plain; great difficulties solved; speculation referred to practice; and men reduced from paradoxes to common sense".

...

The observations which have been made on the scope of Berkeley's argument may serve, at the same time, to illustrate that of Dr. Reid's reply to it, which has been, in general, strangely misunderstood. In order to have a just idea of this, it is necessary always to bear in mind, that it is not directed against the sceptical suggestions of the Pyrrhonists, but against Berkeley's inferences from Locke's principles; or rather, against the principles from which these inferences were deduced. The object of the author is not to bring forward any new proofs that Matter does exist, nor (as has been often very uncandidly affirmed) to cut short all discussion upon this question, by an unphilosophical appeal to popular belief; but to overturn the pretended demonstration, that Matter *does not* exist, by exposing the futility and absurdity of the principles which it assumes as *data.* That from these *data* (which had been received, during a long succession of ages, as incontrovertible articles of faith) both Berkeley and Hume have reasoned with unexceptionable fairness, as well as incomparable acuteness, he acknowledges in every page of his works; and only asserts, that the force of their conclusion is annihilated by the falseness and inconsistency of the hypothesis on which it rests. It is to *reasoning,* therefore, and to *reasoning* alone, that he appeals, in combating their doctrines; and the ground of his objection to these doctrines is, *not* that they evince a blameable freedom and boldness of discussion, but that their authors had suffered themselves too easily to be carried along by the received dogmas of the schools.

The very gross misapprehensions which have taken place with respect to the scope of Dr. Reid's book have probably been owing, in part, to the unfortunate title which he prefixed to it, of *An Inquiry into the Human Mind, on the Principles of Common Sense.* So far, however, from meaning, by that phrase, to intimate a more than due respect for the established opinions of any particular sect or party, it must appear evident, to those who have taken the trouble to read the work, that his sole intention was to disclaim that implicit reverence for the current maxims and current phraseology of the learned, which had so widely misled his two illustrious predecessors, Berkeley and Hume; to assert, in this most important branch of science, an unlimited right of free inquiry; and to set an example of this freedom, by appealing from Locke's fundamental hypothesis (a hypothesis for which no argument can be produced but the authority of schoolmen) to the unbiased *reason* of the human race. It is this *common reason of mankind* which he uniformly represents as the ultimate standard of truth; and of its decisions he forms his estimate, neither from the suffrages of the learned nor of the ignorant, but from those Fundamental Laws of Belief which are manifested in the universal conduct of mankind, in all ages and countries of the world; and to the guidance of which the speculative sceptic must necessarily submit, the very moment he quits the solitude of the closet. It is not, therefore, vulgar prejudice that he wishes to oppose to philosophical speculation, but the essential principles of the human understanding to the gratuitous assumptions of metaphysical theorists. But on this topic I intend to explain myself more fully on a future occasion.

While Reid, however, in his controversy with Hume and Berkeley, thus opposes argument to argument, he does not follow the example of Descartes, in attempting to confirm our belief of the existence of matter, by the aid of deductive evidence. All such evidence, he justly observes, must necessarily take for granted some principles not more certain nor more obvious than the thing to be proved; and therefore, can add nothing to its authority with men who have duly weighed the nature of reasoning and of demonstrative proof. Nor is this all. Where scepticism is founded on a suspicion of the possible fallibility of the human faculties, the very idea of correcting it by an appeal to argument is nugatory; inasmuch as such an appeal virtually takes for granted the paramount authority of those laws of belief which the sceptic calls in question. The belief, therefore, of the existence of Matter, is left by Dr. Reid on the very same footing on which Descartes found it; open, as it then was, and as it must for ever remain, to the sceptical cavils which affect equally every judgment which the human mind is capable of forming; but freed completely from those metaphysical objections which assailed it, as at variance with the conclusions of philosophy.

But although, in so far as the argument of the *Berkeleians* is concerned, Dr. Reid's reasonings appear to me to be unanswerable, I am not completely satisfied that he has stated *the fact* on his own side of the question with sufficient fullness and correctness. …

…

I have already said, that Reid's account of the existence of Matter, although correct so far as it goes, does not embrace all the circumstances of the question. The grounds of this observation I shall endeavour to explain with all possible brevity; but, before proceeding to the discussion, it is necessary to premise some remarks on a principle of our constitution, which may at first sight appear very foreign to the present argument; I mean, *our belief of the permanence or stability of the order of nature.*

That all our physical reasonings, and all those observations on the course of events, which lay the foundation of *foresight* or *sagacity*, imply an expectation, that the order of things will, in time to come, continue similar to what we have experienced it to be in time past, is a fact too obvious to stand in need of illustration; but it is not equally clear *how this expectation arises* at first in the mind. Mr. Hume resolves it into the *association of ideas*, which leads us, after having seen two events often conjoined, to anticipate the second, whenever we see the first, a theory to which a very strong objection immediately presents itself: That a single experiment is sufficient to create as strong a belief of the constancy of the result as ten thousand. When a philosopher repeats an experiment for the sake of greater certainty, his hesitation does not proceed from any doubt, that, in the same circumstances, the same phenomena will be exhibited; but from an apprehension, that he may not have attended duly to all the different circumstances in which the first experiment was made. If the second experiment should differ in its result from the first, he will not suspect that any change has taken place in the laws of nature; but will instantly conclude, that the circumstances attending the two experiments have not been exactly the same.

It will be said, perhaps, that although our belief in this instance is not founded on a repetition of one single experiment, it is founded on a long course of experience with respect to the order of nature in general. We have learned, from a number of cases formerly examined, that this order continues uniform; and we apply this deduction as a rule to guide our anticipations of the result of every new experiment that we make. This opinion is supported by Dr. Campbell in his *Philosophy of Rhetoric;* but it seems to me to afford a very unsatisfactory solution of the difficulty. It plainly differs essentially from Mr. Hume's theory; for it states the fact in such a manner, as excludes the possibility of accounting for it by the *association of ideas;* while, at the same time, it suggests no other principle, by means of which any plausible explanation of it may be obtained. Granting, at present, for the sake of argument, that, after having seen a stone often fall, the associating principle alone might lead me to expect a similar event when I drop another stone; the question still recurs, (supposing my experiments to have been hitherto limited to the descent of heavy bodies): Whence arises my anticipation of the result of a pneumatical, an optical, or a chemical experiment? According, therefore, to Campbell's doctrine, we must here employ a process of analogical reasoning. The course of nature has been found uniform in all our experiments concerning heavy bodies; and therefore we may conclude by analogy, that it will also be uniform in all other experiments we may devise, whatever be the class of phenomena to which they relate. It is difficult to suppose, that such a process of reasoning should occur to children or savages; and yet I apprehend, that a child who had once burned his finger with a candle, would dread the same result, if the same operation were to be repeated. Nor, indeed, would the case be different, in similar circumstances, with one of the lower animals.

...

From these observations it seems to follow, that our expectation of the continuance of the laws of nature is not the result of the Association of Ideas, nor of any other principle generated by experience alone; and Mr. Hume has shown, with demonstrative evidence, that it cannot be resolved into any process of reasoning *a priori*. Till, therefore, some more satisfactory analysis of it shall appear than has yet been proposed, we are unavoidably led to state it as an original law of human belief. In doing so, I am not influenced by any wish to multiply unnecessarily original laws or ultimate truths; nor by any apprehension of the consequences that might result from an admission of anyone of the theories in question. They are all of them, so far as I can see, equally harmless in their tendency, but all of them equally unfounded and nugatory, answering no purpose whatever, but to draw a veil over ignorance, and to divert the attention, by the parade of a theoretical phraseology, from a plain and most important fact in the constitution of the Mind.

In treating of a very different subject, I had occasion, in a former work, to refer to some philosophical opinions of Mr. Turgot, coinciding nearly with those which I have now stated. These opinions are detailed by the author, at considerable length, in the article *Existence* of the French *Encyclopédie*; but a conciser and clearer account of them may be found in Condorcet's discourse, prefixed to his Essay *On the application of analysis to the probability of decisions pronounced by a majority of votes.* From this account it appears, that Turgot resolved "our belief of the existence of the Material World" into our belief of the continuance of "the laws of nature"; or, in other words, that he conceived our belief, in the former of these instances, to amount merely to a conviction of the established order of physical events, and to an expectation that, in the same combination of circumstances, the same event will recur. It has always appeared to me, that something of this sort was necessary to complete Dr. Reid's speculations on the Berkeleian controversy; for although he has shown our notions concerning the primary qualities of bodies to be connected, by an original law of our constitution, with the sensation which they excite in our minds, he has taken no notice of the grounds of our belief that these qualities have an existence *independent* of our perceptions. This belief is plainly the result of *experience;* inasmuch as a *repetition* of the perceptive act must have been prior to any judgment on our part, with respect to the separate and permanent reality of its object. Nor does *experience* itself afford a complete solution of the problem; for, as we are irresistibly led by our perceptions to ascribe to their objects a *future* as well as a present reality, the question still remains, how are we determined by the experience of *the past,* to carry our inference forward to a portion of time which is yet to come? To myself, the difficulty appears to resolve itself, in the simplest and most philosophical manner, into that law of our constitution to which Turgot long ago attempted to trace it.

If this conclusion be admitted, our conviction of the permanent and independent existence of Matter is but a particular case of a more general law of belief extending to all other phenomena. The generalization seems to me to be equally ingenious and just; and while it coincides perfectly in its spirit and tendency with Reid's doctrine on the same point, to render that doctrine at once more precise and more luminous.

...

I have yet another criticism to offer on Dr. Reid's reasonings with respect to *Perception,* a criticism not founded upon any flaw in his argument, but upon his inattention, in enumerating the *Primary Qualities of Matter,* to a very essential distinction among the particulars comprehended in his list; by stating which distinction, he might, in my opinion, have rendered his conclusions much more clear and satisfactory.

Into this oversight Dr. Reid was very naturally led by the common arrangement of his immediate predecessors; most of whom, since the time of Locke, have classed together, under the general title of *Primary Qualities,* Hardness, Softness, Roughness, Smoothness, &c., with *Extension, Figure,* and *Motion.* In this classification he has invariably followed them, both in his *Inquiry into the Human Mind,* and in his *Essays on the Intellectual Powers;* a circumstance the more remarkable, that he has incidentally stated, in different parts of his works, some very important considerations, which seem to point out obviously the necessity of a more strictly logical arrangement.

After observing, on one occasion, that "Hardness and Softness, Roughness and Smoothness, Figure and Motion, do all suppose Extension, and cannot be conceived without it"; he adds, that "he thinks it must, on the other hand, be allowed, that if we had never felt anything hard or soft, rough or smooth, figured or moved, we should never have had a conception of Extension: so that, as there is good ground to believe that the notion of Extension could not be prior to that of other Primary Qualities; so it is certain that it could not be posterior to the notion of any of them, being necessarily implied in them all".

In another passage, the same author remarks, that "though the notion of Space seems not to enter at first into the mind, until it is introduced by the proper objects of sense; yet, being once introduced, it remains in our conception and belief, though the objects which introduced it be removed. We see no absurdity in supposing a body to be annihilated; but the space that contained it remains; and to suppose that annihilated, seems to be absurd".

Among the various inconveniences resulting from this indistinct enumeration of *Primary Qualities*, one of the greatest has been, the plausibility which it has lent to the reasonings of Berkeley and of Hume against the existence of an external world. *Solidity* and *Extension* being confounded together by both, under one common denomination, it seemed to be a fair inference, that whatever can be shown to be true of the one, must hold no less when applied to the other. That their conclusions, even with respect to Solidity, have been pushed a great deal too far, I have already endeavoured to show; the resistance opposed to our compressing force, manifestly implying the existence of something *external*, and altogether *independent of our perceptions*; but still there is a wide difference between the notion of *independent* existence, and that ascribed to *Extension* or *Space*, which, as Dr. Reid observes, carries along with it an irresistible conviction, that its existence is eternal and necessary, equally incapable of being created or annihilated. ...

I am always unwilling to attempt innovations in language; but I flatter myself it will not be considered as a rash or superfluous one after the remarks now made, if I distinguish Extension and Figure by the title of *the Mathematical Affections of Matter*; restricting the phrase *Primary Qualities* to Hardness and Softness, Roughness and Smoothness, and other properties of the same description. The line which I would draw between *Primary* and *Secondary* Qualities is this, that the former necessarily involve the notion of *Extension*, and consequently of *externality* or *outness*; whereas the latter are only conceived as the unknown causes of known sensations; and, when *first apprehended by the mind*, do not imply the existence of anything locally distinct from the subjects of its own consciousness. But these topics I must content myself with merely hinting at on the present occasion.

If these observations be well-founded, they establish *three* very important facts in the history of the human mind. 1. That the notion of the *Mathematical Affections* of Matter presupposes the exercise of our external senses, inasmuch as it is suggested to us by the same sensations which convey the knowledge of its *Primary Qualities*; 2. That this notion involves an irresistible conviction on our part, not only of the external existence of its objects, but of their necessary and eternal existence, whereas, in the case of the Primary Qualities of Matter, our perceptions are only accompanied with a belief that these qualities exist externally and independently of *our* existence as percipient beings, the supposition of their annihilation by the power of the Creator implying no absurdity whatsoever; 3. That our conviction of the necessary existence of Extension or Space, is neither the result of reasoning nor of experience, but is inseparable from the very conception of it; and must therefore be considered as an ultimate and essential law of human thought.

The same conclusion, it is manifest, applies to the notion of *Time*; a notion which, like that of *Space*, presupposes the exercise of our external senses; but which, when it is once acquired, presents irresistibly its object to our thoughts as an existence equally independent of the human mind, and of the material universe. Both these existences, too, swell in the human understanding to infinity - the one to immensity, the other to eternity - nor is it possible for imagination itself to conceive a limit to either. How are these facts to be reconciled with that philosophy which teaches that all our knowledge is derived from experience?

The foregoing reasonings have led us, by a very short, and I hope satisfactory process, to the general conclusion which forms the fundamental principle of the *Kantian system*; a system plainly suggested to the author, by the impossibility he found of tracing any resemblance between *extension* and the *sensations* of which we are conscious. "The notion (or intuition) of *Space*", he tells us, "as well as that of *Time*, is not empirical; that is; it has not its origin in experience. On the contrary, both these notions are supposed, or implied, as *conditions* in all our empirical perceptions; inasmuch as we cannot perceive nor conceive an external object, without representing it to our thoughts as *in space*; nor can we conceive anything, either without us or within us, without representing it to ourselves as in *time*. *Space* and *Time*, therefore, are called, by Kant, the *two forms of our sensibility*. The first is the *general form* of our external senses; the second the *general form* of all our senses, external and internal.

"These notions of Space and of Time, however, although they exist in us *a priori*, are not", according to Kant, "*innate ideas*. If they are anterior to the perceptions of our senses, it is only in the order of reason, and not in the order of time. They have, indeed, their origin in ourselves; but they present themselves to the understanding only in consequence of occasions furnished by our sensations; or (in Kant's language) by our *sensible modifications*. Separated from these modifications, they could not exist; and without them, they would have remained for ever latent and sterile".[6]

The only important proposition which I am able to extract from this jargon is, that as *Extension* and *Duration* cannot be supposed to bear the most distant resemblance to any sensations of which the mind is conscious, the origin of these notions forms a manifest exception to the account given by Locke of the primary sources of our knowledge. This is precisely the ground on which Reid has made his stand against the scheme of Idealism, and I leave it to my readers to judge whether it was

[6] [Stewart quotes from Joseph Marie Degerando's, *Histoire comparée des systèmes de philosophie* (1804), one of the first accounts of the Kantian philosophy.]

not more philosophical to state, as he has done, the *fact*, in simple and perspicuous terms, as a demonstration of the imperfection of Locke's theory, than to have reared upon it a superstructure of technical mystery, similar to what is exhibited in the system of the German metaphysician.

In justice, at the same time, to Kant's merits, I must repeat, that Dr. Reid would have improved greatly the statement of his argument against Berkeley, if he had kept as constantly in the view of his readers, as Kant has done, the essential distinction which I have endeavoured to point out between the *Mathematical Affections* of Matter, and its *Primary Qualities*. Of this distinction he appears to have been fully aware himself, from a passage which I formerly quoted; but he has, in general, slurred it over in a manner which *seemed* to imply, that he considered them both as precisely of the same kind.

I shall only add farther, that the idea or conception of *Motion* involves the idea both of *Extension* and of *Time*. That the idea of *Time* might have been formed, without any ideas either of *Extension* or of *Motion*, is sufficiently obvious; but it is by no means equally clear, whether the idea of *Motion* presupposes that of *Extension*, or that of *Extension* the idea of *Motion*. The question relates to a fact of some curiosity in the Natural History of the Mind; having, for its object, to ascertain, with logical precision, the *occasion* on which the idea of *Extension* is, in the first instance, acquired. But it is a question altogether foreign to the subject of the foregoing discussion. Whichever of the two conclusions we may adopt, the force of Reid's argument against Locke's principle will be found to remain undiminished.

SELECTION 10

Existence of the Deity

It was before observed,[7] that our knowledge of the course of nature is entirely the result of observation and experiment, and that there is no instance in which we perceive such a connexion between two successive events as might enable us to infer the one from the other as a necessary consequence.

From experience, indeed, we learn that there are many events so conjoined, that the one constantly follows the other. It is possible, however, that this connexion, though a constant one as far as our observation has reached, is not a *necessary* connexion; nay, it is possible, for any thing we know to the contrary, that there may be no necessary connexions among any of the phenomena we see; and if there are any such connexions existing, we may rest assured that we shall never be able to discover them.

...

[7] [See selection 6.]

From this view of the subject, with regard to Cause and Effect in physics, Mr. Hume has deduced an objection to the argument *a posteriori* for the existence of the Deity. After having proved that we cannot get the idea of *necessary connexion* from examining the conjunction between any two events, he takes for granted that we have no other idea of cause and effect, than of two *successive* events which are *always conjoined*; that we have therefore no reason to think that anyone event in nature is *necessarily* connected with another, or to infer the operation of Power from the changes we observe in the universe.

In consequence of these alarming inferences, a number of Mr. Hume's opponents have been led to call in question the truth of his general principles with respect to the relation of cause and effect in natural philosophy. But it has always appeared to me that the defect of this part of Mr. Hume's system does not lie in his *premises*, but in the *conclusion* which he has deduced from them; and which, I flatter myself, I shall be able to show cannot be inferred from these premises by a legitimate process of reasoning.

...

But taking for granted the truth of Mr. Hume's premises, let us consider the accuracy of his subsequent reasoning.

In order to form a competent judgment on this point, it is necessary to recollect, that, according to his system, "all our ideas are nothing but copies of our impressions; or, in other words, that it is *impossible* for us to *think* of anything which we have not antecedently *felt*, either by our external or internal senses". Having proved, therefore, that external objects, as they appear to our senses, give us no idea of *power* or of *necessary connexion*, and also that this idea cannot be copied from any internal impression, (that is, cannot be derived from reflection on the operations of our own minds,) he thinks himself warranted to conclude that we have no such idea. "One event", says he, "follows another, but we never observe any tie between them. They seem *conjoined* but never *connected.* And as we can have no idea of anything which never appeared to our outward sense or inward sentiment, the necessary conclusion seems to be, that we have no idea of connexion or power at all, and that these words are absolutely without any meaning when employed either in philosophical reasonings or common life".

Are we therefore to reject, as perfectly unintelligible, a word which is to be found in all languages, because it expresses an idea, for the origin of which we cannot account upon a particular philosophical system? Would it not be more reasonable to suspect that the system was not perfectly complete, than that all mankind should have agreed in employing a word which conveys no meaning?

With respect to Mr. Hume's theory concerning the origin of our ideas, it is the less necessary to enter into particular discussions, as it coincides in the main with the doctrine of Locke to which I have elsewhere stated some objections, which appear to me insurmountable.[8] Upon neither theory is it possible to explain the origin of those simple notions, which are not received immediately by any external sense, or derived from our own consciousness, but which are necessarily formed by the mind while we are exercising our intellectual powers upon their proper objects.

These very slight hints are sufficient to show that we are not entitled to dispute the reality of our idea of Power, because we cannot trace it to any of the senses. The only question is, if it be certain, that we annex any idea to the word *power* different from that of constant succession? The following considerations, among many others, prove that the import of these two expressions is by no means the same.

First, then, it is evident, that, if we had no idea of cause and effect different from that of mere succession, it would appear to us *as* absurd to suppose two events disjoined which we have constantly seen connected, as to suppose a change in external objects to take place without a cause. The fact however is that nobody finds it difficult to conceive that two events which are constantly conjoined *may not* be necessarily connected; whereas it may be safely pronounced to be impossible for a person to bring himself for a moment to believe that *any change* may take place in the *material* universe *without a cause*. I can conceive very easily that the volition in my mind is not the efficient cause of the motions of my hand; but can I conceive that my hand moves without any cause whatever? Nay, I can conceive that no one event in nature is necessarily connected with any other event; but does it therefore follow that I can conceive these events to happen without the operation of a cause? Leibnitz maintained that the volitions of the mind were not the efficient causes of the motions of the body; and compared the connexion between them to that between two clocks so adjusted by an artist that the motions of the one shall always correspond with those of the other. Every person of reflection must acknowledge that, however unwarranted by facts this theory may be, it is still possible it may be true. But if Leibnitz had affirmed not only that there was no connexion between the two clocks, but that the motions in each went on without any cause whatever, his theory would have been not only unsupported by proof, but absurd and inconceivable.

In the *second* place, our experience of the established connexions of physical events is evidently too limited a foundation for our belief that every change must have a cause. Mr. Hume himself, in laying down "the rules by which to judge of causes and effects", observes, in the *first place*, that "Cause and Effect must be contiguous in space and time"; and consequently he apprehended that, according to the general opinion, Matter produces its effects by Impulse alone. If, therefore, every change which had fallen under our notice had been preceded by apparent impulse, experience might have led us to conclude, from observing a

[8] [See selection 5.]

change, that a previous impulse had been given; or, according to Mr. Hume's notion of *a cause*, that a cause had operated to produce this effect. Of the changes, however, which we see, how small a number is preceded by apparent impulse! And yet, in the case of *every* change around us, without exception, we have an irresistible conviction of the operation of some cause. I believe it will be difficult to explain, upon Mr. Hume's principles, how we get this idea of the necessity of a cause in the case of those phenomena in which impulse has apparently no share.

To this we may add, that children at a very early period of life, when their experience is extremely limited, discover an eager curiosity to pry into the causes of the phenomena they observe. Even the attention of the lower animals seems to be roused when they see a body begin to move, or in general any change begin to take place in external objects.

The arguments which are commonly used to prove the necessity of human actions, derive all their plausibility from the general maxim, that *every change requires a cause with which it is necessarily connected.* It is remarkable that this doctrine of the Necessity of the will should form part of the same system with the theory of Cause and Effect which I have now been examining.

The question, however, still recurs, in what manner do we *acquire* the idea of Causation, Power, or Efficiency? But this question, if the foregoing observations be admitted, is comparatively of little consequence, as the doubts which may arise on the subject tend only (without affecting the reality of the idea or notion) to expose the defects of particular philosophical systems.

The most probable account of the matter seems to be, that the idea of Causation or of Power necessarily accompanies the perception of Change in a way somewhat analogous to that in which sensation implies a being who feels, and thought a being who thinks. Is it possible to conceive a person (however limited his experience may be) whose curiosity would not be roused by a *change* taking place in the objects around him? and what is this curiosity but an anxiety to know the *cause* of the *effect*? The mere perception of *change*, therefore, in the material universe, seems sufficient to introduce to the mind the ideas of *cause* and *effect*, and to impress us with a belief that this change *could not* have taken place unless there had been some *cause* for it. Such, I apprehend, would be the conclusion of a man wholly destitute of experience, and who was even ignorant of his own power to move at will the members of his body.

It must indeed be acknowledged, that, after having had experience of our own *power*, we come to associate the idea of *force*, or of an animal *nisus*, with that of *cause*; and hence some have been led to suppose that our only idea of *cause* is derived from our bodily exertions. Hence, too, it is that in natural philosophy our language frequently bears a reference to our own sensations. The ideas of *cause*, however, and of *power*, are more general than that of *force*, and might have been acquired although we had never been conscious of any bodily exertion whatever. There is surely no impropriety in saying that the mind has *power* over the train of its ideas, and over its various faculties, as well as over the members of the body.

...

Upon this part of the subject, indeed, I write with a good deal of diffidence, because the opinion which I have now stated differs considerably from that of some very ingenious and candid persons with whom I have conversed; who think not only that it is from our own voluntary exertions that our *first* ideas of cause and power are derived, but that we have no idea whatever of these which is not borrowed by analogy from our own consciousness.

One of my friends has amused himself with conceiving in what manner a man, who had never had experience of any animal exertion, would reason concerning the phenomena of the material world, and has been led to apprehend that he would consider the different events he saw merely as *antecedents* and *consequents*, without applying to the former in any instance the idea of *causation*.

I have already hinted that my own opinion is different from this; but I perfectly agree with my friend in thinking that this conclusion does not lead the way to any sceptical consequences. To say that our ideas of Power and Cause are derived from our own voluntary exertions, does not affect the reality of these ideas. And although we should grant that a man, who had never been conscious of any voluntary exertion, could never be led to conceive these ideas, or to comprehend the argument for the existence of a Deity, still that argument would apply *universally to our species*, for without such a consciousness no individual ever did, or could exist. Whatever ideas, whatever principles we are necessarily led to acquire by the circumstances in which we are placed, and by the exercise of those faculties which are essential to our preservation, are to be considered as parts of human nature, no less than those which are implanted in the mind at its first formation.

I am aware that this will not be considered by some as a complete answer to the objection; and it will still be urged that, if our only ideas of Cause and Power be derived from our own voluntary exertions, the argument for the existence of a Deity rests merely on an arbitrary association of ideas. We have found from experience that our voluntary exertions are followed by certain changes in the state of external objects, and are accordingly led to suppose, when we see other changes take place, that they have been preceded by some voluntary exertions analogous to those of which we are conscious. I cannot, however, help being of opinion, that the principle which leads us to consider a cause as necessary to produce a *change* in material things, is of a kind very different from the association of ideas. The changes which we and the whole human race are able to produce in the state of terrestrial objects are nothing, either in point of number or magnitude, in comparison of those which we see going on both in the earth and heavens, and I may add in our own bodies, and over which we have no influence. Whence is it then that we connect with *every* change we see, the idea of a cause? From the similarity between our own appearance and that of other men, and from the striking analogy between the human race and other animals, I shall admit that the association of ideas alone might lead us to connect the idea of voluntary exertion with animal motion. But whence is it that we associate the idea of a cause with the fall of a stone, with the ebbing and flowing of the sea, or with the motion of the planets? It will be said that, having learned from our own consciousness and experience the connexion between voluntary exertion and motion, we have recourse to the supposition of some analogous power or force to *account* for every motion we see. But what is it that leads us to think of *accounting* for these motions? Nothing, I apprehend, but that law of our nature which leads us to infer the existence of a cause wherever a change is perceived.

Some authors have compared this law of our nature to our instinctive interpretation of natural signs. As we *perceive* the passions and emotions in the minds of others by means of their looks and gestures, so it has been apprehended that every change we observe is accompanied with a perception of *power* or *cause*. This comparison will not be the less just, although we should proceed on the supposition that our first ideas of power and cause are derived from our own voluntary exertions; for the case is perfectly analogous with respect to the natural expressions of passion and emotion. No modification of countenance could convey the idea of *rage* to a man who had never been conscious of that passion; but after having acquired the idea of this passion from his own consciousness, he is able instinctively to interpret its natural expression.

Although, however, there may be some foundation for the foregoing comparison, it is necessary to remark, that our association of the ideas of *change* and *cause* is of a much more intimate and *indissoluble* nature than our association of any natural sign with the idea signified. Every person must perceive, upon the slightest reflection, that the connexion between any sign and the thing signified, *may be* merely an arbitrary connexion adapted to our particular constitution. Even in the case of Hardness we can discover no connexion whatever between the external quality and the sensation which suggests it. But, in the case of every change in the state of external objects, or of our own bodies, we not only connect with this particular change the idea of some Cause, but we have an irresistible conviction of the *necessity* of a cause. Something not unlike to this takes place with respect to our ideas of Space and Time. We acquire both originally from our perceptions; but having once acquired them, we have an irresistible conviction that both space and time are necessary and self-existent.

Having endeavoured to vindicate against the objections of Mr. Hume the reality of our notion of Power or Efficiency, I proceed to examine more particularly the foundation of our belief, that *every thing that begins to exist must have a cause*. Is this belief founded on *abstract reasoning*, or is it the result of *experience*, or is it an *intuitive Judgment*?

A variety of attempts have been made to demonstrate the truth of this principle from some general metaphysical axioms; in particular by Hobbes, Clarke, and Locke. Mr. Hume, in his *Treatise of Human Nature*, has examined each of their demonstrations, and has shown very clearly that they all take for granted the thing to be proved.

Other philosophers have thought that the principle may be proved by induction, from the particular instances that have fallen under our experience, as we infer from particular facts that cold freezes water, that heat turns it into steam, and that all bodies gravitate to each other.

But this opinion will not bear examination; for the thing to be proved is not a contingent but a necessary truth. ... Now it is manifest that no induction, how extensive soever, can ever lead to the discovery of a *necessary* truth; for experience only informs us of what is, or what has been, not of what must necessarily be; and the evidence of the conclusion must be of the same nature with that of the premises.

But abstracting from this consideration, and viewing this principle merely as a contingent truth, how is it possible to account, by means of experience, for our belief, that *every* change in the state of the universe is actually produced by a cause? In every case in which experience informs us that two things are connected, both of them must have fallen under our observation. But the causes of by far the greater number of phenomena we see are perfectly unknown to us, and therefore we never could learn from experience whether they have causes or not. The only instance in which we have any immediate knowledge of an efficient cause, is in the consciousness we have of our own voluntary actions, and surely this experience is not sufficient to account for the confidence with which we form the general conclusion.

From the foregoing observations we may infer that this principle is not founded on *experience*; and it has been shown clearly by Mr. Hume that it is not *demonstrable* by abstract reasoning, -we must therefore conclude that it is either a prejudice or an *intuitive* judgment.

That it is not a prejudice may be safely inferred from the universal consent of mankind, both learned and unlearned. Mr. Hume was the first person who called it in question, and even he frequently relapses unawares into the common conviction.

...

Upon a review of the observations and reasonings already stated in the course of this inquiry, it can scarcely fail to occur to an attentive reader, that the word *cause* is used both by philosophers and the vulgar in *two* senses, which are widely different. When it is said that every change in nature indicates the operation of a cause, the word *cause* expresses something which is supposed to be *necessarily connected* with the change, and without which it could not have happened. This may be called the *meta-*

physical meaning of the word, and such causes may be called *Metaphysical* or *Efficient causes*.

In natural philosophy, however, when we speak of one thing being the cause of another, all that we mean is, that the two are *constantly conjoined*, so that when we see the one we may expect the other. These conjunctions we learn from experience alone, and without an acquaintance with them we could not accommodate our conduct to the established course of nature. The causes which are the objects of our investigation in *natural* philosophy may, for the sake of distinction, be called *Physical causes*.

...

If this important distinction between Efficient and Physical causes be kept steadily in view, Mr. Hume's doctrine concerning the relation of Cause and Effect in physics, so far from leading to atheism, is more favourable to religious belief than the common inaccurate conceptions entertained on that subject; as it keeps the Deity always in view, not only as the first, but as the constantly operating efficient cause in the material world, (either immediately, or by means of some intelligent instruments,) and as the great connecting principle among all the various phenomena which we observe.

...

But perhaps it may be thought by some that this very conclusion is a sufficient refutation of the supposition from which it is inferred; for how is it possible to conceive that all the events which are constantly taking place in the different parts of the material universe are the immediate effects of the Divine agency?

For my own part, I have no scruple to admit this conclusion in all its extent; for I cannot perceive any absurdity that it involves; and I am happy to find that it is agreeable to the sentiments of some of our best and soundest philosophers.

... Many of the most celebrated theories we meet with in the history both of physics and of metaphysics, have taken their rise from the zeal of philosophers to elude this very conclusion, which appeared to them too extravagant to merit a particular refutation. It was this idea which gave birth to the scheme of Materialism; to the Plastic Nature of Cudworth; to the Mechanical Theories of the Universe proposed by Descartes and Leibnitz; and to various others equally gratuitous and not less extravagant. ...

The different hypotheses to which I have now alluded have been adopted by ingenious men in preference to the simple and sublime doctrine which supposes the order of the universe to be not only at first established, but every moment maintained by the incessant agency of one supreme mind, -a doctrine against which no objection can be stated, but what is founded on prejudices resulting from our own imperfections. How far, indeed, the events we see are actually produced by the immediate hand of God, or how far he may avail himself of the instrumentality of subordinate intelligences, it is impossible for us to determine; but of this we may rest assured, that when he chooses to communicate a certain measure of power to any of his creatures, and employs their operation to accomplish the ends of his providence, it is not because he is himself incompetent to the magnitude, or to the multiplicity of the effects which take place in the universe. And, therefore, the consideration of these effects, how astonishing soever they may be, furnishes no argument in favour of the theories which have already been enumerated.

***

Having treated at considerable length of the foundations of our reasoning from the Effect to the Cause, and of the evidences of Active Power exhibited in the universe, I proceed now to illustrate that principle of our nature which leads us to apprehend intelligence or design when we see a variety of means conspiring to a particular end. In examining this part of our constitution, my object is similar to what I had in view in the speculations in which we have last been engaged, not to bring to light any new or abstruse conclusion, but to vindicate against the cavils of sceptics, a mode of reasoning that is equally familiar to the philosopher and the vulgar, and which is not more intimately connected with our religious belief than with our rational conduct in the common business of life. …

…

Dr. Reid has observed that the argument from Final Causes, when reduced to a syllogism, contains two propositions. First, that design may be traced from its effects: This is the major proposition. The minor is, that there are appearances of design in the universe. The ancient sceptics, he says, granted the first, but denied the second. The moderns (in consequence of the discoveries in natural philosophy) have been obliged to abandon the ground which their predecessors maintained, and have disputed the major proposition.

Among those who have denied the possibility of tracing design from its effects, Mr. Hume is the most eminent; and he seems to have considered his reasonings on this subject as forming one of the most splendid parts of his philosophy; according to him all such inferences are inconclusive, being neither demonstrable by reasoning, nor deducible from experience.

In examining Mr. Hume's argument on this subject, Dr. Reid admits, that the inferences we make of design from its effects, are not the result of reasoning or experience; but still he contends such inferences may be made with a degree of certainty equal to what the human mind is able to attain in any instance whatever. The opinions we form of the talents of other men, nay, our belief that other men are intelligent beings, are founded on this very inference of design from its effects. Intelligence and design are not objects of our senses; and yet we judge of them every moment from external conduct and behaviour, with as little hesitation as we pronounce on the existence of what we immediately perceive.

While Dr. Reid contends in this manner for the authority of this important principle of our constitution, he bestows due praise on Mr. Hume for the acuteness with which he has exposed the inconclusiveness of the common *demonstrations* of the existence of a designing cause, to be found among the writers on natural religion; and he acknowledges the service that, without intending it, he has thereby rendered to the cause of truth; inasmuch as, by the alarming consequences he deduces from his doctrine, he has invited philosophers to an accurate examination of a subject which had formerly been considered in a very superficial manner, and has pointed out to them indirectly the true foundation on which this important article of our belief ought to be placed. With the same view it may be of some use, before we proceed farther, to confirm such of Mr. Hume's principles as appear to be just, by some additional remarks and illustrations.

First, then, it may be observed, (as a strong presumption that our belief of the existence of a designing cause is not the result of reasoning,) that it has prevailed in all nations and ages, among the unlearned, as well as among the learned. Indeed, without a capacity of inferring design from its effects, it would be impossible for us to conduct ourselves in the common affairs of life; a consideration which of itself renders it probable to those who are acquainted with the general analogy of our constitution, that it is not entrusted to the slow and uncertain exercise of our reasoning powers, but that it arises from some intuitive perception of the mind.

In order to feel the full force of these observations, it is necessary to consider, that without a capacity of inferring design from its effects, it would be impossible for us to form any judgment of the intellectual powers, or of the characters of other men, or even to know that they are intelligent beings. The qualities in their minds are not objects of our senses, we only perceive their effects; but these effects indicate to us certain designs and purposes from which they proceed, as certainly as an impression made on an organ of sense indicates the existence of the object. The inferences we make of intelligence and design, as displayed in the universe, are perfectly analogous to this; and whatever sceptical doubts affect our conclusions in the one case, are equally well founded in the other.

...

So far, therefore, we agree with Mr. Hume, in admitting that our inferences of design from its effects, are not the result of reasoning. Still farther, we agree with him in admitting, that these inferences are not the result of experience.

In proof of this it is sufficient to observe, that experience can only inform us of what *is*, and not of what *must be*; or, as Dr. Reid expresses it, experience *can only discover to us what is* CONTINGENTLY *true*; it cannot in any instance lead us to the knowledge of *necessary* truth. Now, our belief that a combination of means conspiring to a particular end implies intelligence, involves a perception of necessary truth. It is not that such a combination has been always or generally found to proceed from an intelligent cause, but that an intelligent cause was necessary to its production, and that the contrary supposition is absurd.

But farther, experience can only inform us of a connexion between a sign and the thing signified, in those cases in which both of these have been separate and distinct objects of our perceptions; but in the instance before us the thing signified is not an immediate object of sense, nor indeed of consciousness; for even in my own case I perceive the existence of mind only from its operations and effects. In other words, my knowledge of the *thing signified* is not *direct*: it is only *relative to the signs* by which it is suggested to the understanding.

In what manner, then, it may be asked, shall we explain the origin of our conviction that the universe is the work of a designing cause, if it be granted that this conviction is neither founded on reasoning nor on experience? According to Mr. Hume, nothing more is necessary than these concessions to show that it is an illusion of the imagination, or a prejudice of the nursery.

But surely the inference is too hasty; for are there not many truths, the contrary of which we feel to be impossible, which are neither demonstrable by reasoning, nor confirmed by experience? Such are all those truths which are perceived by an intuitive judgment of the mind. The authority of these truths is at least on a footing with those truths which rest on demonstration, inasmuch as all demonstration is ultimately founded on them; and it is incomparably superior to that of truths learned from experience, inasmuch as the contrary of *these* is always conceivable, and never implies any absurdity or contradiction.

From the observations already made in the prosecution of this argument, I flatter myself it sufficiently appears, that if there be such a thing as an intuitive perception or judgment of the mind, the inferences we make of design from its effects are entitled to the appellation. A capacity of forming such inferences is plainly an essential part of our constitution; and to dispute their certainty in the common conduct of life, by urging sceptical subtilties in opposition to them, would expose a man to the charge of insanity, as infallibly as if he were to dispute the certainty of a mathematical axiom.[9]

---

[9] [Stewart's observations refer to Hume's *Dialogues on Natural Religion*.]

But leaving these abstract topics, let us for a moment attend to the scope of the sceptical argument as it bears on the evidences of Natural Religion. To those who examine it with attention it must appear obvious, that, if it proves anything, it leads to this general conclusion, that it would be perfectly impossible for the *Deity*, if he *did* exist, to exhibit to man any satisfactory evidence of design by the order and perfection of his works. That every thing we see *is consistent* with the supposition of its being the work of an intelligent author, Philo would (I presume) have granted; and at any rate, supposing the order of the universe to have been as complete as imagination can conceive, it would not obviate in the least the objection stated in the dialogue, inasmuch as this objection is founded not on any appearances of disorder or imperfection, but on the impossibility of rendering intelligence and design manifest to our faculties by the effects they produce. Whether this logical proposition is or is not true, can be decided only by an appeal to the judgment of the human understanding in analogous circumstances. If I were thrown ashore on a desert island, and were anxious to leave behind me some memorial which might inform those who should afterwards visit the same spot, that it had once been inhabited by a human being, what expedient could I employ but to execute some work of art; -to rear a dwelling, to enclose a piece of ground, or to arrange a number of stones in such a symmetrical order that their position could not be ascribed to chance? This would surely be a language intelligible to all nations, whether civilized or savage; and which, without the help of reasoning, would convey its meaning with the force of a perception. …

Now all this seems wonderfully applicable to the subject before us. If the universe had really been created by a powerful and intelligent being, whose pleasure it was to proclaim to human reason his existence and attributes, what means could have been devised more effectual for this purpose than those actually employed! A display of order, of beauty, of contrivance, obvious to the apprehensions of the most unlearned, and commanding more and more our admiration and our wonder as our faculties improve, and as our knowledge extends. These evidences of power, of wisdom, and of goodness may be regarded as *natural and universal signs* by which the Creator reveals himself to his creatures. There is accordingly, "No speech where their voice is not heard. Their line is gone through all the earth, and their words to the end of the world".

That in these remarks I have done no injustice to Philo's reasoning, appears from a remarkable passage which occurs in a subsequent part of the dialogue, where, in my opinion, he yields without reserve the only point for which it was of much importance for a sceptic to contend. The logical subtleties formerly quoted about *experience* and *belief*, (even supposing them to remain unanswered,) are but little calculated to shake the authority of principles on which we are every moment called on to act in the business of life. I shall transcribe in Philo's words the passage I allude to, premising only, that, for this memorable concession, (so contrary in its spirit to the sceptical cavils of the ancient Epicureans,) we are chiefly indebted to the lustre thrown on the order of nature by the physical researches of the two last centuries.

"Supposing there were a God who did not discover himself immediately to our senses, were it possible for him to give stronger proofs of his existence than what appear on the whole face of nature? What indeed could such a divine being do but copy the present economy of things; render many of his artifices so plain that no stupidity could mistake them; afford glimpses of still greater artifices which demonstrate his prodigious superiority over our narrow apprehensions, and conceal, altogether a great many from such imperfect creatures?"

Another concession extorted from Philo by the discoveries of modern science is still more important. I need not point out its coincidence with some remarks already made: "A purpose, an intention, a design, strikes everywhere the most careless, the most stupid thinker, and no man can be so hardened in absurd systems as at all times to reject it. *That nature does nothing in vain,* is a maxim established in all the schools, merely from the contemplation of the works of nature, without any religious purpose; and from a firm conviction of its truth, an anatomist who had observed a new organ or canal would never be satisfied till he had also discovered its use and intention. One great foundation of the Copernican system is the [Aristotelic] maxim, *That nature acts by the simplest methods, and chooses the most proper means to any end*; and astronomers often, without thinking of it, lay this strong foundation of piety and religion. The same thing is observable in other parts of philosophy; and thus all the sciences almost lead us insensibly to acknowledge a first intelligent author; and their authority is often so much the greater, as they do not directly profess that intention".

"But", (says Mr. Hume in one of his *Philosophical Essays,)* "it is only when two *species* of objects are found to be constantly conjoined that we can infer the one from the other; and were an effect presented which was entirely singular, and could not be comprehended under any known *species,* I do not see that we could form any conjecture or inference at all concerning its cause. If experience and observation and analogy be indeed the only guides which we can reasonably follow in inferences of this nature, both the effect and cause must bear a similarity and resemblance to other effects and causes which we know, and which we have found in many instances to be conjoined with each other". If I understand the scope and import of this reasoning, nothing more is necessary for its refutation but to explain its meaning. To what, then, does it amount? Merely to this! "That if we had been accustomed to see worlds produced, some by design, and others without it, and had observed that such a world as this which we inhabit was always the effect of design, we might then, from past experience, conclude that it was in this way our world was produced; but having no such experience we have no means of forming any conclusion about it".

The argument, it is manifest, proceeds entirely on the supposition, that our inferences of design are in every ease the result of experience, the contrary of which has been already sufficiently shown; and which indeed, (as Dr. Reid has remarked,) "if it be admitted as a general truth, leads to this conclusion, that no man can have any evidence of the existence of any intelligent being but himself".

Four

Intellectual Powers

SELECTION 11

Attention

When we are deeply engaged in conversation, or occupied with any speculation that is interesting to the mind, the surrounding objects either do not produce in us the perceptions they are fitted to excite, or these perceptions are instantly forgotten. A clock, for example, may strike in the same room with us, without our being able next moment to recollect whether we heard it or not.

...

It has been proved by optical writers that, in perceiving the distances of visible objects from the eye, there is a judgment of the understanding antecedent to the perception. In some cases this judgment is founded on a variety of circumstances combined together: the conformation of the organ necessary for distinct vision; the inclination of the optic axes; the distinctness or indistinctness of the minute parts of the object; the distances of the intervening objects from each other, and from the eye; and perhaps on other circumstances besides these. And yet, in consequence of our familiarity with such processes from our earliest infancy, the perception seems to be instantaneous, and it requires much reasoning to convince persons unaccustomed to philosophical speculations, that the fact is otherwise.

Another instance of a still more familiar nature, may be of use for the farther illustration of the same subject. It is well known that our thoughts do not succeed each other at random, but according to certain laws of association, which modern philosophers have been at much pains to investigate. It frequently, however, happens, particularly when the mind is animated by conversation, that it makes a sudden transition from one subject to another, which at first view appears to be very remote from it, and that it requires a considerable degree of reflection, to enable the person himself by whom the transition was made, to ascertain what were the intermediate ideas. ...

In the instances which have been last mentioned, we have also a proof that a perception, or an idea, which passes through the mind, without leaving any trace in the memory, may yet serve to introduce other ideas connected with it by the laws of association. Other proofs of this important fact shall be mentioned afterwards.

When a perception or an idea passes through the mind, without our being able to recollect it next moment, the vulgar themselves ascribe our want of memory to a want of attention. Thus, in the instance already mentioned of the clock, a person upon observing that the minute hand had just passed twelve, would naturally say, that he did not attend to the clock when it was striking. There seems, therefore, to be a certain effort of mind upon which, even in the judgment of the vulgar, memory in some measure depends, and which they distinguish by the name of attention.

...

But although the connexion between attention and memory has been frequently remarked in general terms, I do not recollect that the power of attention has been mentioned by any of the writers on pneumatology, in their enumeration of the faculties of the mind; nor has it been considered by anyone, so far as I know, as of sufficient importance to deserve a particular examination. ...

With respect to the nature of this effort, it is perhaps impossible for us to obtain much satisfaction. We often speak of greater and less degrees of attention, and, I believe, in these cases, conceive the mind (if I may use the expression) to exert itself with different degrees of energy. I am doubtful, however, if this expression conveys any distinct meaning. For my own part, I am inclined to suppose, (though I would by no means be understood to speak with confidence,) that it is essential to memory, that the perception or the idea that we would wish to remember, should remain in the mind for a certain space of time, and should be contemplated by it exclusively of every thing else; and that attention consists partly (perhaps entirely) in the effort of the mind, to detain the idea or the perception, and to exclude the other objects that solicit its notice.

...

The wonderful effect of practice in the formation of habits, has been often, and justly, taken notice of as one of the most curious circumstances in the human constitution. A mechanical operation, for example, which we at first performed with the utmost difficulty, comes in time to be so familiar to us, that we are able to perform it without the smallest danger of mistake; even while the attention appears to be completely engaged with other subjects. The truth seems to be, that in consequence of the association of ideas, the different steps of the process present themselves successively to the thoughts, without any recollection on our part, and with a degree of rapidity proportioned to the length of our experience, so as to save us entirely the trouble of hesitation and reflection, by giving us every moment a precise and steady notion of the effect to be produced.

In the case of some operations which are very familiar to us, we find ourselves unable to attend to, or to recollect the acts of the will by which they were preceded; and accordingly, some philosophers of great eminence have called in question the existence of such volitions, and have represented our habitual actions as involuntary and mechanical. But surely the circumstance of our inability to recollect our volitions does not authorize us to dispute their possibility, any more than our inability to attend to the process of the mind in estimating the distance of an object from the eye, authorizes us to affirm that the perception is instantaneous. Nor does it add any force to the objection to urge, that there are instances in which we find it difficult, or perhaps impossible, to check our habitual actions by a contrary volition. For it must be remembered that this contrary volition does not remain with us steadily during the whole operation; but is merely a general intention or resolution, which is banished from the mind, as soon as the occasion presents itself with which the habitual train of our thoughts and volitions is associated.

It may indeed be said, that these observations only prove the possibility that our habitual actions may be voluntary. But if this be admitted, nothing more can well be required; for surely if these phenomena are clearly explicable from the known and acknowledged laws of the human mind, it would be unphilosophical to devise a new principle, on purpose to account for them. The doctrine, therefore, which I have laid down with respect to the nature of habits, is by no means founded on hypothesis, as has been objected to me by some of my friends; but, on the contrary, the charge of hypothesis falls on those who attempt to explain them, by saying that they are *mechanical or automatic;* a doctrine which, if it is at all intelligible, must be understood as implying the existence of some law of our constitution, which has been hitherto unobserved by philosophers; and to which, I believe, it will be difficult to find anything analogous in our constitution.

In the foregoing observations I have had in view a favourite doctrine of Dr. Hartley's, which has been maintained also of late by a much higher authority, I mean Dr. Reid.

"Habit", says this ingenious author, "differs from instinct, not in its nature, but in its origin; the last being natural, the first acquired. Both operate without will or intention, without thought, and therefore may be called mechanical principles". In another passage, he expresses himself thus: "I conceive it to be a part of our constitution, that what we have been accustomed to do, we acquire not only a facility but a proneness to do on like occasions; so that it requires a particular will or effort to forbear it, but to do it requires, very often, no will at all".

...

I cannot help thinking it more philosophical to suppose, that those actions which are originally voluntary, always continue so; although, in the case of operations which are become habitual in consequence of long practice, we may not be able to recollect every different volition. …

The only plausible objection which, I think, can be offered to the principles I have endeavoured to establish on this subject, is founded on the astonishing and almost incredible rapidity they necessarily suppose in our intellectual operations. When a person, for example, reads aloud, there must, according to this doctrine, be a separate volition preceding the articulation of every letter; and it has been found by actual trial, that it is possible to pronounce about two thousand letters in a minute. Is it reasonable to suppose that the mind is capable of so many different acts in an interval of time so very inconsiderable?

With respect to this objection it may be observed, in the first place, that all arguments against the foregoing doctrine with respect to our habitual exertions, in so far as they are founded on the inconceivable rapidity which they suppose in our intellectual operations, apply equally to the common doctrine concerning our perception of distance by the eye. …

It may contribute to remove, still more completely, some of the scruples which are naturally suggested by the foregoing doctrine, to remark, that as the great use of attention and memory is to enable us to treasure up the results of our experience and reflection for the future regulation of our conduct, it would have answered no purpose for the author of our nature to have extended their province to those intervals of time which we have no occasion to estimate in the common business of life. All the intellectual processes I have mentioned are subservient to some particular end, either of perception or of action; and it would have been perfectly superfluous, if, after this end were gained, the steps which are instrumental in bringing it about were all treasured up in the memory. Such a constitution of our nature would have had no other effect but to store the mind with a variety of useless particulars.

…

Before we leave the subject of Attention, it is proper to take notice of a question which has been stated with respect to it; whether we have the power of attending to more than one thing at one and the same instant; or, in other words, whether we can attend at one and the same instant to objects which we can attend to separately? This question has, if I am not mistaken, been already decided by several philosophers in the negative; and I acknowledge, for my own part, that although their opinion has not only been called in question by others, but even treated with some degree of contempt as altogether hypothetical, it appears to me to be the most reasonable and philosophical that we can form on the subject.

There is, indeed, a great variety of cases, in which the mind apparently exerts different acts of attention at once; but from the instances which have already been mentioned, of the astonishing rapidity of thought, it is obvious that all this may be explained without supposing these acts to be co-existent; and I may even venture to add, it may all be explained in the most satisfactory manner, without ascribing to our intellectual operations a greater degree of rapidity than that with which we know from the fact that they are sometimes carried on. The effect of practice in increasing this capacity of apparently attending to different things at once, renders this explanation of the phenomenon in question more probable than any other. ...

The same doctrine leads to some curious conclusions with respect to vision. Suppose the eye to be fixed in a particular position, and the picture of an object to be painted on the retina. Does the mind perceive the complete figure of the object at once, or is this perception the result of the various perceptions we have of the different points in the outline? With respect to this question, the principles already stated lead me to conclude, that the mind does at one and the same time perceive every point in the outline of the object, (provided the whole of it be painted on the retina at the same instant,) for perception, like consciousness, is an involuntary operation. As no two points, however, of the outline are in the same direction, every point by itself constitutes just as distinct an object of attention to the mind, as if it were separated by an interval of empty space from all the rest. If the doctrine, therefore, formerly stated be just, it is impossible for the mind to attend to more than one of these points at once; and as the perception of the figure of the object implies a knowledge of the relative situation of the different points with respect to each other, we must conclude, that the perception of figure by the eye, is the result of a number of different acts of attention. These acts of attention, however, are performed with such rapidity, that the effect, with respect to us, is the same as if the perception were instantaneous.

In farther confirmation of this reasoning, it may be remarked, that if the perception of visible figure were an immediate consequence of the picture on the retina, we should have, at the first glance, as distinct an idea of a figure of a thousand sides, as of a triangle or a square. The truth is, that when the figure is very simple, the process of the mind is so rapid, that the perception seems to be instantaneous; but when the sides are multiplied beyond a certain number, the interval of time necessary for these different acts of attention becomes perceptible.

It may perhaps be asked what I mean by a *point* in the outline of a figure, and what it is that constitutes this point *one* object of attention? The answer, I apprehend is, that this point is the *minimum visible*. If the point be less, we cannot perceive it; if it be greater, it is not all seen in one direction.

If these observations be admitted, it will follow, that without the faculty of memory, we could have had no perception of visible figure.

SELECTION 12

Abstraction

The origin of appellatives, or, in other words, the origin of those classes of objects which, in the schools, are called *genera* and *species*, has been considered by some philosophers as one of the most difficult problems in metaphysics. The account of it which is given by Mr. Smith, in his Dissertation on the Origin of Languages, appears to me to be equally simple and satisfactory.

"The assignation", says he, "of particular names, to denote particular objects, that is, the institution of nouns substantive, would probably be one of the first steps towards the formation of Language. The particular cave, whose covering sheltered the savage from the weather; the particular tree, whose fruit relieved his hunger; the particular fountain, whose water allayed his thirst, would first be denominated by the words, *Cave, Tree, Fountain;* or by whatever other appellations he might think proper, in that primitive jargon, to mark them. Afterwards, when the more enlarged experience of this savage had led him to observe, and his necessary occasions obliged him to make mention of, other caves, and other trees, and other fountains, he would naturally bestow upon each of those new objects the same name by which he had been accustomed to express the similar object he was first acquainted with. And thus, those words, which were originally the proper names of individuals, would each of them insensibly become the common name of a multitude".

"It is this application", he continues, "of the name of an individual to a great number of objects, whose resemblance naturally recalls the idea of that individual, and of the name which expresses it, that seems originally to have given occasion to the formation of those classes and assortments, which, in the schools, are called *genera* and *species;* and of which the ingenious and eloquent Rousseau finds himself so much at a loss to account for the origin. What constitutes a *species*, is merely a number of objects, bearing a certain degree of resemblance to one another, and, on that account, denominated by a single appellation, which may be applied to express any one of them".

...

The classification of different objects supposes a power of attending to some of their qualities or attributes, without attending to the rest; for no two objects are to be found without some specific difference; and no assortment or arrangement can be formed among things not perfectly alike, but by losing sight of their distinguishing peculiarities, and limiting the attention to those attributes which belong to them in common. Indeed, without this power of attending separately to things which our senses present to us in a state of union, we never could have had any idea of *number;* for, before we can consider different objects as forming a multitude, it is necessary that we should be able to apply to all of them one common name; or, in other words, that we should reduce them all to the same genus. The various objects, for example, animate and inanimate, which are, at this moment before me, I may class and number in a variety of different ways, according to the view of them that I choose to take. I may reckon successively the number of sheep, of cows, of horses, of elms, of oaks, of beeches; or I may first reckon the number of animals, and then the number of trees; or I may at once reckon the number of all the organized substances which my senses present to me. But whatever be the principle on which my classification proceeds, it is evident that the objects, numbered together, must be considered in those respects only in which they agree with each other; and that, if I had no power of separating the combinations of sense, I never could have conceived them as forming a plurality.

This power of considering certain qualities or attributes of an object apart from the rest; or, as I would rather choose to define it, the power which the understanding has, of separating the combinations which are presented to it, is distinguished by logicians by the name of *abstraction*. It has been supposed, by some philosophers, (with what probability I shall not now inquire,) to form the characteristical attribute of a rational nature. That it is one of the most important of all our faculties, and very intimately connected with the exercise of our reasoning powers, is beyond dispute. And, I flatter myself, it will appear from the sequel of this chapter, how much the proper management of it conduces to the success of our philosophical pursuits, and of our general conduct in life.

The subserviency of Abstraction to the power of Reasoning, and also its subserviency to the exertions of a Poetical or Creative Imagination, shall be afterwards fully illustrated. At present, it is sufficient for my purpose to remark, that as Abstraction is the groundwork of classification, without this faculty of the mind we should have been perfectly incapable of general speculation, and all our knowledge must necessarily have been limited to individuals; and that some of the most useful branches of science, particularly the different branches of mathematics, in which the very subjects of our reasoning are abstractions of the understanding, could never have possibly had an existence. With respect to the subserviency of this faculty to poetical imagination, it is no less obvious that, as the poet is supplied with all his materials by experience, and as his province is limited to combine and modify things which really exist, so as to produce new wholes of his own; so every exertion which he thus makes of his powers, presupposes the exercise of abstraction in decomposing and separating actual combinations. And it was on this account that, in the chapter on Conception, I was led to make a distinction between that faculty, which is evidently simple and uncompounded, and the power of Imagination, which (at least in the sense in which I employ the word in these inquiries) is the result of a combination of various other powers.

I have introduced these remarks, in order to point out a difference between the abstractions which are subservient to reasoning, and those which are subservient to imagination. And, if I am not mistaken, it is a distinction which has not been sufficiently attended to by some writers of eminence. In every instance in which imagination is employed in forming new wholes, by decompounding and combining the perceptions of sense, it is evidently necessary that the poet or the painter should be able to state to himself the circumstances abstracted, as separate objects of conception. But this is by no means requisite in every case in which abstraction is subservient to the power of reasoning; for it frequently happens, that we can reason concerning one quality or property of an object abstracted from the rest, while, at the same time, we find it impossible to conceive it separately. Thus, I can reason concerning extension and figure, without any reference to colour, although it may be doubted, if a person possessed of sight can make extension and figure steady objects of conception, without connecting with them one colour or another. Nor is this always owing (as it is in the instance now mentioned) merely to the association of ideas, for there are cases, in which we can reason concerning things separately, which it is impossible fur us to suppose any being so constituted as to conceive apart. Thus we can reason concerning length, abstracted from any other dimension; although, surely, no understanding can make length, without breadth, an object of conception. And, by the way, this leads me to take notice of an error, which mathematical teachers are apt to commit, in explaining the first principles of geometry. By dwelling long on Euclid's first definitions, they lead the student to suppose that they relate to notions which are extremely mysterious, and to strain his powers in fruitless attempts to conceive, what cannot possibly be made an object of conception. If these definitions were omitted, or very slightly touched upon, and the attention at once directed to geometrical reasonings, the student would immediately perceive, that although the lines in the diagrams are really extended in two dimensions, yet that the demonstrations relate only to one of them; and that the human understanding has the faculty of reasoning concerning things separately, which are always presented to us, both by our powers of perception and conception, in a state of union. Such abstractions, in truth, are familiar to the most illiterate of mankind, and it is in this very way that they are insensibly formed. When a tradesman speaks of the length of a room, in contradistinction to its breadth, or when he speaks of the distance between any two objects, he forms exactly the same abstraction, which is referred to by Euclid in his second definition, and which most of his commentators have thought it necessary to illustrate by prolix metaphysical disquisitions.

I shall only observe farther, with respect to the nature and province of this faculty of the mind, that notwithstanding its essential subserviency to every act of classification, yet it might have been exercised, although we had only been acquainted with one individual object. Although, for example, we had never seen but one rose, we might still have been able to attend to its colour, without thinking of its other properties. This has led some philosophers to suppose, that another faculty besides abstraction, to which they have given the name of generalization, is necessary to account for the formation of genera and species; and they have endeavoured to show, that although generalization without abstraction is impossible, yet that we might have been so formed, as to be able to abstract, without being capable of generalizing. The grounds of this opinion, it is not necessary for me to examine, for any of the purposes which I have at present in view.[1]

***

I formerly explained in what manner the words, which in the infancy of language were proper names, became gradually appellatives, in consequence of which extension of their signification, they would express, when applied to individuals, those qualities only which are common to the whole genus. Now it is evident, that with respect to individuals of the same genus, there are two classes of truths; the one, particular truths relating to each individual apart, and deduced from a consideration of its peculiar and distinguishing properties; the other, general truths deduced from a consideration of their common qualities, and equally applicable to all of them. Such truths may be conveniently expressed by means of general terms, so as to form propositions, comprehending under them as many particular truths as there are individuals comprehended under the general terms. It is farther evident, that there are two ways in which such general truths may be obtained; either by fixing the attention on one individual, in such a manner that our reasoning may involve no circumstances but those which are common to the whole genus, or, (laying aside entirely the consideration of things,) by means of the general terms with which language supplies us. In either of these cases, our investigations must necessarily lead us to general conclu-

---

[1] The words Abstraction and Generalization are commonly, but improperly, used as synonymous; and the same inaccuracy is frequently committed in speaking of abstract or general ideas, as if the two expressions were convertible. A person who had never seen but one rose, (it has been already remarked,) might yet have been able to consider its *colour* apart from its other qualities; and, therefore, (to express myself in conformity to common language,) there may be such a thing as an idea which is at once abstract and particular. After having perceived this quality as belonging to a variety of individuals, we can consider it without reference to any of them, and thus form the notion of redness or whiteness in general, which may be called a *general abstract idea*. The words *abstract* and *general*, therefore, when applied to ideas, are as completely distinct from each other as all two words to be found in the language.

It is indeed true, that the formation of every general notion presupposes abstraction; but it is surely improper, on this account, to call a general term an abstract term, or a general idea an abstract idea.

sions. In the first case, our attention being limited to those circumstances in which the subject of our reasoning resembles all other individuals of the same genus, whatever we demonstrate with respect to this subject must be true of every other to which the same attributes belong. In the second case, the subject of our reasoning being expressed by a generic word, which applies in common to a number of individuals, the conclusion we form must be as extensive in its application, as the name of the subject is in its meaning. The former process is analogous to the practice of geometers, who, in their most general reasonings, direct the attention to a particular diagram; the latter to that of algebraists, who carry on their investigations by means of symbols.[2] In cases of this last sort, it may frequently happen from the association of ideas, that a general word may recall some one individual to which it is applicable, but this is so far from being necessary to the accuracy of our reasoning, that excepting in some cases, in which it may be useful to check us in the abuse of general terms, it always has a tendency more or less to mislead us from the truth. As the decision of a judge must necessarily be impartial, when he is only acquainted with the relations in which the parties stand to each other, and when their names are supplied by letters of the alphabet, or by the fictitious names of Titius, Caius, and Sempronius; so, in every process of reasoning, the conclusion we form is most likely to be logically just, when the attention is confined solely to signs, and when the imagination does not present to it those individual objects which may warp the judgment by casual associations.

To these remarks, it may not be improper to add, that although, in our speculations concerning individuals, it is possible to carry on processes of reasoning, by fixing our attention on the objects themselves, without the use of language; yet it is also in our power to accomplish the same end, by substituting for these objects words or other arbitrary signs. The difference between the employment of language in such cases, and in our speculations concerning classes or genera, is, that in the former case the use of words is, in a great measure, optional; whereas, in the latter, it is essentially necessary. …

…

[T]he assent we give to the conclusion of a syllogism does not result from any examination of the notions expressed by the different propositions

---

[2] These two methods of obtaining general truths proceed on the same principles, and are, in fact, much less different from each other than they appear to be at first view. When we carry on a process of general reasoning, by fixing our attention on a particular individual of a genus, this individual is to be considered merely as a sign or representative, and differs from any other sign only in this, that it bears a certain resemblance to the things it denotes. The straight lines which are employed in the fifth book of Euclid to represent magnitudes in general, differ from the algebraical expressions of these magnitudes, in the same respects in which picture writing differs from arbitrary characters.

of which it is composed, but is an immediate consequence of the relations in which the words stand to each other. The truth is, that in every syllogism the inference is only a particular instance of the general axiom, that whatever is true universally of any sign, must also be true of every individual which that sign can be employed to express. Admitting, therefore, that every process of reasoning may be resolved into a series of syllogisms, it follows that this operation of the mind furnishes no proof of the existence of anything corresponding to general terms, distinct from the individuals to which these terms are applicable.

These remarks, I am very sensible, do by no means exhaust the subject, for there are various modes of reasoning to which the syllogistic theory does not apply. But in all of them, without exception, it will be found, on examination, that the evidence of our conclusions appears immediately from the consideration of the words in which the premises are expressed, without any reference to the things which they denote. The imperfect account which is given of deductive evidence, in the received systems of logic, makes it impossible for me, in this place, to prosecute the subject any farther.

After all that I have said on the use of language as an instrument of reasoning, I can easily foresee a variety of objections which may occur to the doctrine I have been endeavouring to establish. But, without entering into a particular examination of these objections, I believe I may venture to affirm, that most, if not all, of them take their rise from confounding reasoning or deduction, properly so called, with certain other intellectual processes which it is necessary for us to employ in the investigation of truth. That it is frequently of essential importance to us, in our speculations, to withdraw our attention from words, and to direct it to the things they denote, I am very ready to acknowledge. All that I assert is, that in so far as our speculations consist of that process of the mind which is properly called reasoning, they may be carried on by words alone; or, which comes to the same thing, that every process of reasoning is perfectly analogous to an algebraical operation. What I mean by "the other intellectual processes distinct from reasoning, which it is necessary for us sometimes to employ in the investigation of truth", will, I hope, appear clearly from the following remarks.

In algebraical investigations, it is well known that the practical application of a general expression, is frequently limited by the conditions which the hypothesis involves, and that in consequence of a want of attention to this circumstance, some mathematicians of the first eminence have been led to adopt the most paradoxical and absurd conclusions. Without this cautious exercise of the judgment, in the interpretation of the algebraical language, no dexterity in the use of the calculus will be sufficient to preserve us from error. Even in algebra, therefore, there is an application of the intellectual powers perfectly distinct from any process of reasoning, and which is absolutely necessary for conducting us to the truth.

In geometry we are not liable to adopt the same paradoxical conclusions as in algebra, because the diagrams to which our attention is directed, serve as a continual check on our reasoning powers. These diagrams exhibit to our very senses, a variety of relations among the quantities under consideration, which the language of algebra is too general to express, in consequence of which we are not conscious of any effort of the judgment distinct from a process of reasoning. As every geometrical investigation, however, may be expressed algebraically, it is manifest that in geometry, as well as in algebra, there is an exercise of the intellectual powers distinct from the logical process, although in the former science it is rendered so easy by the use of diagrams as to escape our attention.

The same source of error and of absurdity which exists in algebra, is to be found in a much greater degree in the other branches of knowledge. Abstracting entirely from the ambiguity of language, and supposing also our reasonings to be logically accurate, it would still be necessary for us, from time to time, in all our speculations, to lay aside the use of words, and to have recourse to particular examples or illustrations, in order to correct and to limit our general conclusions. To a want of attention to this circumstance, a number of the speculative absurdities which are current in the world, might, I am persuaded, be easily traced.

Besides, however, this source of error, which is in some degree common to all the sciences, there is a great variety of others from which mathematics are entirely exempted, and which perpetually tend to lead us astray in our philosophical inquiries. Of these, the most important is that ambiguity in the signification of words, which renders it so difficult to avoid employing the same expressions in different senses, in the course of the same process of reasoning. This source of mistake, indeed, is apt in a much greater degree to affect our conclusions in metaphysics, morals, and politics, than in the different branches of natural philosophy, but, if we except mathematics, there is no science whatever in which it has not a very sensible influence. In algebra, we may proceed with perfect safety through the longest investigations, without carrying our attention beyond the signs, till we arrive at the last result. But in the other sciences, excepting in those cases in which we have fixed the meaning of all our terms by accurate definitions, and have rendered the use of these terms perfectly familiar to us by very long habit, it is but seldom that we can proceed in this manner without danger of error. In many cases, it is necessary for us to keep up during the whole of our investigations, a scrupulous and constant attention to the signification of our expressions; and in most cases, this caution in the use of words is a much more difficult effort of the mind than the logical process. But still this furnishes no exception to the general doctrine already delivered; for the attention we find it necessary to give to the import of our words, arises only from the accidental circumstance of their ambiguity, and has no essential connexion with that process of the mind which is properly called reasoning, and which consists in the inference of a conclusion from premises. In all the sciences, this process of the mind is perfectly analogous to an algebraical operation; or, in other words, (when the meaning of our expressions is once fixed by definitions,) it may be carried on entirely by the use of signs, without attending during the time of the process to the thing signified.

The conclusion to which the foregoing observations lead, appears to me to be decisive of the question, with respect to the objects of our thoughts when we employ general terms; for, if it be granted that words, even when employed without any reference to their particular signification, form an instrument of thought sufficient for all the purposes of reasoning, the only shadow of an argument in proof of the common doctrine on the subject, (I mean that which is founded on the impossibility of explaining this process of the mind on any other hypothesis,) falls to the ground. Nothing less, surely, than a conviction of this impossibility, could have so long reconciled philosophers to an hypothesis unsupported by any direct evidence, and acknowledged even by its warmest defenders to involve much difficulty and mystery.

It does not fall within my plan to enter, in this part of my work, into a particular consideration of the practical consequences which follow from the foregoing doctrine. I cannot, however, help remarking the importance of cultivating, on the one hand, a talent for ready and various illustration; and, on the other, a habit of reasoning by means of general terms. The former talent is necessary, not only for correcting and limiting our general conclusions, but for enabling us to apply our knowledge, when occasion requires, to its real practical use. The latter serves the double purpose of preventing our attention from being distracted during the course of our reasonings, by ideas which are foreign to the point in question; and of diverting the attention from those conceptions of particular objects and particular events which might disturb the judgment, by the ideas and feelings which are apt to be associated with them, in consequence of our own casual experience.

...

It appears farther, from the remarks which have been made, that the perfection of philosophical language, considered either as an instrument of thought, or as a medium of communication with others, consists in the use of expressions, which, from their generality, have no tendency to awaken the powers of conception and imagination; or, in other words, it consists in its approaching, as nearly as possible, in its nature, to the language of Algebra. ...

***

It has been already shown that, without the use of signs, all our knowledge must necessarily have been limited to individuals, and that we should have been perfectly incapable both of classification and general reasoning. Some authors have maintained, that without the power of generalization, (which I have endeavoured to show means nothing more than the capacity of employing general terms,) it would have been impossible for us to have carried on any species of reasoning whatever. But I cannot help thinking that this opinion is erroneous, or, at least, that it is very imperfectly stated. The truth is, it appears to me to be just in one sense of the word *reasoning*, but false in another; and I even suspect it is false in that sense of the word in which it is most commonly employed. Before, therefore, it is laid down as a general proposition, the meaning we are to annex to this very vague and ambiguous term should be ascertained with precision.

It has been remarked by several writers, that the expectation which we feel of the continuance of the laws of nature, is not founded upon reasoning, and different theories have of late been proposed to account for its origin. Mr. Hume resolves it into the association of ideas. Dr. Reid, on the other hand, maintains that it is an original principle of our constitution which does not admit of any explanation, and which, therefore, is to be ranked among those general and ultimate facts, beyond which philosophy is unable to proceed. Without this principle of expectation, it would be impossible for us to accommodate our conduct to the established course of nature; and accordingly, we find that it is a principle coeval with our very existence, and in some measure common to man with the lower animals.

...

As we are enabled, by our instinctive anticipation of physical events, to accommodate our conduct to what we foresee is to happen, so we are enabled, in many cases, to increase our power, by employing physical causes as instruments for the accomplishment of our purposes; nay, we can employ a series of such causes, so as to accomplish very remote effects. We can employ the agency of air to increase the heat of a furnace; the furnace to render iron malleable; and the iron to all the various purposes of the mechanical arts. Now, it appears to me that all this may be conceived and done without the aid of language: and yet, assuredly, to discover a series of means subservient to a particular end, or, in other words, an effort of mechanical invention, implies, according to the common doctrines of philosophers, the exercise of our reasoning powers. In this sense, therefore, of the word reasoning, I am inclined to think that it is not essentially connected with the faculty of generalization, or with the use of signs.

...

In general, it may be remarked that, in so far as our thoughts relate merely to individual objects, or to individual events, which we have actually perceived, and of which we retain a distinct remembrance, we are not under the necessity of employing words. It frequently, however, happens, that when the subjects of our consideration are particular, our reasoning with respect to them may involve very general notions; and, in such cases, although we may conceive without the use of words the things about which we reason, yet we must necessarily have recourse to language in carrying on our speculations concerning them. If the *subjects* of our reasoning be general, (under which description I include all our reasonings, whether more or less comprehensive, which do not relate merely to individuals,) words are the sole objects about which our thoughts are employed. According as these words are comprehensive or limited in their signification, the conclusions we form will be more or less general; but this accidental circumstance does not in the least affect the nature of the intellectual process, so that it may be laid down as a proposition which holds without any exception, that, in every case in which we extend our speculations beyond individuals, language is not only a useful auxiliary, but is the sole instrument by which they are carried on.

...

It appears sufficiently from the reasonings which I offered in the preceding section, how important are the advantages which the philosopher acquires, by quitting the study of particulars, and directing his attention to general principles. I flatter myself it appears farther, from the same reasonings, that it is in consequence of the use of language alone, that the human mind is rendered capable of these comprehensive speculations.

In order, however, to proceed with safety in the use of general principles, much caution and address are necessary, both in establishing their truth, and in applying them to practice. Without a proper attention to the circumstances by which their application to particular cases must be modified, they will be a perpetual source of mistake and of disappointment, in the conduct of affairs, however rigidly just they may be in themselves, and however accurately we may reason from them. If our general principles happen to be false, they will involve us in errors, not only of conduct but of speculation; and our errors will be the more numerous, the more comprehensive the principles are on which we proceed.

To illustrate these observations fully, would lead to a minuteness of disquisition inconsistent with my general plan, and I shall therefore, at present, confine myself to such remarks as appear to be of most essential importance.

And, in the first place, it is evidently impossible to establish solid general principles, without the previous study of particulars; in other words, it is necessary to begin with the examination of individual objects, and individual events, in order to lay a ground-work for accurate classification, and for a just investigation of the laws of nature. It is in this way only that we can expect to arrive at general principles, which may be safely relied on, as guides to the knowledge of particular truths;

and unless our principles admit of such a practical application, however beautiful they may appear to be in theory, they are of far less value than the limited acquisitions of the vulgar. The truth of these remarks is now so universally admitted, and is indeed so obvious in itself, that it would be superfluous to multiply words in supporting them; and I should scarcely have thought of stating them in this chapter, if some of the most celebrated philosophers of antiquity had not been led to dispute them, in consequence of the mistaken opinions which they entertained concerning the nature of universals. Forgetting that *genera* and *species* are mere arbitrary creations which the human mind forms, by withdrawing the attention from the distinguishing qualities of objects, and giving a common name to their resembling qualities, they conceive universals to be real existences, or (as they expressed it) to be the essences of individuals; and flattered themselves with the belief, that by directing their attention to these essences in the first instance, they might be enabled to penetrate the secrets of the universe, without submitting to the study of nature in detail. These errors, which were common to the Platonists and the Peripatetics, and which both of them seem to have adopted from the Pythagorean school, contributed, perhaps more than anything else, to retard the progress of the ancients in physical knowledge. The late learned Mr. Harris is almost the only author of the present age who has ventured to defend this plan of philosophizing, in opposition to that which has been so successfully followed by the disciples of Lord Bacon.

The conclusion to which we are led by the foregoing observations is, that the foundation of all human knowledge must be laid in the examination of particular objects and particular facts; and that it is only as far as our general principles are resolvable into these primary elements, that they possess either truth or utility. It must not, however, be understood to be implied in this conclusion, that all our knowledge must ultimately rest on our own proper experience. If this were the case, the progress of science, and the progress of human improvement, must have been wonderfully retarded; for if it had been necessary for each individual to form a classification of objects, in consequence of observations and abstractions of his own, and to infer from the actual examination of particular facts, the general truths on which his conduct proceeds, human affairs would at this day remain nearly in the same state to which they were brought by the experience of the first generation. In fact, this is very nearly the situation of the species in all those parts of the world in which the existence of the race depends on the separate efforts which each individual makes in procuring for himself the necessaries of life, and in which, of consequence, the habits and acquirements of each individual must be the result of his own personal experience. In a cultivated society, one of the first acquisitions which children make is the use of language; by which means they are familiarized, from their earliest years, to the consideration of classes of objects, and of general truths; and before that time of life at which the savage is possessed of the knowledge necessary for his own preservation, are enabled to appropriate to themselves the accumulated discoveries of ages.

Notwithstanding, however, the stationary condition in which the race must, of necessity, continue, prior to the separation of arts and professions, the natural disposition of the mind to ascend from particular truths to general conclusions, could not fail to lead individuals, even in the rudest state of society, to collect the results of their experience, for their own instruction and that of others. But without the use of general terms, the only possible way of communicating such conclusions, would be by means of some particular example, of which the general application was striking and obvious. In other words, the wisdom of such ages will necessarily be expressed in the form of fables or parables, or in the still simpler form of proverbial instances, and not in the scientific form of general maxims. In this way, undoubtedly, much useful instruction, both of a prudential and moral kind, might be conveyed: at the same time, it is obvious that, while general truths continue to be expressed merely by particular exemplifications, they would afford little or no opportunity to one generation to improve on the speculations of another; as no effort of the understanding could combine them together, or employ them as premises, in order to obtain other conclusions more remote and comprehensive. For this purpose, it is absolutely necessary that the scope or moral of the fable should be separated entirely from its accessory circumstances, and stated in the form of a general proposition.

From what has now been said, it appears how much the progress of human reason, which necessarily accompanies the progress of society, is owing to the introduction of general terms, and to the use of general propositions. In consequence of the gradual improvements which take place in language as an instrument of thought, the classifications both of things and facts with which the infant faculties of each successive race are conversant, are more just and more comprehensive than those of their predecessors; the discoveries which, in one age, were confined to the studious and enlightened few, becoming in the next the established creed of the learned; and in the third, forming part of the elementary principles of education. Indeed, among those who enjoy the advantages of early instruction, some of the most remote and wonderful conclusions of the human intellect are, even in infancy, as completely familiarized to the mind, as the most obvious phenomena which the material world exhibits to their senses.

If these remarks be just, they open an unbounded prospect of intellectual improvement to future ages; as they point out a provision made by nature to facilitate and abridge more and more the process of study, in proportion as the truths to be acquired increase in number. Nor is this prospect derived from theory alone. It is encouraged by the past history of all the sciences, in a more particular manner by that of mathematics and physics, in which the state of discovery, and the prevailing methods of instruction, may at all times be easily compared together.

SELECTION 13

Association of Ideas

That one thought is often suggested to the mind by another, and that the sight of an external object often recalls former occurrences and revives former feelings, are facts which are perfectly familiar even to those who are the least disposed to speculate concerning the principles of their nature. In passing along a road which we have formerly travelled in the company of a friend, the particulars of the conversation in which we were then engaged are frequently suggested to us by the objects we meet with. In such a scene, we recollect that a particular subject was started; and, in passing the different houses, and plantations, and rivers, the arguments we were discussing when we last saw them recur spontaneously to the memory. The connexion which is formed in the mind between the words of a language and the ideas they denote; the connexion which is formed between the different words of a discourse we have committed to memory; the connexion between the different notes of a piece of music in the mind of the musician, are all obvious instances of the same general law of our nature.

The influence of perceptible objects in reviving former thoughts and former feelings, is more particularly remarkable. After time has, in some degree, reconciled us to the death of a friend, how wonderfully are we affected the first time we enter the house where he lived! Everything we see - the apartment where he studied - the chair upon which he sat, recall to us the happiness we have enjoyed together; and we should feel it a sort of violation of that respect we owe to his memory, to engage in any light or indifferent discourse when such objects are before us. In the case, too, of those remarkable scenes which interest the curiosity, from the memorable persons or transactions which we have been accustomed to connect with them in the course of our studies, the fancy is more awakened by the actual perception of the scene itself, than by the mere conception or imagination of it. Hence the pleasure we enjoy in visiting classical ground, in beholding the retreats which inspired the genius of our favourite authors, or the fields which have been dignified by exertions of heroic virtue. ...

...

This influence of perceptible objects in awakening associated thoughts and associated feelings, seems to arise in a great measure from their permanent operation as exciting or suggesting causes. When a train of thought takes its rise from an idea or conception, the first idea soon disappears, and a series of others succeeds, which are gradually less and less related to that with which the train commenced; but in the case of perception, the exciting cause remains steadily before us, and all the thoughts and feelings which have any relation to it, crowd into the mind in rapid succession, strengthening each other's effects, and all conspiring in the same general impression.

...

To this tendency which one thought has to introduce another, philosophers have given the name of the *Association of Ideas;* and as I would not wish, excepting in a case of necessity, to depart from common language, or to expose myself to the charge of delivering old doctrines in a new form, I shall continue to make use of the same expression. I am sensible, indeed, that the expression is by no means unexceptionable, and that, if it be used (as it frequently has been) to comprehend those laws by which the succession of all our thoughts and of all our mental operations is regulated, the word *idea* must be understood in a sense much more extensive than it is commonly employed in. It is very justly remarked by Dr. Reid, that "memory, judgment, reasoning, passions, affections, and purposes; in a word, every operation of the mind, excepting those of sense, is excited occasionally in the train of our thoughts, so that if we make the train of our thoughts to be only a train of ideas, the word *idea* must be understood to denote all these operations". In continuing, therefore, to employ upon this subject that language which has been consecrated by the practice of our best philosophical writers in England, I would not be understood to dispute the advantages which might be derived from the introduction of a new phrase, more precise and more applicable to the fact.

The ingenious author whom I last quoted, seems to think that the *association of ideas* has no claim to be considered as an original principle, or as an ultimate fact in our nature. "I believe", says he, "that the original principles of the mind, of which we can give no account, but that such is our constitution, are more in number than is commonly thought. But we ought not to multiply them without necessity. That trains of thinking which by frequent repetition have become familiar, should spontaneously offer themselves to our fancy, seems to require no other original quality but the power of habit".

With this observation I cannot agree, because I think it more philosophical to resolve the power of habit into the association of ideas, than to resolve the association of ideas into habit.

The word *habit,* in the sense in which it is commonly employed, expresses that facility which the mind acquires in all its exertions, both animal and intellectual, in consequence of practice. We apply it to the dexterity of the workman, to the extemporary fluency of the orator, to the rapidity of the arithmetical accountant. That this facility is the effect of practice, we know from experience to be a fact, but it does not seem to be an ultimate fact, nor incapable of analysis.

In the Essay on Attention, I showed that the effects of practice are produced partly on the body, and partly on the mind. The muscles which we employ in mechanical operations become stronger, and become more obedient to the will. This is a fact, of which it is probable that philosophy will never be able to give any explanation.

But even in mechanical operations, the effects of practice are produced partly on the mind; and, as far as this is the case, they are resolvable into what philosophers call the *association of ideas*, or into that general fact which Dr. Reid himself has stated, "that trains of thinking, which, by frequent repetition, have become familiar, spontaneously offer themselves to the mind". In the case of habits which are purely intellectual, the effects of practice resolve themselves completely into this principle: and it appears to me more precise and more satisfactory, to state the principle itself as a law of our constitution, than to slur it over under the concise appellation of *habit*, which we apply in common to mind and to body.

...

The facts which I stated in the former Section, to illustrate the tendency of a perception, or of an idea, to suggest ideas related to it, are so obvious as to be matter of common remark. But the relations which connect all our thoughts together, and the laws which regulate their succession, were but little attended to before the publication of Mr. Hume's writings.

It is well known to those who are in the least conversant with the present state of metaphysical science, that this eminent writer has attempted to reduce all the principles of association among our ideas to three: Resemblance, Contiguity in time and place, and Cause and Effect. The attempt was great, and worthy of his genius; but it has been shown by several writers since his time, that his enumeration is not only incomplete, but it is even indistinct, so far as it goes.

It is not necessary for my present purpose that I should enter into a critical examination of this part of Mr. Hume's system; or that I should attempt to specify those principles of association which he has omitted. Indeed, it does not seem to me that the problem admits of a satisfactory solution; for there is no possible relation among the objects of our knowledge, which may not serve to connect them together in the mind; and therefore although one enumeration may be more comprehensive than another, a perfectly complete enumeration is scarcely to be expected.

...

I have already said that the view of the subject which I propose to take, does not require a complete enumeration of our principles of association. There is, however, an important distinction among them, to which I shall have occasion frequently to refer, and which, as far as I know, has not hitherto attracted the notice of philosophers. The relations upon which some of them are founded are perfectly obvious to the mind; those which are the foundation of others, are discovered only in consequence of particular efforts of attention. Of the former kind are the relations of Resemblance and Analogy, of Contrariety, of Vicinity in time and place, and those which arise from accidental coincidences in the sound of different words. These, in general, connect our thoughts together, when they are suffered to take their natural course, and when we are conscious of little or no active exertion. Of the latter kind, are the relations of Cause and Effect, of Means and End, of Premises and Conclusion; and those others which regulate the train of thought in the mind of the philosopher when he is engaged in a particular investigation.

...

Notwithstanding, however, the immediate dependence of the train of our thoughts on the laws of association, it must not be imagined that the will possesses no influence over it. This influence, indeed, is not exercised directly and immediately as we are apt to suppose on a superficial view of the subject; but it is, nevertheless, very extensive in its effects, and the different degrees in which it is possessed by different individuals, constitute some of the most striking inequalities among men, in point of intellectual capacity.

Of the powers which the mind possesses over the train of its thoughts, the most obvious is its power of singling out anyone of them at pleasure, of detaining it, and of making it a particular object of attention. By doing so, we not only stop the succession that would otherwise take place, but in consequence of our bringing to view the less obvious relations among our ideas, we frequently divert the current of our thoughts into a new channel. If, for example, when I am indolent and inactive, the name of Sir Isaac Newton accidentally occur to me, it will perhaps suggest one after another the names of some other eminent mathematicians and astronomers, or of some of his illustrious contemporaries and friends, and a number of them may pass in review before me, without engaging my curiosity in any considerable degree. In a different state of mind, the name of Newton will lead my thoughts to the principal incidents of his life, and the more striking features of his character; or, if my mind be ardent and vigorous, will lead my attention to the sublime discoveries he made, and gradually engage me in some philosophical investigation. To every object, there are others which bear obvious and striking relations; and others, also, whose relation to it does not readily occur to us, unless we dwell upon it for some time, and place it before us in different points of view.

But the principal power we possess over the train of our ideas, is founded on the influence which our habits of thinking have on the laws of Association; an influence which is so great, that we may often form a pretty shrewd judgment concerning a man's prevailing turn of thought, from the transitions he makes in conversation or in writing. It is well known, too, that by means of habit, a particular associating principle may be strengthened to such a degree, as to give us a command of all the different ideas in our mind which have a certain relation to each other, so that when anyone of the class occurs to us, we have almost a certainty that it will suggest the rest. What confidence in his own powers must a speaker possess, when he rises without premeditation in a popular assembly, to amuse his audience with a lively or a humorous speech! Such a confidence, it is evident, can only arise from a long experience of the strength of particular associating principles.

To how great a degree this part of our constitution may be influenced by habit, appears from facts which are familiar to everyone. A man who has an ambition to become a punster, seldom or never fails in the attainment of his object; that is, he seldom or never fails in acquiring a power which other men have not, of summoning up on a particular occasion a number of words different from each other in meaning, and resembling each other more or less in sound. I am inclined to think that even genuine wit is a habit acquired in a similar way; and that, although some individuals may from natural constitution be more fitted than others to acquire this habit, it is founded in every case on a peculiarly strong association among certain classes of our ideas, which gives the person who possesses it a command over those ideas which is denied to ordinary men. But there is no instance in which the effect of habits of association is more remarkable, than in those men who possess a facility of rhyming. That a man should be able to express his thoughts perspicuously and elegantly, under the restraints which rhyme imposes, would appear to be incredible if we did not know it to be fact. Such a power implies a wonderful command both of ideas and of expressions, and yet daily experience shows that it may be gained with very little practice. Pope tells us with respect to himself, that he could express himself not only more concisely, but more easily, in rhyme than in prose.

Nor is it only in these trifling accomplishments that we may trace the influence of habits of association. In every instance of invention, either in the fine arts, in the mechanical arts, or in the sciences, there is some new idea, or some new combination of ideas, brought to light by the inventor. This, undoubtedly, may often happen in a way which he is unable to explain; that is, his invention may be suggested to him by some lucky thought, the origin of which he is unable to trace. But when a man possesses a habitual fertility of invention in any particular art or science, and can rely, with confidence, on his inventive powers, whenever he is called upon to exert them, he must have acquired, by previous habits of study, a command over certain classes of his ideas, which enables him at pleasure to bring them under his review. …

***

The association of ideas has a tendency to warp our speculative opinions chiefly in the three following ways:

> First, by blending together in our apprehensions, things which are really distinct in their nature, so as to introduce perplexity and error into every process of reasoning in which they are involved.
>
> Secondly, by misleading us in those anticipations of the future from the past, which our constitution disposes us to form, and which are the great foundation of our conduct in life.
>
> Thirdly, by connecting in the mind erroneous opinions, with truths which irresistibly command our assent, and which we feel to be of importance to human happiness.

A short illustration of these remarks will throw light on the origin of various prejudices, and may perhaps suggest some practical hints with respect to the conduct of the understanding.

I. I formerly had occasion to mention several instances of very intimate associations formed between two ideas which have no necessary connexion with each other. One of the most remarkable is, that which exists in every person's mind between the notions of *colour* and of *extension*. The former of these words expresses (at least in the sense in which we commonly employ it) a sensation in the mind, the latter denotes a quality of an external object; so that there is, in fact, no more connexion between the two notions than between those of pain and of solidity; and yet, in consequence of our always perceiving extension, at the same time at which the sensation of colour is excited in the mind, we find it impossible to think of that sensation without conceiving extension along with it.

Another intimate association is formed in every mind between the ideas of *space* and of *time*. When we think of an interval of duration, we always conceive it as something analogous to a line, and we apply the same language to both subjects. We speak of a *long* and *short time*, as well as of a *long* and *short distance*, and we are not conscious of any metaphor in doing so. Nay, so very perfect does the analogy appear to us, that Boscovich mentions it as a curious circumstance, that extension should have three dimensions, and duration only one.

This apprehended analogy seems to be founded wholly on an association between the ideas of space and of time, arising from our always measuring the one of these quantities by the other. We measure time by motion, and motion by extension. In an hour, the hand of the clock moves over a certain space; in two hours, over double the space, and so on. Hence the ideas of space and of time become very intimately united, and we apply to the latter the words *long* and *short*, *before* and *after*, in the same manner as to the former.

The apprehended analogy between the relation which the different notes in the scale of music bear to each other, and the relation of superiority and inferiority in respect of position among material objects, arises also from an accidental association of ideas.

...

In the instances which have now been mentioned, our habits of combining the notions of two things become so strong, that we find it impossible to think of the one, without thinking at the same time of the other. Various other examples of the same species of combination, although perhaps not altogether so striking in degree, might easily be collected from the subjects about which our metaphysical speculations are employed. The *sensations*, for instance, which are excited in the mind by external objects, and the *perceptions* of material qualities which follow these sensations, are to be distinguished from each other only by long habits of patient reflection. A clear conception of this distinction may be regarded as the key to all Dr. Reid's reasonings concerning the process of nature in perception, and till it has once been rendered familiar to the reader, a great part of his writings must appear unsatisfactory and obscure. In truth, our progress in the philosophy of the human mind depends much more on that severe and discriminating judgment, which enables us to separate ideas which nature or habit have immediately combined, than on acuteness of reasoning or fertility of invention. And hence it is that metaphysical studies are the best of all preparations for those philosophical pursuits which relate to the conduct of life. In none of these do we meet with casual combinations so intimate and indissoluble as those which occur in metaphysics, and he who has been accustomed to such discriminations as this science requires, will not easily be imposed on by that confusion of ideas which warps the judgments of the multitude in moral, religious, and political inquiries.

...

II. The association of ideas is a source of speculative error, by misleading us in those anticipations of the future from the past, which are the foundation of our conduct in life.

The great object of philosophy, as I have already remarked more than once, is to ascertain the laws which regulate the succession of events, both in the physical and moral worlds; in order that, when called upon to act in any particular combination of circumstances, we may be enabled to anticipate the probable course of nature from our past experience, and to regulate our conduct accordingly.

As a knowledge of the established connexions among events is the foundation of sagacity and of skill, both in the practical arts and in the conduct of life, nature has not only given to all men a strong disposition to remark, with attention and curiosity, those phenomena which have been observed to happen nearly at the same time, but has beautifully adapted to the uniformity of her own operations, the laws of association in the human mind. By rendering *contiguity in time* one of the strongest of our associating principles, she has conjoined together in our thoughts the same events which we have found conjoined in our experience, and has thus accommodated (without any effort on our part) the order of our ideas to that scene in which we are destined to act.

The degree of experience which is necessary for the preservation of our animal existence, is acquired by all men without any particular efforts of study. The laws of nature, which it is most material for us to know, are exposed to the immediate observation of our senses, and establish, by means of the principle of association, a corresponding order in our thoughts, long before the dawn of reason and reflection, or at least long before that period of childhood to which our recollection afterwards extends.

This tendency of the mind to associate together events which have been presented to it nearly at the same time, although on the whole it is attended with infinite advantages, yet, like many other principles of our nature, may occasionally be a source of inconvenience, unless we avail ourselves of our reason and of our experience in keeping it under proper regulation. Among the various phenomena which are continually passing before us, there is a great proportion whose vicinity in time does not indicate a constancy of conjunction; and unless we be careful to make the distinction between these two classes of connexions, the order of our ideas will be apt to correspond with the one as well as with the other, and our unenlightened experience of the past will fill the mind, in numberless instances, with vain expectations, or with groundless alarms concerning the future. This disposition to confound together accidental and permanent connexions, is one great source of popular superstitions. Hence the regard which is paid to unlucky days, to unlucky colours, and to the influence of the planets; apprehensions which render human life to many a continued series of absurd terrors. ...

Such spectres can be dispelled by the light of philosophy only, which, by accustoming us to trace established connexions, teaches us to despise those which are casual; and, by giving a proper direction to that bias of the mind which is the foundation of superstition, prevents it from leading us astray.

In the instances which we have now been considering, events come to be combined together in the mind merely from the accidental circumstance of their contiguity in time, at the moment when we perceived them. Such combinations are confined, in a great measure, to uncultivated and unenlightened minds, or to those individuals who, from nature or education, have a more than ordinary facility of association. But there are other accidental combinations which are apt to lay hold of the most vigorous understandings, and from which, as they are the natural and necessary result of a limited experience, no superiority of intellect is sufficient to preserve a philosopher in the infancy of physical science.

As the connexions among physical events are discovered to us by experience alone, it is evident that, when we see a phenomenon preceded by a number of different circumstances, it is impossible for us to determine, by any reasoning *a priori*, which of these circumstances are to be regarded as the *constant*, and which as the *accidental*, antecedents of the effect. If, in the course of our experience, the same combination of circumstances is always exhibited to us without any alteration, and is invariably followed by the same result, we must for ever remain ignorant whether this result be connected with the whole combination, or with one or more of the circumstances combined; and therefore, if we are anxious upon any occasion to produce a similar effect, the only rule that we can follow with perfect security, is to imitate in every particular circumstance the combination which we have seen. It is only where we have an opportunity of separating such circumstances from each other, of combining them variously together, and of observing the effects which result from these different experiments, that we can ascertain with precision the general laws of nature, and strip physical causes of their accidental and unessential concomitants.

...

III. ... The remarks which have been already made are sufficient to show how necessary it is for us, in the formation of our philosophical principles, to examine with care all those opinions which, in our early years, we have imbibed from our instructors, or which are connected with our local situation. Nor does the universality of an opinion among men who have received a similar education, afford any presumption in its favour, for however great the deference is which a wise man will always pay to common belief, upon those subjects which have employed the unbiased reason of mankind, he certainly owes it no respect in so far as he suspects it to be influenced by fashion or authority. Nothing can be more just than the observation of Fontenelle, that "the number of those who believe in a system already established in the world, does not in the least add to its credibility, but that the number of those who doubt of it has a tendency to diminish it".

The same remarks lead, upon the other hand, to another conclusion of still greater importance, that notwithstanding the various false opinions which are current in the world, there are some truths which are inseparable from the human understanding, and by means of which the errors of education, in most instances, are enabled to take hold of our belief.

A weak mind, unaccustomed to reflection, and which has passively derived its most important opinions from habits or from authority, when, in consequence of a more enlarged intercourse with the world, it finds that ideas which it had been taught to regard as sacred, are treated by enlightened and worthy men with ridicule, is apt to lose its reverence for the fundamental and eternal truths on which these accessory ideas are grafted, and easily falls a prey to that sceptical philosophy which teaches that all the opinions, and all the principles of action by which mankind are governed, may be traced to the influence of education and example. Amidst the infinite variety of forms, however, which our versatile nature assumes, it cannot fail to strike an attentive observer, that there are certain indelible features common to them all. In one situation, we find good men attached to a republican form of government; in another, to a monarchy; but in all situations we find them devoted to the service of their country and of mankind, and disposed to regard with reverence and love the most absurd and capricious institutions which custom has led them to connect with the order of society. The different appearances, therefore, which the political opinions and the political conduct of men exhibit, while they demonstrate to what a wonderful degree human nature may be influenced by situation and by early instruction, evince the existence of some common and original principles which fit it for the political union, and illustrate the uniform operation of those laws of association to which, in all the stages of society, it is equally subject.

Similar observations are applicable, and indeed in a still more striking degree, to the opinions of mankind on the important questions of religion and morality. The variety of systems which they have formed to themselves concerning these subjects, has often excited the ridicule of the sceptic and the libertine; but if, on the one hand, this variety shows the folly of bigotry, and the reasonableness of mutual indulgence; the curiosity which has led men in every situation to such speculations, and the influence which their conclusions, however absurd, have had on their character and their happiness, prove no less clearly on the other, that there must be some principles from which they all derive their origin, and invite the philosopher to ascertain what are these original and immutable laws of the human mind.

...

The manner in which the association of ideas operates in producing new principles of action, has been explained very distinctly by different writers. Whatever conduces to the gratification of any natural appetite, or of any natural desire, is itself desired on account of the end to which it is subservient; and by being thus habitually associated in our apprehension with agreeable objects, it frequently comes, in process of time, to be regarded as valuable in itself, independently of its utility. It is thus that wealth becomes, with many, an ultimate object of pursuit; although, at first, it is undoubtedly valued merely on account of its subserviency to the attainment of other objects. In like manner, men are led to desire dress, equipage, retinue, furniture, on account of the estimation in which they are supposed to be held by the public. Such desires are called by Dr. Hutcheson *secondary* desires, and their origin is explained by him in the way which I have mentioned. ...

Our moral judgments, too, may be modified, and even perverted to a certain degree, in consequence of the operation of the same principle. In the same manner in which a person who is regarded as a model of taste may introduce, by his example, an absurd or fantastical dress; so a man of splendid virtues may attract some esteem also to his imperfections; and, if placed in a conspicuous situation, may render his vices and follies objects of general imitation among the multitude.

...

It must, I think, in justice be acknowledged, that this theory concerning the origin of our affections, and of the moral sense, is a most ingenious refinement upon the selfish system, as it was formerly taught; and that, by means of it, the force of many of the common reasonings against that system is eluded. Among these reasonings, particular stress has always been laid on the instantaneousness with which our affections operate, and the moral sense approves or condemns; and on our total want of consciousness, in such cases, of any reference to our own happiness. The modern advocates for the selfish system admit the fact to be as it is stated by their opponents, and grant that, after the moral sense and our various affections are formed, their exercise, in particular cases, may become completely disinterested; but still they contend, that it is upon a regard to our own happiness that all these principles are originally grafted. The analogy of avarice will serve to illustrate the scope of this theory. It cannot be doubted that this principle of action is artificial. It is on account of the enjoyments which it enables us to purchase that money is originally desired; and yet, in process of time, by means of the agreeable impressions which are associated with it, it comes to be desired for its own sake, and even continues to be an object of our pursuit, long after we have lost all relish for those enjoyments which it enables us to command.

Without meaning to engage in any controversy on the subject, I shall content myself with observing in general, that there must be some limit beyond which the theory of association cannot possibly be carried; for the explanation which it gives of the formation of new principles of action, proceeds on the supposition that there are other principles previously existing in the mind. The great question then is, when are we arrived at this limit; or, in other words, when are we arrived at the simple and original laws of our constitution?

In conducting this inquiry philosophers have been apt to go into extremes. Lord Kames and some other authors have been censured, and perhaps justly, for a disposition to multiply original principles to an unnecessary degree. It may be questioned whether Dr. Hartley and his followers have not sometimes been misled by too eager a desire of abridging their number.

Of these two errors the former is the least common and the least dangerous. It is the least common, because it is not so flattering as the other to the vanity of a theorist; and it is the least dangerous, because it has no tendency, like the other, to give rise to a suppression or to a misrepresentation of facts, or to retard the progress of the science by bestowing upon it an appearance of systematical perfection, to which in its present state it is not entitled.

Abstracting, however, from these inconveniences which must always result from a precipitate reference of phenomena to general principles, it does not seem to me that the theory in question has any tendency to weaken the foundation of morals. It has, indeed, some tendency, in common with the philosophy of Hobbes and of Mandeville, to degrade the dignity of human nature, but it leads to no sceptical conclusions concerning the rule of life. For, although we were to grant that all our principles of action are acquired, so striking a difference among them must still be admitted, as is sufficient to distinguish clearly those universal laws which were intended to regulate human conduct, from the local habits which are formed by education and fashion. It must still be admitted that while some active principles are confined to particular individuals, or to particular tribes of men, there are others which, arising from circumstances in which all the situations of mankind must agree, are common to the whole species. Such active principles as fall under this last description, at whatever period of life they may appear, are to be regarded as a part of human nature no less than the instinct of suction; in the same manner as the acquired perception of distance by the eye, is to be ranked among the perceptive powers of man, no less than the original perceptions of any of our other senses.

...

... That the casual associations which the mind forms in childhood and in early youth, are frequently a source of inconvenience and of misconduct, is sufficiently obvious; but that this tendency of our nature increases, on the whole, the sum of human enjoyment, appears to me to be indisputable, and the instances in which it misleads us from our duty and our happiness, only prove to what important ends it might be subservient, if it were kept under proper regulation.

Nor do these representations of life (admitting them in their full extent) justify the practical inferences which have been often deduced from them, with respect to the vanity of our pursuits. In every case, indeed, in which our enjoyment depends upon association, it may be said in one sense that it arises from the mind itself; but it does not therefore follow that the external object which custom has rendered the cause or the occasion of agreeable emotions, is indifferent to our happiness. The effect which the beauties of nature produce on the mind of the poet is wonderfully heightened by association, but his enjoyment is not on that account the less exquisite; nor are the objects of his admiration of the less value to his happiness, that they derive their principal charms from the embellishments of his fancy.

...

It is the business of education not to counteract, in any instance, the established laws of our constitution, but to direct them to their proper purposes. That the influence of early associations on the mind might be employed, in the most effectual manner, to aid our moral principles, appears evidently from the effects which we daily see it produce, in reconciling men to a course of action which their reason forces them to condemn; and it is no less obvious that, by means of it, the happiness of human life might be increased, and its pains diminished, if the agreeable ideas and feelings which children are so apt to connect with events and with situations which depend on the caprice of fortune, were firmly associated in their apprehensions with the duties of their stations, with the pursuits of science, and with those beauties of nature which are open to all.

Five

Active Powers

SELECTION 14

Philosophy of the Active Powers of Man—Introduction

In prosecuting our inquiries into the Active and the Moral Powers of Man, I propose, *first*, to attempt a classification and analysis of the most important principles belonging to this part of our constitution; and, *secondly*, to treat of the various branches of our duty. Under the former of these heads, my principal aim will be to illustrate the essential distinction between those active principles which originate in man's rational nature, and those which urge him, by a blind and instinctive impulse, to their respective objects.

In general, it may be here remarked, that the word *action* is properly applied to those exertions which are consequent on volition, whether the exertion be made on external objects, or be confined to our mental operations. Thus we say the mind is active when engaged in study. In ordinary discourse, indeed, we are apt to confound together action and motion. As the operations in the minds of other men escape our notice, we can judge of their activity only from the sensible effects it produces; and hence we are led to apply the character of activity to those whose bodily activity is the most remarkable, and to distinguish mankind into two classes, the active and the speculative. In the present instance, the word *active* is used in its most extensive signification, as applicable to every voluntary exertion.

According to the definition now given of the word *action*, the primary sources of our activity are the circumstances in which the acts of the will originate. Of these there are some which make a part of our constitution, and which, on that account, are called Active Principles. Such are hunger, thirst, the appetite which unites the sexes, curiosity, ambition, pity, resentment. These active principles are also called powers of the will, because, by stimulating us in *various* ways to action, they afford exercise to our sense of duty and our other rational principles of action, and give occasion to our voluntary determinations as free agents.

The study of this part of our constitution, although it may at first view seem to lie more open to our examination than the powers of the understanding, is attended with some difficulties peculiar to itself. For this various reasons may be assigned; among which there are two that seem principally to claim our attention: 1. When we wish to examine the nature of any of our intellectual principles we can at all times subject the faculty in question to the scrutiny of *reflection*, and can institute whatever experiments with respect to it may be necessary for ascertaining its general laws. It is characteristical of all our operations, purely intellectual, to leave the mind cool and undisturbed, so that the *exercise* of the faculties concerned in them does not prevent us from an analytical investigation of their theory. The case is very different with our active powers, particularly with those which, from their violence and impetuosity, have the greatest influence on human happiness. When we are under the dominion of the power, or, in plainer language, when we are hurried by *passion* to the pursuit of a particular end, we feel no inclination to speculate concerning the mental phenomena. When the tumult subsides, and our curiosity is awakened concerning the past, the moment for observation and experiment is lost, and we are obliged to search for our facts in an imperfect recollection of what was viewed, even in the *first* instance, through the most troubled and deceitful of all *media*.

Something connected with this is the following remark of Mr. Hume: 'Moral philosophy has this peculiar disadvantage, which is not to be found in natural, that, in collecting its experiments, it cannot make them purposely, with premeditation, and after such a manner as to satisfy itself concerning every particular difficulty that may arise. When I am at a loss to know the effects of one body upon another in any situation, I need only put them in that situation, and observe what results from it. But should I endeavour to clear up, after the same manner, any doubts in moral philosophy, by placing myself in the same case with that which I consider, 'tis evident, that this reflection and premeditation would so disturb the operation of my natural principles, as must render it impossible to form any just conclusion from the phenomenon. We must therefore glean up our experiments in this science from a cautious observation of human life, and take them as they appear in the common course of the world, by men's behaviour in company, in affairs, and in their pleasures'.

Another circumstance which adds much to the difficulty of this branch of study, is the great variety of our active principles, and the endless diversity of their combinations in the characters of men. The same action may proceed from very different, and even opposite motives in the case of two individuals, and even in the same individual on different occasions; or, an action which in one man proceeds from a single motive, may, in another, proceed from a number of motives conspiring together and modifying each other's effects. The philosophers who have speculated on this subject, have in general been misled by an excessive love of simplicity, and have attempted to explain the phenomena from the smallest possible number of data. Overlooking the real complication of our active principles, they have sometimes fixed on a single one, (good or bad, according as they were disposed to think well or ill of human nature,) and have deduced from it a plausible explanation of all the varieties of human character and conduct.

Our inquiries on this subject must be conducted in one of two ways, either by studying the characters of other men, or by studying our own. In the former way, we may undoubtedly collect many useful hints, and many facts to confirm or to limit our conclusions; but the conjectures we form concerning the motives of others are liable to so much uncertainty, that it is chiefly by attending to what passes in our own minds that we can reasonably hope to ascertain the general laws of our constitution as active and moral beings.

Even this plan of study, however, as I already hinted, requires uncommon perseverance, and still more uncommon candour. The difficulty is great of attending to any of the operations of the mind; but this difficulty is much increased in those cases in which we are led by vanity or timidity to fancy that we have an interest in concealing the truth from our own knowledge.

Most men, perhaps, are disposed, in consequence of these and some other causes, to believe themselves better than they really are; and a few, there is reason to suspect, go into the opposite extreme, from the influence of false systems of philosophy or religion, or from the gloomy views inspired by a morbid melancholy.

When to these considerations we add the endless metaphysical disputes on the subject of the will, and of man's free agency, it may easily be conceived that the field of inquiry upon which we are now to enter abounds with questions not less curious and intricate than any of those which have been hitherto under our review. In point of practical importance some of them will be found in a still higher degree entitled to our attention.

In the further prosecution of this subject, I shall avoid, as much as possible, all technical divisions and classifications, and shall content myself with the following enumeration of our Active Principles, which I hope will be found sufficiently distinct and comprehensive for our purposes.

1. Appetites
2. Desires
3. Affections
4. Self-love
5. The Moral Faculty

The three first may be distinguished (for a reason which will afterwards appear) by the title of *Instinctive or Implanted Propensities*; the two last by the title of *Rational and Governing Principles of Action*.[1]

---

[1] In the above enumeration I have departed widely from Dr. Reid's language. (See his *Essays on the Active Powers*, Essay III., Parts i., ii., iii.) This great philosopher, with whom I am always unwilling to differ, refers our active principles to three classes, the Mechanical, the Animal, and the Rational; using all these three words

SELECTION 15

Perception of Right and Wrong

The controversy concerning the origin of our moral ideas took its rise in modern times, in consequence of the writings of Mr. Hobbes. According to him we approve of virtuous actions, or of actions beneficial to society, from self-love, as we know that whatever promotes the interest of society, has on that *very* account an indirect tendency to promote our own. He further taught, that, as it is to the institution of government we are indebted for all the comforts and the confidence of social life, the laws which the civil magistrate enjoins are the ultimate standards of morality.

Dangerous as these doctrines are, some apology may be made for the author from the unfortunate circumstances of the times in which he lived. He had been a witness of the disorders which took place in England at the time of the dissolution of the monarchy by the death of Charles the First; and, in consequence of his mistaken speculations on the politics of that period, he contracted a bias in favour of despotical

---

with what I think a very exceptionable latitude. My reasons for objecting to the use he makes of the words animal and rational will appear in the sequel. On this occasion I shall only observe, that the word *mechanical*, (under which he comprehends our *instincts and habits*,) cannot, in my opinion, be properly applied to any of our active principles. It is indeed used, in this instance, merely as a term of distinction; but it *seems* to imply some theory concerning the nature of the principles comprehended under it, and is apt to suggest incorrect notions on the subject. If I had been disposed to examine this part of our constitution with all the minute accuracy of which it is susceptible, I should have preferred the following arrangement to that which I have adopted, as well as to that proposed by Dr. Reid. 1. Of our *original* principles of action. 2. Of our *acquired* principles of action. The original principles of action may be subdivided into the *animal* and the *rational*; to the former of which classes our *instincts* ought undoubtedly to be referred, as well as our *appetites*. In Dr. Reid's arrangement, nothing appears more unaccountable, if not capricious, than to call our appetites *animal* principles, because they are common to man and to the brutes; and, at the same time, to distinguish our *instincts* by the title of *mechanical*; when, of all our active propensities, there are none in which the nature of man bears so strong an analogy to that of the lower animals as in these instinctive impulses. Indeed, it is from the condition of the brutes that the word *instinct* is transferred to that of man by a sort of figure or metaphor.

Our *acquired* principles of action comprehend all those propensities to act which we acquire from habit. Such are our artificial appetites and artificial desires, and the various factitious motives of human conduct generated by association and fashion. At present, it being useless for any of the purposes which I have in view to attempt so comprehensive and detailed an examination of the subject, I shall confine myself to the general enumeration already mentioned. As our appetites, our desires, and our affections, whether original or acquired, stand in the same common relation to the Moral Faculty, (the illustration of which is the chief object of this volume,) I purposely avoid those slighter and less important

government, and was led to consider it as the duty of a good citizen to strengthen, as much as possible, the hands of the civil magistrate, by inculcating the doctrines of passive obedience and non-resistance. It was with this view that he was led to maintain the philosophical principles which have been already mentioned. He seems likewise to have formed a very unfavourable idea of the clerical order, from the instances which his own experience afforded of their turbulence and ambition; and on that account he wished to subject the consciences of men immediately to the secular powers. In consequence of this, his system, although offensive in a very high degree to all sound moralists, provoked in a more peculiar manner the resentment of the clergy, and drew on the author a great deal of personal obloquy, which neither his character in private life, nor his intentions as a writer, appear to have merited.

Among the antagonists of Hobbes, the most eminent by far was Dr. Cudworth; and indeed modern times have not produced an author who was better qualified to do justice to the very important argument he undertook, by his ardent zeal for the best interests of mankind, by his singular vigour and comprehensiveness of thought, and by the astonishing treasures he had collected of ancient literature.

That our ideas of right and wrong are not derived from positive law Cudworth concluded from the following argument: "Suppose such a law to be established, it must either be right to obey it, and wrong to disobey it, or indifferent whether we obey or disobey it. But a law which it is indifferent whether we obey or not, cannot, it is evident, be the source of moral distinctions; and, on the contrary supposition, if it is right to obey the law, and wrong to disobey it, these distinctions must have had an existence antecedent to the law". In a word, it is from *natural* law that *positive* law derives all its force.

...

At the time when Cudworth wrote, no accurate classification had been attempted of the principles of the Human Mind. His account of the office of reason, accordingly, in enabling us to perceive the distinction between right and wrong, passed without censure, and was understood merely to imply, that there is an eternal and immutable distinction between right and wrong, no less than between truth and falsehood; and that both these distinctions are perceived by our rational powers, or by those powers which raise us above the brutes.

The publication of Locke's *Essay* introduced into this part of science a precision of expression unknown before, and taught philosophers to distinguish a variety of powers which had formerly been very generally confounded. With these great merits, however, his work has capital defects, and perhaps in no part of it are these defects more important

---

subdivisions which might be thought to savour unnecessarily of scholastic subtlety.

than in the attempt he has made to deduce the origin of our knowledge entirely from *Sensation* and *Reflection*. To the former of these sources he refers the ideas we receive by our external senses, of colours, sounds, hardness, &c. To the latter, the ideas we derive from consciousness of our own mental operations of memory, imagination, volition, pleasure, pain, &c. These, according to him, are the sources of all our simple ideas; and the only power that the mind possesses is to perform certain operations of analysis, combination, comparison, &c., on the materials with which it is thus supplied.

It was this system of Locke's which led him to those dangerous opinions that were formerly mentioned concerning the nature of moral distinctions, which he seems to have considered as entirely the offspring of education and fashion. Indeed, if the words *right* and *wrong* neither express simple ideas, nor relations discoverable by reason, it will not be found easy to avoid adopting this conclusion.

In order to reconcile Locke's account of the origin of our ideas with the immutability of moral distinctions, different theories were proposed concerning the nature of virtue. According to one,[2] for example, it was said to consist in a conduct conformable to *truth*; according to another,[3] in a conduct conformable to the *fitness of things*. The great object of all these theories may be considered as the same, to remove right and wrong from the class of simple ideas, and to resolve moral rectitude into a conformity with some relation perceived by reason or by the understanding.

Dr. Hutcheson saw clearly the vanity of these attempts, and hence he was led, in compliance with the language of Locke's Philosophy, to refer the origin of our moral ideas to a particular power of perception, to which he gave the name of the *Moral Sense*. "All the ideas", says he, "or the materials of our reasoning or judging, are received by some immediate powers of Perception, internal or external, which we may call *Senses*. ... Reasoning or Intellect seems to raise no new species of ideas, but to discover or discern the Relations of those received".

According to this system, as it has been commonly explained, our perceptions of right and wrong are *impressions* which our minds are made to receive from particular actions, similar to the relishes and aversions given us for particular objects of the external and internal senses.

...

Mr. Hume, whose philosophy coincides in this respect with Dr. Hutcheson's, has expressed himself on this subject still more explicitly. ...

... The words *Right* and *Wrong* (according to him) signify nothing in the objects themselves to which they are applied, any more than the words sweet and bitter, pleasant and painful, but only certain effects in

---

[2] Mr. Wollaston
[3] Dr. Clarke

the mind of the spectator. As it is improper, therefore, (according to the doctrines of some modern philosophers,) to say of an object of taste that it is sweet, or of heat that it is in the fire, so it is equally improper to say of actions that they are right or wrong. It is absurd to speak of morality as a thing independent and unchangeable, inasmuch as it arises from an arbitrary relation between our constitution and particular objects. The distinction of moral good and evil is founded on the pleasure or pain which results from the view of any sentiment or character; and, as that pleasure or pain cannot be unknown to the person who feels it, it follows that there is just so much vice or virtue in any character as everyone places in it; and that it is impossible in this particular we can ever be mistaken.

...

With respect to this sceptical philosophy as it is taught in the writings of Hume, it appears evidently, from what has been already said, to be founded entirely on the supposition that our perception of the moral qualities of actions has some analogy to our perception of the sensible qualities of matter; and therefore it becomes a very interesting inquiry for us to examine how far this supposition is agreeable to fact. Indeed this is the most important question that can be stated with respect to the theory of morals; and yet I confess it appears to me that the obscurity in which it is involved arises chiefly, if not wholly, from the use of indefinite and ambiguous terms.

That moral distinctions are perceived by a sense is implied in the definition of a sense already quoted from Dr. Hutcheson, "All the ideas, or the materials of our reasoning or judging, are received by some immediate powers of Perception, internal or external, which we may call *Senses*. Reasoning or Intellect seems to raise no new species of ideas, but to discover or discern the Relations of those received". If this definition be admitted, there cannot be a doubt that the origin of our moral ideas must be referred to a sense; at least there can be no doubt upon this point among those who hold, with Cudworth and with Price, that the words right and wrong express simple ideas. ...

...

It may be farther observed, in justification of Dr. Hutcheson, that the sceptical consequences deduced from his supposition of a *Moral Sense*, do not necessarily result from it. Unfortunately, most of his illustrations were taken from the *secondary* qualities of matter, which since the time of Descartes, philosophers have been in general accustomed to refer to the mind, and not to the external object. But if we suppose our perception of right and wrong to be analogous to the perception of extension and figure and other *primary* qualities, the reality and immutability of moral distinctions seem to be placed on a foundation sufficiently satisfactory to a candid inquirer. That our notions of primary qualities are necessarily accompanied with a conviction of their separate and independent existence was formerly shown; and, therefore, to compare our perception of right and wrong to our perception of extension and of figure, although it may not perhaps be very accurate or philosophical, does not imply any scepticism with respect to the immutability of moral distinctions; at least does not justify those sceptical inferences which Mr. Hume has endeavoured to deduce from Dr. Hutcheson's language.

The definition, however, of a Sense which Dr. Hutcheson has given is by far too general, and was plainly suggested to him by Locke's account of the Origin of our ideas. The words Cause and Effect, Duration, Number, Equality, Identity, and many others, express simple ideas as well as the words Right and Wrong; and yet it would surely be absurd to ascribe each of them to a particular power of Perception. Notwithstanding this circumstance, as the expression *Moral Sense* has now the sanction of use, and as, when properly explained, it cannot lead to any bad consequences, it may be still retained without inconvenience in ethical disquisitions. It has been much in fashion among moralists since the time of Shaftesbury and Hutcheson, nor was it an innovation introduced by them; for the ancients often speak of a *Sensus Recti et Honesti*; and, in our own language, *a Sense of Duty* is a phrase not only employed by philosophers, but habitually used in common discourse.

To what part of our constitution then shall we ascribe the origin of the ideas of right and wrong? Dr. Price (returning to the antiquated phraseology of Cudworth) says - to the *Understanding*, and endeavours to show, in opposition to Locke and his followers, that "the power which understands, or the faculty that discerns truth, is itself a source of new ideas".

This controversy turns solely on the meaning of words. The origin of our ideas of Right and Wrong is manifestly the same with that of the other simple ideas already mentioned; and, whether it be referred to the Understanding or not, seems to be a matter of mere arrangement, provided it be granted that the words right and wrong express qualities of actions, and not merely a power of exciting certain agreeable or disagreeable emotions in our minds.

It may perhaps obviate some objections against the language of Cudworth and Price, to remark that the word *Reason* is used in senses which are extremely different: sometimes to express the whole of those powers which elevate man above the brutes, and constitute his rational nature (more especially, perhaps, his intellectual powers); sometimes to express the power of deduction or argumentation. The former is the sense in which the word is used in common discourse; and it is in this sense that it seems to be employed by those writers who refer to it the origin of our moral ideas. Their antagonists, on the other hand, understand in general, by Reason, the power of deduction or argumentation; a use of the word which is not unnatural, from the similarity between the words reason and reasoning, but which is not agreeable to its ordinary meaning. "No hypothesis", says Dr. Campbell, "hitherto invented hath shown that, by means of the discursive faculty, without the aid of any other mental power, we could ever obtain a notion either of the beautiful or the good". The remark is undoubtedly true; and it may be applied to all those systems which ascribe to *Reason* the origin of our moral ideas, if the expressions reason and discursive faculty be used as synonymous. But if the word Reason be used in a more general sense to denote merely our rational and intellectual nature, there does not seem to be much impropriety in ascribing to it the origin of those simple notions which are not excited in the mind by the immediate operation of the senses, but which arise in consequence of the exercise of the intellectual powers upon their various objects.

A variety of intuitive judgments might be mentioned involving simple ideas, which it is impossible to trace to any origin but to the power which enables us to form these judgments. Thus it is surely an intuitive truth, that the sensations of which I am conscious, and all those I remember, belong to one and the same being, which I call *myself*. Here is an intuitive judgment involving the simple idea of *Identity*. In like manner, the changes which I perceive in the universe impress me with a conviction that some cause must have operated to produce them. Here is an intuitive judgment involving the simple idea of *Causation*. When we consider the adjacent angles made by a straight line standing upon another, and perceive that their sum is equal to two right angles, the judgment we form involves the simple idea of *Equality*. To say, therefore, that Reason, or the Understanding, is a source of new ideas, is not so exceptionable a mode of speaking as has some times been supposed. According to Locke, *Sense* furnishes our ideas, and *Reason* perceives their agreements or disagreements; whereas, in point of fact, these agreements or disagreements are in many instances simple ideas, of which no analysis can be given, and of which the origin must therefore be referred to reason, according to Locke's own doctrine.

...

The opinion we form, however, on this point, is of little moment, provided it be granted that the words Right and Wrong express qualities of actions. When I say of an act of justice that it is *right*, do I mean merely that the act excites pleasure in my mind, as a particular colour pleases my eye, in consequence of a relation which it bears to my organ? Or do I mean to assert *a truth* which is as independent of my constitution as the equality of the three angles of a triangle to two right angles? Scepticism may be indulged in both cases, about mathematical and about moral truth, but in neither case does it admit of a refutation by argument.

For my own part, I can as easily conceive a rational being so formed as to believe the three angles of a triangle to be equal to *one* right angle, as to believe that if he had it in his power it would be *right* to sacrifice the happiness of other men to the gratification of his own animal appetites, or that there would be no *injustice* in depriving an industrious old man of the fruits of his own laborious acquisitions. The exercise of our reason in the two cases is very different; but in both cases we have a perception of *truth*, and are impressed with an irresistible conviction that the truth is immutable and independent of the will of any being whatever.

SELECTION 16

Man's Free Agency

All the foregoing inquiries concerning the moral constitution of man, proceed on the supposition that he has a *freedom of choice between good and evil*, and that, when he deliberately performs an action which he knows to be wrong, he renders himself justly obnoxious to punishment. That this supposition is agreeable to the common apprehensions of mankind will not be disputed.

From very early times indeed the truth of the supposition has been called in question by a few speculative men, who have contended that the actions we perform are the necessary result of the constitutions of our minds, operated on by the circumstances of our external situation; and that what we call moral delinquencies are as much a part of our destiny as the corporeal or intellectual qualities we have received from Nature. The argument in support of this doctrine has been proposed in various forms, and has been frequently urged with the confidence of demonstration.

This question about Predestination and Free-will has furnished, in all ages and countries, inexhaustible matter of contention, both to Philosophers and Divines. In the ancient schools of Greece it is well known how generally and how keenly it was agitated. Among the Mahometans it constitutes one of the principal points of division between the followers of Omar and those of Ali; and among the ancient Jews it was the subject of endless dispute between the Pharisees and the Sadducees. It is scarcely necessary for me to add, what violent controversies it has produced, and still continues to produce, in the Christian world.

As this controversy, like most others in metaphysics, has been involved in much unnecessary perplexity by the ambiguity of language, a few brief remarks on some *equivocal terms* connected with the question at issue, may perhaps add something to the perspicuity and precision of the following reasonings. In stating these remarks, however, I shall not scrupulously confine myself to such as are to bear on my intended argument, but shall avail myself of every opportunity that may occur of correcting those inaccurate modes of speaking which have any connexion, however distant, with this important article in the Philosophy of the Human Mind.

The word *Volition* is defined by Locke to be "an act of the mind, knowingly exerting that dominion it takes itself to have over any part of the man, by employing it ill, or withholding it from any particular action". Dr. Reid defines it more briefly to be, "the determination of the mind to do or not to do something which we conceive to be in our power". He remarks, at the same *time*, that "this definition is not strictly logical, inasmuch as *the determination of the mind* is only another term for volition. But it ought to be observed, that the most simple acts of the mind do not admit of being logically defined. The only way to form a precise notion of them is to reflect attentively upon them as we feel them in ourselves. Without this reflection no definition can enable us to reason about them with correctness".

It is necessary to form a distinct notion of what is meant by the word *Volition*, in order to understand the import of the word *Will*; for this last word properly expresses that *power* of the mind of which volition is the *act*, and it is only by attending to what we experience, while we are conscious of the act, that we can understand anything concerning the nature of the power.

The word *Will*, however, is not always used in this its proper acceptation, but is frequently substituted for *Volition*; as when I say that my hand moves in obedience to my *Will*. This indeed happens to the names of most of the powers of the mind; that the same word is employed to express the *power* and the *act*. Thus Imagination signifies both the power and the act of imagining; Abstraction signifies both the power and the act of abstracting, and so in other instances. But although the word *Will* may, without departing from the usual forms of speech, be used indiscriminately for the power and the act, the word *Volition* applies only to the latter; and it would undoubtedly contribute to the distinctness of our reasonings to restrict the signification of the word *Will* entirely to the former.

It is not necessary, I apprehend, to enlarge any more on the meaning of these terms. It is to be learned only from careful reflection on what passes in our own minds, and to multiply words upon the subject would only involve it in obscurity.

There is, however, a state of the mind perfectly distinct, both from the power and the act of willing, with which they have been frequently confounded, and of which it may therefore be proper to mention the characteristical marks. The state I refer to is properly called *Desire*, the distinction between which and *Will* was first clearly pointed out by Mr. Locke. "I find the *Will*", says he, "often confounded with several of the affections, especially *Desire*, and that by men who would not willingly be thought not to have had very distinct notions of things, and not to have writ very clearly about them". "This", he justly adds, "has been no small occasion of obscurity and mistake in this matter, and therefore is, as much as may be, to be avoided". The substance of his remarks on the appropriate meaning of these two terms amounts to the two following propositions: 1. That at the same moment a man may desire one thing and will another; 2. That at the same moment a man may have contrary desires, but cannot have contrary wills. The notions, therefore, which ought to be annexed to the words *will* and *desire* are essentially different.

...

In another paragraph of the chapter quoted above, Locke justly objects to the terms in which the question concerning Liberty and Necessity is commonly stated, *whether man's will be free or no*? This question he pronounces to be "*unreasonable and unintelligible*; inasmuch as *liberty*, which is but a *power*, belongs only to agents, and cannot be an attribute or modification of the *will*, which is also but a *power*".

To this remark of Locke it may be added, that, instead of speaking (according to common phraseology) of the influence of motives on the *will*, it would be much more correct to speak of the influence of motives on the *agent*. We are apt to forget what *the will* is, and to consider it as something inanimate and passive, the state of which can be altered only by the action of some external cause. The habitual use of the metaphorical word *motives*, to denote the intentions or purposes which accompany our voluntary actions, or, in other words, the *ends* which we have in view in the exercise of the power entrusted to us, has a strong tendency to confirm us in this error, by leading us to assimilate in fancy the *volition* of a mind to the *motion* of a body; and the circumstances which give rise to this volition to the *vis motrix* by which the motion is produced.

It was probably in order to facilitate the reception of his favourite scheme of Necessity, that Hobbes was led to substitute, instead of the old division of our faculties into the powers of the Understanding and those of the Will, a new division of his own, in which the name of *Cognitive* powers was given to the former, and that of *Motive* powers to the latter. To familiarize the ears of superficial readers to this phraseology was of itself one great step towards securing their suffrages against the supposition of man's free agency. To say that the *will* is determined by *motive* powers is to employ a language which virtually implies a recognition of the very point in dispute. Accordingly, Mr. Belsham[4] is at pains to keep the metaphorical origin of the word *motive* in the view of his readers, by prefixing to his argument, in favour of the scheme of necessity, the following definition:

> "*Motive*, in this discussion, is to be understood in its most extensive sense. It expresses whatever MOVES or influences the mind in its choice".

According to Mr. Locke, the ideas of *liberty* and of *power* are very nearly the same. "Everyone", he observes, "finds in himself a power to begin or forbear, continue or put an end to several actions in himself. From the

[4] [Thomas Belsham (1750–1829). English theologian, leader of the Unitarian movement, and philosopher of the Associationist school. Stewart refers here to his *Elements of the Philosophy of the Mind* (1801).]

consideration of the extent of this power of the mind over the actions of the man, which everyone finds in himself, arise the ideas of' Liberty and Necessity". And a few sentences afterwards: "The idea of liberty is the idea of a power in any agent to do or forbear any particular action, according to the determination or thought of the mind, whereby either of them is preferred to the other. Where either of them is not in the power of the agent, to be produced by him according to his volition, there he is not at Liberty but under Necessity". That these definitions are not perfectly correct will appear hereafter. They approach, indeed, very nearly to the definitions of Liberty and Necessity given by Hobbes, Collins, and Edwards; whereas Locke, in order to do justice to his own decided opinion on the subject, ought to have included also in his idea of Liberty, a *power* over the determinations of his will.

It is owing in a great measure to this close connexion between the ideas of *Free-will* and of *Power*, and to the pleasure with which the consciousness of *power* is always accompanied, that we feel so painful a mortification in perusing those systems in which our free agency is called in question. Dr. Priestley himself, as well as his great oracle, Dr. Hartley, has acknowledged, that "he was not a ready convert to the doctrine of Necessity, and that he gave up his liberty with great reluctance". But whence this reluctance to embrace a doctrine so "great and glorious", but from its repugnance to the natural feelings and natural wishes of the human mind?

In addition to the foregoing considerations, the following detached hints may be of use in guarding us against some logical oversights which have misled a large proportion of the ingenious men who have engaged in this controversy.

In the case of inanimate matter, when I say that the motion produced is proportional to the impressed force, I only assert an identical proposition; for my only notion of *the quantity of a force* is from the effects it produces. In like manner, in the case of *motives*, I may, if I choose, define the *strength* of a motive by its prevailing over other motives in determining the will, and then lay it down as a proposition, that the will is determined by the strongest motive. In this case likewise it is evident that I only assert an identical proposition; a proposition, however, extremely apt to mislead, in consequence of its applying to mind the word *strength*, which, from its ordinary and proper application to the forces that move *inert* matter, suggests a theory concerning the influence of motives which takes for granted the thing to be proved. Let us consider what is meant, when it is said that the will is *necessarily* determined by motives. Is it to be understood that the connexion is similar to that between a force impressed on a body and the subsequent motion? But of the nature of this connexion I am as ignorant as of the other. In both cases I only see the fact. It is remarkable that the advocates for Necessity have attempted to explain the actions of voluntary agents by the phenomena of motion, and that some other metaphysicians (in particular Kepler and Lord

Monboddo) have attempted to explain the phenomena of motion by the operations of voluntary agents. In both cases philosophers saw the difficulties attending that set of phenomena to which they confined their attention, and endeavoured to explain them by the analogy of another class of facts not so immediately under their consideration at the moment, without recollecting that both the one and the other are equally placed beyond our comprehension.

Although, however, the connexion between an impressed force and the subsequent motion be as inexplicable as the connexion between the motive and the subsequent action, I would not be understood to insinuate that the two cases are at all parallel. In the case of motion, although I cannot trace the necessary connexion between it and the impressed force, I am certain that the motion is the effect of *some cause* with which it is necessarily connected; for every change that takes place in an inanimate object, suggests to me the notion of a cause. But in the case of the determinations of a voluntary agent, *he* is himself the author of them; nor could anything have led philosophers to look out for any other causes of them, but an apprehended analogy between volition in a mind and motion in a body.

The argument for Necessity derives all its force from the maxim, "*that every change requires a cause*". But this maxim, although true with respect to inanimate matter, does not apply to intelligent agents, which cannot be conceived without the power of self-determination. Upon an accurate analysis, indeed, of the meaning of words, it will be found that the idea of an *efficient cause* implies the idea of *mind*, and consequently, that it is absurd to ascribe the volitions of *mind* to the efficiency of causes foreign to itself. It is curious that Mr. Hume, who has in one part of his system denied the certainty of the maxim just now mentioned, has, in another part of it, adopted the scheme of necessity, although that scheme derives all its plausibility from an undue and unwarrantable extension of this very maxim.[5]

---

[5] From these observations it seems to me to follow, that, whatever may be the nature of the relation between a *motive* and an *action*, there is no reason for concluding it to be at all analogous to that between a *cause* and its *effect*. In farther proof of this some authors have remarked, that the latter connexion is always constant and uniform, whereas we know that the same motive may at different times lead to very different actions. (See the very ingenious *Essays, Philosophical and Literary*, of the late learned and excellent Dr. James Gregory.) But this answer is not satisfactory; and as it places the point in dispute on an improper ground, it may be useful to show in what its fallacy consists. By giving up an argument which will not bear examination we strengthen a good cause, no less than by producing additional evidence in its support.

Six

Language

SELECTION 17

Natural and Artificial Signs

Having treated at some length of the chief Faculties and Powers which constitute what is commonly called the Human Understanding, I now proceed to the examination of some auxiliary faculties and principles essential to our intellectual improvement, or intimately connected with it.

The form and posture of the human body, and its various organs of perception, have an obvious reference to man's rational nature, and are beautifully fitted to encourage and facilitate the culture of his Mind. A similar remark may be extended to many other parts of our constitution, both external and internal; but there are two which more particularly claim our attention: the power of expressing our thoughts by Language, and the principle of Imitation.

The connexion of language with the subjects which have been under our review in the former volumes of this work is sufficiently obvious. It is to the use of artificial signs (as was formerly shown)[1] that we are indebted for all our general conclusions; and without it our knowledge would have been entirely limited to individuals. It is also to the use of artificial signs, that we are indebted for all that part of our information which is not the immediate result of our own personal experience; and for that transmission of intellectual acquisitions from one race to another, which lays the foundation of the progressive improvement of the species.

In treating of Language, I shall begin with a few remarks on *Natural Language*, without which (as Dr. Reid has well observed) the formation of an artificial language would have been impossible. The justness of this remark appears manifest from the following considerations: that the establishment of *artificial* signs must have been the effect of convention; and that, without signs of one kind or another to serve as a *medium* of communication, no convention could have taken place. It may be laid down, therefore, as a first principle, that the formation of an artificial

---

[1] [See selection 12.]

language presupposes the use of natural signs. These consist in certain expressions of the countenance, certain gestures of the body, and certain tones of the voice. Each of these classes of natural signs well deserves a separate consideration, but I must confine myself here to a few very general and miscellaneous hints.

I

The language of the face consists in the play of the muscles of which it is composed, particularly of the muscles connected with the *eyes* and the *mouth*, and in the change of colour arising from the motion of the blood. The expression of the countenance, therefore, depends partly on *colour*, and partly on *movement*; of which two circumstances it may be remarked, by the way, that the *former* is far less subject to the restraints of the will than the *latter*, a change of colour often betraying an emotion when the features are perfectly quiescent.

. . .

There seems to be in man a power of interpreting instinctively certain expressions of the countenance, certain gestures of the body, and certain tones of the voice. This has, indeed, been much disputed by Priestley and other writers, who have attempted to resolve the whole into experience and observation; but I think there is a variety of considerations which (under proper limitations) go far to justify the common opinion on the subject. It is sufficient for my present purpose to mention one or two of these. I shall have occasion to resume the same argument, at greater length, in treating of Imitation.[2]

1. A child is able at a very early period to understand the meaning of smiles and frowns, of a soothing or threatening tone of voice; long, at least, before it can be supposed capable of so much observation as to remark the connexion between a passion and its external effect. If the interpretation of natural signs be the result of experience, whence is it that children understand their meaning at a much earlier period than they do that of arbitrary signs? If it were merely the effect of observation, the fact would be reversed, inasmuch as it is obviously more easy to remember the sound of a word than the most simple modification of the human countenance. Nor is there anything more wonderful in this instinctive interpretation of certain natural signs than in many other phenomena which infants exhibit; nor perhaps *so* wonderful as that instinctive terror with which nature has certainly endowed some of the brutes for the destined enemies of their respective tribes. It deserves, too, to be remarked, with respect to the lower animals, that they, as well as man, express what passes in their minds by natural signs; and there is

---

[2] [See selection 18.]

even some reason for apprehending, that some of them understand instinctively certain natural signs which we employ.

2. If natural signs be interpreted in consequence of experience only, why are we more *affected* by natural signs than by artificial ones? A peasant who has never heard but one language spoken, has as much reason to associate the word *love* or *hatred* with the sentiment it denotes, as to associate these passions with their natural expressions: and yet the effects of the two species of signs are widely different. For the farther confirmation or limitation of this conclusion, it would be worth while to institute some experiments expressly, if such a case as that recorded by Cheselden should again fall under the examination of an equally intelligent observer.

As ideas multiply, the imperfections of natural language are felt; and men find it necessary to invent artificial signs, of which the meaning is fixed by mutual agreement. In proportion as artificial language improves, the language of nature declines, insomuch that, in such a state of society as ours, it requires a great deal of reflection and study to recover the use of it. This study is, in a considerable degree, the foundation of the arts both of the Actor and of the Orator.

...

Notwithstanding, however, the decline of natural language in consequence of the use of artificial signs, the acquaintance which we still have with the former (however imperfect) is of essential service in teaching children the meaning of the latter. This may be easily exemplified, by first reading over to a child one of the simplest of Æsop's *Fables*, without taking your eye from the book, or using any inflection of voice; and afterwards telling him the same story, with the commentary of your face, and gestures, and tones. ...

From the observations already made it seems to follow, that there are natural signs of the operations and passions of mind, which are interpreted instinctively by all who see them. At the same time, I am ready to grant that there are many expressions of countenance of which the meaning is learnt from experience alone; expressions which may justly be called *natural signs*, inasmuch as their connexion with the things signified is the effect of the natural constitution of the human frame, and as they must, therefore, have exhibited the same appearance in all ages and nations; but which, notwithstanding, are of a very different class from those hitherto considered, being intelligible to those alone who have turned their attention, in some degree, to the study of *Character*. A single instance will be sufficient, both for the illustration and proof of this remark.

When a variety of ideas are passing rapidly through the mind, the eyes are constantly in motion; for every time our thoughts change from one object to another, there is a corresponding movement in the organ. I do not say that it is impossible to prevent this effect from taking place, by a particular exertion of the will, but only that this is the natural and ordinary effect of the general laws of our constitution. Revolve, for example, quickly in your mind the names of a number of your acquaintance, or travel over in imagination the different parts of a country with whose geography you are acquainted; you will be sensible of a motion in your eyes every time that you change your idea, either of the person or place. Hence persons of a lively fancy or of a busy mind acquire what is called a *quick eye*. On the contrary, when the attention is much engaged with one object, or when the succession of ideas is slow, as in a deep melancholy, or in a mind occupied with some inquiry which requires patient and collected meditation, the eyes are either completely fixed, or their motions are slow and heavy. ...

...

In the instances which have just been mentioned, the connexion between the mind and the external appearance, is plainly the *effect* of the operation of the mind on the body. Whether there are not other connexions resulting from the operation of the body on the mind is a question of greater difficulty. At the same time there seems to be but little doubt, that *general* inferences concerning the intellectual capacity, may be drawn with some confidence from the form and size of the scull, and from other circumstances connected with the original organization of that part of the body. No parent, for example, fails to feel some apprehension about the intellect of a child whose head is uncommonly large, or whose scull departs widely from the common form. In this last case, the observation is as old as the time of Homer, according to whose idea the head of Thersites (a person whom the Poet represents as of a very unsound understanding) seems to have somewhat resembled a cone. It has been imagined by some that, corresponding to the varieties of intellectual and moral character, there are certain inequalities or prominences on the surface of the scull: and it certainly is a legitimate object of experimental inquiry to ascertain how far this opinion is agreeable to fact. Any conclusions on this point, cautiously obtained by induction, would undoubtedly form an interesting accession to what Bacon calls the *Doctrina de Fœdere*. But, hitherto, the inquiry has produced nothing more than bold and gratuitous assertions; and the little we know with certainty of the indications of character as they are exhibited on the exterior of the head, has been inferred, not from the surface of the *cranium*, but from the forms which the face assumes from the play of the muscles. How far the particular rules on this subject, given by Lavater[3] and others, have a solid foundation in experience, I do not pretend to decide. I confess, indeed, I strongly suspect that it is only very gross estimates

[3] [Johann Caspar Lavater (1741–1801), Swiss theologian, philosopher and poet. Author of *Physiognomische Fragmente zur Beforderung der Menschenkenntnis und Menschenliebe* (1774–80, *Essays on Physiognomy*).]

which can be formed on those mathematical proportions which can be measured by a pair of compasses; and that the traces of the more delicate peculiarities of mind are too complicated and too fugitive to be comprehended in the terms of any verbal description. On the other hand, I will not affirm that these traces may not be distinctly visible to those who, by long practice, have acquired a sort of new sense, or rather a new perceptive faculty, analogous to what physicians acquire by long experience, for the more delicate and evanescent symptoms of disease. It seems to be owing to this that so little satisfaction can be obtained from the writings of the ancients, concerning the principles on which their art of physiognomy proceeded, while we have complete evidence of the great success with which they cultivated the study.

There is yet another class of signs which may be considered as *natural*, inasmuch as they have been found to present themselves to the common sense of mankind in a great variety of instances, as the most obvious and intelligible signs they could employ for particular purposes. Such, for example, is the universal practice of showing respect for another person, by stepping aside upon the road, in order to make way for him; of rising up when he enters, or when he leaves an apartment; of bending the head forward as a token of assent or approbation; of shaking the head as a sign of dissent or disapprobation; and many others of a similar kind. In general it may be remarked, that wherever a particular sign is in use among unconnected nations, however arbitrary and capricious it may at first appear, it must have some foundation in nature, or reason, or fancy; although perhaps we may be unable to give a satisfactory account of its origin. Thus the agreement, among so many different tribes, in various quarters of the globe, to employ a branch of a tree as an emblem of peace, has probably been suggested by the natural weapon of the savage - the *club* - the emblem exhibiting the materials, or the means of hostility, and, at the same time, a disposition to forbearance and accommodation. ...

When different savage tribes have occasion to carry on any intercourse, whether friendly or hostile, with one another, the imperfections of natural signs will force them to call to their aid the use of such conventional signs as may be necessary to make themselves mutually understood; which conventional signs, when once introduced, will become permanent acquisitions to both parties. In this way it is easy to conceive how signs, the most capricious and arbitrary, may spread over such a continent as America, where the hunting grounds of some of the tribes are compared in point of extent to the kingdom of France. And, in fact, it would appear, from some late accounts, that, in the new world, there exists a sort of mute *Lingua Franca* by which the different tribes hold communication with each other.

In a very interesting, and (as may be presumed from the authority under which it is published) a very authentic historical account of the Indian nations, we are given to understand that there actually exists a system of visible signs, intelligible wherever Indians are to be found, over the whole American continent. "The Indians", it is said, "have a language of signs, by which they communicate on occasions when speaking is not prudent or proper, as, for instance, when they are about to meet an enemy, and by speaking they would run the risk of being discovered. By this means they also make themselves understood to those nations of Indians whose language they are not acquainted *with, for all the Indian nations understand each other in this way*. It is also, in many cases, a saving of words, which the Indians are much intent on, believing that too much talking disgraces a man. When, therefore, they will relate something extraordinary in a few words, they make use of corresponding signs, which is very entertaining to those who listen and attend to them, and who are acquainted both with the language and the signs, being very much as if somebody were to explain a picture set before them".

...

These facts seem to me to be not only curious, but to form a new and not unimportant accession to the Philosophy of the Mind. They illustrate, in a very striking manner, the instinctive propensity in our species to communicate their ideas to each other; and the variety of expedients (some of them by no means obvious) to accomplish this end, which necessity suggests to man even in his rudest state. The existence of an artificial language, consisting of visible signs, intelligible among *all* the Indian nations spread over the American Continent, is a fact which I do not recollect to have met with in any prior account of these interesting communities; and, if duly reflected on, may serve to diminish our wonder at the invention of oral speech, an art to which many philosophers of high name have affirmed that the human faculties would have been altogether incompetent, without an express revelation for the purpose. Surely the ingenuity displayed in these visible signs is at least equal to what is requisite for giving audible names to surrounding objects, and for some of the succeeding steps in the formation of speech. The truth of this position will, I hope, be still more clearly evinced by some of the following speculations.

II

It was before remarked, that, as ideas multiply, the imperfections of natural language are felt, and men find it necessary to invent artificial signs, of which the meaning is fixed by mutual agreement. Dumb people, who associate much together, soon invent a language of their own, consisting of visible signs; and the same thing happens in those convents and boarding schools, where a severe discipline prevents a free communication by means of ordinary speech.

Artificial signs may be divided into the *visible* and the *audible*. To the former class belong those signals by fire, which were so much in use among the ancients. The Greeks are even said to have invented a method of expressing, by the number and arrangement of torches, every letter of the alphabet, so that a guard on one eminence could converse with another at a distance, by spelling his words. A full and curious description of this method may be found in Polybius.

Another instance of a visible language occurs in that system of signals which is said to have been introduced into the British navy by James II; and in the still more recent invention of the telegraph,[4] a contrivance which has been found to admit of a far more extensive and important application than could have been anticipated *a priori*; and which is probably still susceptible of farther improvements, tending to enlarge and accelerate the mutual intercourse of mankind.

If men had been destitute of the organs of speech, or of the sense of hearing, there can be no doubt that they might have contrived, by means of an alphabet of visible signs, to express all their ideas and feelings; as we see done by school-boys, who, for their amusement, denote the different letters by certain conformations and movements of the fingers. Such a language, however, is attended with great inconveniences. It is useless in the dark, or when the person we are conversing with is removed to a considerable distance; nor does it enable us to call his attention, if his eye should happen to be otherwise engaged. To this may be added, that it is not susceptible of that rapidity which is necessary for the purposes of life. In all these respects, audible signs possess important advantages, more particularly in the last, in consequence of the wonderful adaptation of our powers of articulation to the perceptive powers of the human ear, an organ, we may remark in passing, which is always open to the reception of sounds. It has been found that two thousand letters, when combined into words, may be pronounced in a minute of time, so that the sound of each letter may be distinctly heard. The infinite variety of modifications of which the voice is capable, enable us to add, in some measure, the expressiveness of natural signs to the conventional meaning of arbitrary words; while its musical modulations render language a vehicle of pleasure as well as information.

Among all nations, accordingly, audible signs form the established medium of intellectual communication, and the materials (as indeed the etymology of the words denotes) of what is commonly called LANGUAGE or SPEECH; a wonderful art, infinitely diversified in the principles on which it has proceeded in different instances, and admitting of all possible degrees of perfection, from the uncouth jargon of a savage tribe, to the graces of which the most cultivated languages are susceptible, in the hands of the orator or the poet.

---

[4] [Stewart means the optical telegraph, the forerunner of the railway semaphore, got ready by Claude Chappé in 1793.]

SELECTION 18

Sympathetic Imitation

The *power* by which the imitation is, in certain cases, accomplished, although a subject not less interesting than the corresponding *propensity*, has not yet, as far as I know, attracted the notice of any philosopher whatever.

It was before observed, that the powers of imitation displayed, in so extraordinary a degree by the mimic, seem to be only a continuation of capacities possessed by all men in the first years of their existence; but which, in most individuals, are in a great measure lost from disuse soon after the period of infancy. The consideration, therefore, of some circumstances connected with this peculiar talent, may perhaps throw light on the general or common principles of the human frame.

When a mimic attempts to copy the countenance of a person whom he never saw before, what are the means which he employs in order to effectuate his purpose? Shall we suppose that his efforts are merely tentative and experimental; or, in other words, that he tries successively every possible modification of his features, till he finds, at last, by the information of a mirror, that he has succeeded in the imitation of the original? Nobody can for a moment believe this to be the case, who has attended in the slightest degree to the subject. On the contrary, it is a fact universally known, that the imitation is often perfectly successful in the very first trial; and that it is not from a mirror, but from his own internal consciousness, that the mimic judges of its correctness. I acknowledge, at the same time, that the fact is sometimes otherwise, and that instances occur, in which the best mimics are found to make many successive efforts before they accomplish their end; or in which, after all their efforts, the attempt proves ultimately abortive. But it will not be disputed that the former statement holds in general, where the propensity to mimicry is strong; and even where exceptions take place, there is commonly, from the first, such an approximation to the resemblance aimed at, as sufficiently demonstrates, that, how much soever experience may be useful in finishing the portrait, the most important part of the process must be referred to causes of a different description.

... I am disposed to lay peculiar stress on this last consideration, because superficial inquirers, *in their zeal to explain away the phenomena commonly ascribed to* INSTINCT, have, of late, been strangely led to conclude, that wherever experience can be shown to have *any* share in directing our actions, it is idle to have recourse to the operation of any other cause. In this way, it is a very easy matter to establish their doctrine, because, in general, Nature has done nothing more, either for man, or for the lower animals, than was absolutely necessary for enabling them to turn their experience to account, seldom giving a perfectly precise determination to their efforts, but invariably performing for both, the essential office which Lord Bacon would have called the *Abscissio Infiniti*; and confining their experiments within such narrow limits as are suited to their respective capacities. Thus the lamb, although the moment after it is dropped it is guided by nature (probably through the medium of the sense of smelling) to the neighbourhood of that organ where its nourishment is to be found, rarely, if ever, fixes, till after repeated trials, on one of the teats. An ear for music, in our own species, is unquestionably, in a very great measure, the gift of nature; yet, where such a capacity exists, how wonderfully may it be improved by culture! Something analogous to this seems to take place in the act of bodily imitation, nature directing our efforts *near* the mark, and leaving the task of hitting it with precision to our own industry. In such cases, the most interesting problem for the examination of the philosopher, is *not*, whether experience does not contribute *something* to render the operations of instinct effectual, (a point about which, in general, there can be little doubt,) but whether experience is of itself sufficient to explain the *whole* difficulty, a question upon which I am inclined to think, that they who have considered the subject the most deeply will be the slowest to pronounce a decided opinion in the affirmative. ...

...

As in all our common voluntary exertions we have only to *will* the end, and the *means* are arranged without our co-operation, I conclude, that in mimicry the mimic forms a lively *conception* of the features he wishes to copy; and, by repeated efforts, succeeds in producing the desired effect. The case is similar when he imitates voices. He remembers and conceives strongly what he wishes to imitate, and the muscles necessary for that purpose are, as in other cases, put into action in obedience to his will. The same thing happens when a singer, who has a correct ear, catches a musical air, after hearing it once played or sung by another person. ...

The inference I draw from these facts is this: That, in the case of the mimic, many of the muscles of the countenance, which in other men are immovable, have acquired from exercise a certain degree of mobility, so that when the mimic wishes to assume a particular look, he has only to will the end, and his wish is immediately accomplished.

It is not, however, always that the mimic succeeds at first. Some who are still living must remember to have heard the late Lord Cullen (the most perfect of all mimics) mention the difficulty he experienced in seizing the features of Lord Kames, when, after many fruitless efforts, he succeeded all at once, in the course of a tour with a friend in the Highlands of Scotland. The moment he had acquired the command of the hitherto dormant set of muscles on which the effect depended, he knew, *by consciousness*, that he had hit the resemblance; and he appealed to his companion in the carriage for the fidelity of the portrait. It certainly became, in process of time, one of the most accurate of all his imitations.

With this power of imitation, our interpretation of natural signs, *so far as it is the result of an instinct for which experience alone will not account*, seems to me to have an intimate connexion. The following very slight hints will be sufficient to show that this idea is not altogether groundless.

That our interpretation of natural signs is, in no case, the result of *pure* or *unmixed instinct*, is abundantly obvious. Indeed, I do not know of any philosopher who has been so hardy as to maintain explicitly the contrary opinion; who has asserted, (for example,) that the natural signs of *Rage*, in the countenance of another person, would convey an idea of that passion to a man who had never experienced its workings within his own breast. The real problem with respect to this very interesting part of the human constitution is, in truth, of a very different nature from what most theorists seem of late to have supposed; and the solution of it (if I do not greatly deceive myself) lies deeper in the Philosophy of the Mind, than they are willing to allow.

Among those who contend, that experience alone furnishes a sufficient explanation of the phenomenon in question, two different suppositions may be formed with respect to the manner in which it operates; and to these suppositions I cannot even in imagination add a third. In the first place, it may be conceived, that an infant, having learned *in its own case*, that a smile is the natural effect or sign of a happy and affectionate state of mind, is induced by the *principle of association*, when it sees a smile on the countenance of its nurse, to ascribe it to emotions similar to those which it has itself experienced. Or, secondly, it may be thought, that, having uniformly observed the smiles of its nurse to be a prelude to the agreeable sensations it is accustomed to receive through the medium of her kindness, it comes, in process of time, to interpret their meaning, and to anticipate her tenderness, in the same manner in which it learns by experience, at a more advanced period of life, to interpret the meaning of conventional language.

With respect to the first of these theories, it seems sufficient to observe, that, in order to bestow upon it even the shadow of plausibility, it must be supposed farther, that the infant has the aid of a mirror, to enable it to know the *existence* of its own smiles, and what sort of *appearance* these smiles exhibit to the eye. That the particular modification of features connected with this expression is itself accompanied with an agreeable bodily sensation, I think highly probable; but this throws no light whatever on the present difficulty, till it is farther explained by what process the child learns to identify what it *feels*, or is *conscious of*, in its own countenance, with what it *sees* on the countenance of another.

It is to the other hypothesis, however, that Dr. Priestley[5] plainly leans, as may be inferred from the following very explicit statement given by

[5] [Joseph Priestley (1733–1804), English chemist, philosopher and theologian. Stewart refers to his *Examination of Dr. Reid's 'Inquiry into the Human Mind on the Principles of Common Sense'* (1774).]

himself: "I do not hesitate to say, that if it were possible always to beat and terrify a child with a placid countenance, so as never to assume that appearance but in these circumstances, and always to soothe him with what we call an angry countenance, this natural connexion of ideas would be reversed, and we should see the child frighted with a smile, and delighted with a frown".

As this view of the subject places the interpretation of *Natural* and *Conventional* signs exactly on the same footing, it obviously suggests to us the two following queries, as preliminary subjects of consideration. Till these queries are answered in a satisfactory manner, Dr. Priestley's solution of the difficulty is of no value whatsoever; and yet, he has not even alluded to either, in the course of his argument. *1st,* Whence is it, that we interpret *natural* signs so much earlier than *conventional* signs? And, *2nd,* To what cause is it owing, that their *effects* are so widely different on the human frame? It is scarcely necessary for me to mention, as an additional objection, that this theory overlooks altogether that *physico-moral* sympathy which, through the medium of the body, harmonizes different minds with each other; and which, as it is one of the most important, so it is one of the most incontestable facts connected with the theory of our common nature.

SELECTION 19

Philosophy vs. Philology

In carrying back our thoughts to the infancy of a cultivated language, a difficulty occurs, which, however obviously it may seem to present itself, I do not recollect to have seen taken notice of by any writer on the Human Mind; and which, as it leads the attention to various questions closely connected with the main design of this volume, as well as with the particular discussion which has been last under our review, I shall point out and illustrate at some length.

In the case of objects which fall under the cognizance of any of our external senses, it is easy to conceive the origin of the different classes of words composing a conventional dialect; to conceive, for example, that two savages should agree to call this animal a *Horse,* and that tree *an Oak.* But, in words relating to things intellectual and moral, in what manner was the conventional connexion at first established between the sign and the thing signified? In what manner (to take one of the simplest instances) was it settled, that the name of *imagination* should be given to one operation of the mind; that of *recollection* to a second; that of *deliberation* to a third; that of *sagacity,* or *foresight,* to a fourth? Or, supposing the use of these words to be once introduced, how was their meaning to be explained to a novice, altogether unaccustomed to think upon such subjects.

1. In answer to this question, it is to be observed, in the first place, that the meaning of many words, of which it is impossible to exhibit any sensible prototypes, is gradually collected by a species of *induction,* which is more or less successfully conducted by different individuals, according to the degree of their attention and judgment. The connexion in which an unknown term stands in relation to the other words combined with it in the same sentence, often affords a key for its explanation in that particular instance; and in proportion as such instances are multiplied in the writings and conversation of men well acquainted with propriety of speech, the means are afforded of a progressive approximation towards its precise import. A familiar illustration of this process presents itself in the expedient which a reader naturally employs for decyphering the meaning of an unknown word in a foreign language, when he happens not to have a dictionary at hand. The first sentence where the word occurs affords, it is probable, sufficient foundation for a vague conjecture concerning the notion annexed to it by the author; some idea or other being necessarily substituted in its place, in order to make the passage at all intelligible. The next sentence where it is involved renders this conjecture a little more definite; a third sentence contracts the field of doubt within still narrower limits; till, at length, a more extensive induction fixes completely the signification we are in quest of. There cannot be a doubt, I apprehend, that it is in some such way as this, that children slowly and imperceptibly enter into the abstract and complex notions annexed to numberless words in their mother tongue, of which we should find it difficult or impossible to convey the sense by formal definitions.

2. The strong tendency of the mind to express itself metaphorically, or analogically, on all abstract subjects, supplies another help to facilitate the acquisition of language. The prevalence of this tendency among rude nations has been often remarked; and has been commonly accounted for, partly from the warmth of imagination supposed to be peculiarly characteristical of savages, and partly from the imperfections of their scanty vocabularies. The truth, however, is, that the same disposition is exhibited by man in every stage of his progress; prompting him uniformly, whenever the enlargement of his knowledge requires the use of a new word for the communication of his meaning, instead of coining at once a sound altogether arbitrary, to assist, as far as possible, the apprehension of his hearers, either by the happy employment of some old word in a metaphorical sense, or by grafting etymologically on some well-known stock, a new *derivative,* significant to his own fancy of the thought he wishes to impart.

To this bias of the mind to enrich language, rather by a modification of old materials, than by the creation of new ones, it is owing that the number of primitive or radical words, in a cultivated tongue, bears so small a proportion to the whole amount of its vocabulary. …

…

I have stated the difficulty attending the origin of words expressive of things which do not fall under the cognizance of any of our senses; and I have also remarked the disposition of the Mind, on such occasions, to have recourse to metaphors borrowed from the Material World. It is in this proneness of the fancy to employ analogical language, in order to express notions purely intellectual, that a provision seems to have been made by nature, for an intercourse between different Minds, concerning things abstracted from Matter; inasmuch as the very same circumstances which open an easier vent to the utterance of the speaker, must necessarily contribute powerfully (by what Lord Bacon would have called the *abscissio infiniti*) to assist and prompt the apprehension of the hearer. The moment that the terms *attention, imagination, abstraction, sagacity, foresight, penetration, acuteness, inclination, aversion, deliberation,* are pronounced, a great step towards their interpretation is made in the mind of every person of common understanding; and although this analogical reference to the Material World adds greatly to the difficulty of analyzing, with philosophical rigour, the various faculties and principles of our nature, yet it cannot be denied, that it facilitates, to a wonderful degree, the mutual communications of mankind concerning them, in so far as such communications are necessary in the ordinary business of life. Even to the philosopher himself, it is probably, in the first instance, indispensably requisite, as a preparation for a more accurate survey of the Mind. It serves, at least, to circumscribe the field of his attention within such narrow limits, as may enable him, with greater ease, to subject it to the examination of the power of *reflection*; and, in this way, renders *fancy* subservient to the ultimate correction of her own illusions. ...

And here, I cannot help pausing a little, to remark how much more imperfect language is, than is commonly supposed, when considered as an organ of mental intercourse. We speak of *communicating*, by means of words, our ideas and our feelings to others, and we seldom reflect sufficiently on the latitude with which this metaphorical phrase ought to be understood. Even in conversing on the plainest and most familiar subjects, however full and circumstantial our statements may be, the words which we employ, if examined with accuracy, will be found to do nothing more than to suggest *hints* to our hearers, leaving by far the principal part of the process of interpretation to be performed by the Mind itself. In this respect, the effect of *words* bears some resemblance to the *stimulus* given to the memory and imagination, by an outline or a shadow, exhibiting the profile of a countenance familiar to the Eye. The most minute narratives, accordingly, are by no means, in every instance, the most intelligible and satisfactory; as the most faithful copies after nature do not always form the best portraits. In both cases, the skill of the artist consists in a happy selection of particulars, which are *expressive* or *significant*.

"Language", it is commonly said, "is the express image of thought"; and that it may be said with sufficient propriety to be so, I do not dispute, when the meaning of the proposition is fully explained. The mode of expression, however, it ought to be remembered, is figurative; and, therefore, when the proposition is assumed as a principle of reasoning, it must not be rigorously or literally interpreted. This has too often been overlooked by writers on the Human Mind. Even Dr. Reid himself, cautious as he is in general, with respect to the ground on which he is to build, has repeatedly appealed to this maxim, without any qualification whatsoever; and, by thus adopting it, agreeably to its letter, rather than to its spirit, has been led, in various instances, to lay greater stress on the structure of speech, than (in my opinion) it can always bear in a philosophical argument.

As a necessary consequence of this assumption, it has been, not unnaturally, inferred by logicians that every word, which is not wholly useless in the vocabulary, is the sign of an *idea*; and that these *ideas* (which the common systems lead us to consider as the representatives of *things*) are the immediate instruments, or (if I may be allowed such a phrase) *the intellectual tools* with which the Mind carries on the operation of thinking. In reading, for example, the enunciation of a proposition, we are apt to fancy that for *every word* contained in it there is an *idea* presented to the understanding; from the combination and comparison of which *ideas*, results that act of the mind called *Judgment*. So different is all this from the fact, that our words, when examined separately, are often as completely insignificant as the letters of which they are composed; deriving their meaning solely from the connexion, or relation, in which they stand to others. Of this, a very obvious example occurs, in the case of terms which have a *variety* of acceptations, and of which the import, in every particular application, must be collected from the whole sentence of which they form a part. When I consult Johnson's *Dictionary*, I find many words of which he has enumerated forty, fifty, or even sixty different significations; and, after all the pains he has taken to distinguish these from each other, I am frequently at a loss how to avail myself of his definitions. Yet, when a word of this kind occurs to me in a book, or even when I hear it pronounced in the rapidity of discourse, I at once select, without the slightest effort of conscious thought, the precise meaning which it was intended to convey. How is this to be explained but by the light thrown upon the problematical term by the general import of the sentence? (A species of interpretation easily conceivable, where I have leisure to study the context deliberately, but which, in the circumstances I have now supposed, implies a quickness in the exercise of the intellectual powers, which, the more it is examined, will appear the more astonishing.) It is constant habit alone that keeps these intellectual processes out of view; giving to the mind such a celerity in its operations, as eludes the utmost vigilance of our attention; and exhibiting to the eyes of common observers, the use of speech, as a much simpler, and less curious phenomenon than it is in reality.

...

In instances of this sort, it will be generally found, upon an accurate examination, that the intellectual act, as far as we are able to trace it, is altogether simple, and incapable of analysis; and that the elements into which we flatter ourselves we have resolved it, are nothing more than the *grammatical elements of speech*; the logical doctrine about *the comparison of ideas* bearing a much closer affinity to the task of a school-boy in *parsing* his lesson, than to the researches of philosophers, able to form a just conception of the mystery to be explained.

These observations are general, and apply to every case in which language is employed. When the subject, however, to which it relates, involves notions which are abstract and complex, the process of interpretation becomes much more complicated and curious; involving, at every step, that species of mental induction which I have already endeavoured to describe. In reading, accordingly, the most perspicuous discussions, in which such notions form the subject of the argument, little instruction is received, till we have made the reasonings *our own*, by revolving the steps again and again in our thoughts. The fact is, that, in cases of this sort, the function of language is not so much to *convey* knowledge (according to the common phrase) from one mind to another, as to bring two minds into *the same train of thinking*; and to confine them, as nearly as possible, to the same track. Many authors have spoken of the wonderful *mechanism of speech*; but none has hitherto attended to the far more wonderful *mechanism* which it puts into action behind the scene.

The speculations of Mr. Horne Tooke[6] (whatever the conclusions were to which he meant them to be subservient) afford, in every page, illustrations of these hints, by showing how imperfect and disjointed a thing *speech* must have been in its infant state, prior to the development of those various *component parts*, which now appear to be essential to its existence. ...

***

If the different considerations, stated in the preceding chapter, be carefully combined together, it will not appear surprising that, in the judgment of a great majority of individuals, the common analogical phraseology concerning the mind should be mistaken for its genuine philosophical theory. It is only by the patient and persevering exercise of Reflection on the subjects of Consciousness, that this popular prejudice can be gradually surmounted. In proportion as the thing typified grows familiar to the thoughts, the metaphor will lose its influence on the fancy; and while the signs we employ continue to discover, by their etymology, their historical origin, they will be rendered, by long and accurate use, virtually equivalent to literal and specific appellations. A

[6] [John Horne Tooke (1736-1812). English lawyer and philologer author of EPEA PTEROENTA *or the Diversions of Purley* (1786–1805).]

thousand instances, perfectly analogous to this, might be easily produced from the figurative words and phrases which occur every moment in ordinary conversation. They who are acquainted with Warburton's account of the natural progress of writing, from hieroglyphics to apparently arbitrary characters, cannot fail to be struck with the similarity between the history of this art, as traced by him, and the gradual process by which metaphorical terms come to be stripped of that literal import which, at first, pointed them out to the selection of our rude progenitors. Till this process be completed, with respect to the words denoting the powers and operations of the understanding, it is vain to expect any success in our inductive researches concerning the principles of the human frame.

In thus objecting to metaphorical expressions, as solid *data* for our conclusions in the science of Mind, I would not be understood to represent them as of no use to the speculative inquirer. To those who delight to trace the history of language, it may, undoubtedly, form an interesting, and not unprofitable employment, to examine the circumstances by which they were originally suggested, and the causes which may have diversified them in the case of different nations. To the philologer it may also afford an amusing and harmless gratification (by tracing, to their unknown roots, in some obscure and remote dialects, those words which, in his mother tongue, generally pass for primitives) to show, that even the terms which denote our most refined and abstracted thoughts, were borrowed originally from some object of external perception. This, indeed, is nothing more than what the considerations already stated would have inclined us to expect *a priori*; and which, how much soever it may astonish those who have been accustomed to confine their studies to grammar alone, must strike every philosopher, as the natural and necessary consequence of that progressive order in which the mind becomes acquainted with the different objects of its knowledge, and of those general laws which govern human thought in the employment of arbitrary signs. While the philologer, however, is engaged in these captivating researches, it is highly necessary to remind him, from time to time, that his *discoveries* belong to the same branch of literature with that which furnishes a large proportion of the materials in our common lexicons and etymological dictionaries; that after he has told us (for example) that *imagination* is borrowed from an optical *image*, and *acuteness* from a Latin word, denoting the sharpness of a material instrument, we are no more advanced in studying the theory of the human intellect, than we should be in our speculations concerning the functions of money, or the political effects of the national debt, by learning from Latin etymologists, that the word *pecunia*, and the phrase *æs alienum* had both a reference, in their first origin, to certain circumstances in the early state of Roman manners.

...

... Mr. Tooke evidently assumes, as a principle, that in order to ascertain with precision the philosophical import of any word, it is necessary to trace its progress historically through all the successive meanings which it has been employed to convey, from the moment that it was first introduced into our language; or, if the word be of foreign growth, that we should prosecute the etymological research, till we ascertain the literal and primitive sense of the root from whence it sprung. It is in this literal and primitive sense alone, that according to him a philosopher is entitled to employ it, even in the present advanced state of science; and whenever he annexes to it a meaning at all different, he imposes equally on himself and on others. To me, on the contrary, it appears that to appeal to etymology in a philosophical argument, (excepting, perhaps, in those cases where the word itself is of philosophical origin,) is altogether nugatory, and can serve, at the best, to throw an amusing light on the laws which regulate the operations of human fancy. ...

I shall only mention another example in which Mr. Tooke has followed out, with still greater intrepidity, his general principle to its most paradoxical and alarming consequences.

"TRUE, as we now write it; or TREW, as it was formerly written; means simply and merely, that which is TROWED. And instead of being a rare commodity upon earth, except only in words, there is nothing but TRUTH in the world.

"That every man in his communication with others, should speak that which he TROWETH, is of so great importance to mankind, that it ought not to surprise us, if we find the most extravagant praises bestowed upon TRUTH. But TRUTH supposes mankind; *for whom*, and *by whom*, alone the word is formed, and *to whom* only it is applicable. If no man, no TRUTH. There is, therefore, no such thing as eternal, immutable, everlasting TRUTH; unless mankind, *such as they are at present*, be also eternal, immutable, and everlasting".

But what connexion, it may be asked, have these quotations with the question about the Origin of Human Knowledge? The answer will appear obvious to those who have looked into the theories which have been built on the general principle just referred to; a principle which it seems to have been the main object of Mr. Tooke's book to confirm, by an induction of particulars; and which if it were admitted as sound, would completely undermine the foundations both of logic and of ethics. In truth, it is from this general principle, combined with a fact universally acknowledged among philosophers, (the impossibility of speaking about *mind* or its phenomena, without employing a metaphorical phraseology,) that so many of our late philologists and grammarians, dazzled, as it should seem, with the novelty of these *discoveries*, have shown a disposition to conclude, (as Diderot and Helvetius formerly did from other premises,) that the only real knowledge we possess relates to the objects of our external senses; and that we can annex no idea to the word *mind* itself, but that of *matter* in the most subtle and attenuated form which imagination can lend it. ...

...

I have already, on various occasions, observed that the question concerning the *nature of mind* is altogether foreign to the opinion we form concerning the *theory of its operations*; and that granting it to be of a material origin, it is not the less evident, that all our knowledge of it is to be obtained by the exercise of the powers of Consciousness and of Reflexion. As this distinction, however, has been altogether overlooked by these profound etymologists, I shall take occasion, to propose, as a problem not unworthy of their attention, an examination of the circumstances which have led men, in all ages, to apply to the sentient and thinking principle within us, some appellation synonymous with *spiritus* or πνεῦμα and, in other cases, to liken it to *a spark of fire*, or some other of the most impalpable and mysterious modifications of matter. ... This figurative language, with respect to Mind, has been considered by some of our later metaphysicians as a convincing proof, that the doctrine of its materiality is agreeable to general belief; and that the opposite hypothesis has originated in the blunder of confounding what is very minute with what is immaterial.

To me, I must confess, it appears to lead to a conclusion directly opposite. For whence this disposition to attenuate and subtilize, to the very verge of existence, the atoms or elements supposed to produce the phenomena of thought and volition, but from the repugnance of the scheme of Materialism to our natural apprehensions, and from a secret anxiety to guard against a literal interpretation of our metaphorical phraseology? Nor has this disposition been confined to the vulgar. Philosophical materialists themselves have only refined farther on the popular conceptions, by entrenching themselves against the objections of their adversaries in the modern discoveries concerning *light* and *electricity*, and other inscrutable causes manifested by their effects alone. In some instances, they have had recourse to the supposition of the possible existence of Matter, under forms incomparably more subtle than what it probably assumes in these, or in any other class of physical phenomena; a hypothesis which it is impossible to describe better than in the words of La Fontaine:

> Quintessence d'atome, extrait de la lumière.

It is evident, that in using this language they have only attempted to elude the objections of their adversaries, by keeping the absurdity of their theory a little more out of the view of superficial inquirers; divesting Matter completely of all those properties by which it is known to our senses; and substituting, instead of what is commonly meant by that word, infinitesimal or evanescent entities, in the pursuit of which imagination herself is quickly lost.

The prosecution of this remark would, if I be not mistaken, open a view of the subject widely different from that which modern materialists have taken. But as it would lead me too far aside from my present design, I shall content myself with observing here, that the reasonings which have been lately brought forward in their support, by their new philological allies, have proceeded upon *two* errors, extremely common even among our best philosophers: first, the error of confounding the historical progress of an art with its theoretical principles when advanced to maturity; and, secondly, that of considering language as a much more exact and complete picture of thought, than it is in any state of society, whether barbarous or refined. With both of these errors, Mr. Tooke appears to me to be chargeable in an eminent degree. Of the latter, I have already produced various instances; and of the former, his whole work is one continued illustration. After stating, for example, the beautiful result of his researches concerning conjunctions, the leading inference which he deduces from it is, that the common arrangement of the parts of speech in the writings of grammarians, being inaccurate and unphilosophical must contribute greatly to retard the progress of students in the acquisition of particular languages: whereas nothing can be more indisputable than this, that his speculations do not relate, in the least, to the analysis of a language, after it has assumed a regular and systematical form; but to the gradual steps by which it proceeded to that state from the inartificial jargon of savages. They are speculations, not of a metaphysical, but of a purely philological nature; belonging to that particular species of disquisition which I have elsewhere called *theoretical history*.[7] To prove that conjunctions are a derivative part of speech, and that at first their place was supplied by words which are confessedly pronouns or articles, does not prove that they ought not to be considered as a separate part of speech *at present*, any more than Mr. Smith's theory with respect to the gradual transformation of proper names into appellatives, proves that proper names and appellatives are now radically and essentially the same; or that the employment of substantives to supply the place of adjectives, (which Mr. Tooke tells us is one of the signs of an imperfect language,) proves that no grammatical distinction exists between these two parts of speech, in such tongues as the Greek, the Latin, or the English. Mr. Tooke, indeed, has not hesitated to draw this last inference also; but, in my own opinion, with nearly as great precipitation as if he had concluded, because savages supply the want of forks by their fingers, that therefore a finger and a fork are the same thing. ...

***

[7] [See selection 24.]

Of Mr. Tooke's opinion on the nature of *General Reasoning*, we are not as yet fully informed; nor has he even explained himself concerning the logical principles of mathematical science. He has, indeed, given us to understand, that he conceived the whole of his second volume to be levelled at the imaginary power of *Abstraction*; and towards the close of it, he expresses himself, in pretty confident terms, as having completely accomplished his object: "You have now instances of my doctrine in, I suppose, about a thousand words. Their number may be easily increased. But I trust these are sufficient to discard that imagined operation of the mind which has been called *abstraction*; and to prove, that what we call by that name is merely one of the contrivances of language for the purpose of more speedy communication".

In what manner Mr. Tooke connects this very copious induction with the inference he deduces from it, I must confess myself unable to comprehend. For my own part, I can perceive no logical connexion whatsoever between his premises and his conclusion; nor do his numerous examples appear to me to establish any one general truth, but the influence of fancy and of casual association on the structure of speech. Not that I consider this as a conclusion of little moment; for of the reciprocal influence of speech on our speculative judgments, I am fully aware; and perhaps, if I wished for an illustration of the fact, I should be tempted to refer to the train of thought which has given birth to the second volume of the *Diversions of Purley*, as the most remarkable example of it that has yet occurred in literary history. ...

...

Strongly impressed with the prevalence of errors similar to those which have misled Mr. Tooke to so unprecedented a degree, a philosophical grammarian,[8] of the first eminence, long ago recommended the total proscription of figurative terms from all abstract discussions. To this proposal D'Alembert objects, that it would require the creation of a new language, unintelligible to all the world: for which reason, he advises philosophers to adhere to the common modes of speaking; guarding themselves, as much as possible, against the false judgments which they may have a tendency to occasion. To me it appears that the execution of the design would be found, by any person who should attempt it, to be wholly impracticable, at least in the present state of metaphysical science. If the new nomenclature were coined out of merely arbitrary sounds, it would be altogether ludicrous; if analogous, in its formation, to that lately introduced into chemistry, it would, in all probability, systematize a set of hypotheses, as unfounded as those which we are anxious to discard.

---

[8] [César Chesneau Du Marsais (1676-1756). Author of a *Traité des tropes* (1730) and of several articles on grammar and education in the French *Encyclopédie*. Stewart refers to the article *Abstraction*.]

Neither of these writers has hit on the only effectual remedy against this inconvenience: to *vary*, from time to time, the metaphors we employ, so as to prevent anyone of them from acquiring an undue ascendant over the others, either in our own minds, or in those of our readers. It is by the exclusive use of some favourite figure, that careless thinkers are gradually led to mistake a simile or distant analogy for a legitimate theory.

…

After these remarks, it is almost superfluous to add that it is, in many cases, a fortunate circumstance, when the words we employ have lost their pedigree; or (what amounts nearly to the same thing) when it can be traced by those alone who are skilled in ancient and in foreign languages. Such words have in their favour the sanction of immemorial use; and the obscurity of their history prevents them from misleading the imagination, by recalling to it the sensible objects and phenomena to which they owed their origin. The notions, accordingly, we annex to them may be expected to be peculiarly precise and definite, being entirely the result of those habits of induction which I have shown to be so essentially connected with the acquisition of language.

…

When I study the intellectual powers of Man, in the writings of Hartley, of Priestley, of Darwin, or of Tooke, I feel as if I were examining the sorry mechanism that gives motion to a puppet. If, for a moment, I am carried along by their theories of human knowledge, and of human life, I seem to myself to be admitted behind the curtain of what I had once conceived to be a magnificent theatre; and, while I survey the tinsel frippery of the wardrobe, and the paltry decorations of the scenery, am mortified to discover the trick which had cheated my eye at a distance. This surely is not the characteristic of truth or of nature; the beauties of which invite our closest inspection, deriving new lustre from those microscopical researches which deform the most finished productions of art. If, in our physical inquiries concerning the Material World, every step that has been hitherto gained has at once exalted our conceptions of its immensity, and of its order, can we reasonably suppose, that the genuine philosophy of the Mind is to disclose to us a spectacle less pleasing, or less elevating, than fancy or vanity had disposed us to anticipate?

In dismissing this subject, it is, I hope, scarcely necessary to caution my readers against supposing, that the scope of the remarks now made is to undervalue the researches of Mr. Tooke and his followers. My wish is only to mark out the limits of their legitimate and very ample province. As long as the philologer confines himself to discussions of grammar and of etymology, his labours, while they are peculiarly calculated to gratify the natural and liberal curiosity of men of erudition, may often furnish important data for illustrating the progress of laws, of arts, and of manners; for clearing up obscure passages in ancient writers; or for tracing the migrations of mankind, in ages of which we have no historical records. And although, without the guidance of more steady lights than their own, they are more likely to bewilder than to direct us in the study of the Mind, they may yet supply many useful materials towards a history of its natural progress; more particularly towards a history of Imagination, considered in its relation to the principles of Criticism. …

Seven

Taste

SELECTION 20

Formation of Taste

I have already said that, notwithstanding the attempts which a few philosophers have made to ascertain the nature of Taste, the prevailing notions concerning it are far from being correct or definite. Of this, no doubt can be entertained by those who have observed the manner in which it is classed by some of the latest writers on the Human Mind, in their analysis of our Intellectual Faculties; or who recollect the definitions given of it in our most popular books of criticism. It is sufficient for me to mention that of Dr. Blair, according to which, its characteristical quality is said to consist in "a power of receiving pleasure from the beauties of nature and of art". From the following lines, too, it would appear that the idea of it entertained by Akenside was nearly the same:

> What then is Taste, but these internal powers,
> Active and strong, and *feelingly alive*
> *To each fine impulse?*

It is in consequence of this *gift* that we are supposed to be susceptible of the pleasures resulting from a poem, a picture, a landscape, a well-proportioned building, a regular set of features; and it is to those individuals who possess it, that Nature is understood to have confined exclusively the right of pronouncing judgment in the fine arts, and even on the beauties of her own productions.

If these ideas be just, it evidently follows, that the degree of our taste is proportioned to the degree of pleasure we are fitted to receive from its appropriate objects. The fact, however, is certainly different. Many whose taste is indisputably good, contemplate with little interest what they acknowledge to be beautiful; while others, in whom the slightest pretension to taste would be justly treated with ridicule, are affected, on the same occasion, with rapture and enthusiasm. Nor are the words Taste and Sensibility by any means conceived to be synonymous in the common apprehensions of mankind. On the contrary, a more than ordinary share of the latter quality is apt to be regarded as pretty strong evidence of some deficiency in the former.

That Taste does not consist in sensibility alone, appears farther from this, that it is susceptible of improvement from culture, in a higher degree, perhaps, than any other power of the mind; whereas the acuteness of all our feelings is diminished by a repetition of the impression. …

These general observations are sufficient to show, that the definition of Taste, formerly quoted, is at least incomplete; and that this power must necessarily include other elements in its composition.

In order to ascertain what these elements are, the first step seems to be, to examine that particular class of *objects* with which Taste is conversant. …

From the train of thought pursued in a former Essay,[1] it appeared that, even in those objects of taste which are presented to the mind, by the sense of Seeing alone, an indefinite variety of circumstances of very different kinds, may conspire in producing that agreeable effect, to the cause of which we give the name of Beauty: colours, forms, motion, proportion, fitness, symmetry, variety, utility, with all the modifications of which they are susceptible; together with the numberless charms attached to moral expression, or arising from associations established by custom, between the material world and our complicated frame. It appeared farther, that in such instances, the pleasing emotion (heightened, as it frequently is, by the concomitant pleasures of Sound) continues still, as far as our consciousness can judge of it, to be simple and uncompounded, and that all the different sources from which it proceeds are naturally united, and identified in our conceptions, with the organic impressions on the eye or on the ear.

It is scarcely necessary to remark that it is not by reasoning *a priori,* that we can hope to make any progress in ascertaining and separating the respective effects of the various ingredients which may be thus blended in the composition of Beauty. In analyzing these, we must proceed on the same general principles by which we are guided in investigating the physical and chemical properties of material substances; that is, we must have recourse to a series of observations and experiments on beautiful objects of various kinds; attending diligently to the agreeable or the disagreeable effects we experience, in the case of these diversified combinations. The conclusions thus formed may, it is obvious, enable us afterwards to recompound the same elements, according to our own fancy, so as to diversify or to increase the pleasure produced; while they furnish an agreeable exercise to the intellectual powers, in tracing the beauties, both of nature and of art, to their general laws.

In all these experiments and observations, it is of importance to add, the result is judged of by attending to our own feelings; as, in our researches concerning *heat,* we appeal to the thermometer. By habits of this kind, therefore, it is reasonable to expect that we may acquire a power of remarking those slighter impressions, whether pleasant or painful, which are overlooked by ordinary observers; in the same

[1] [*On the Beautiful,* chap. II]

manner as the touch of a blind man appears to improve, in consequence of the peculiar attention which he is led to bestow on the perceptions of the hand. Our sensibility to beauty does not, in this way, become really more exquisite and delightful than before; but, by attracting our notice in a greater degree, it is rendered a nicer and more delicate instrument for assisting the judgment in its estimate of facts.

Nor is it only in analyzing the pleasing ingredients which enter into the composition of beautiful objects, that observations and experiments are necessary to those who wish to study the principles of Beauty, with a view to their practical applications. Whether their aim may be to produce new combinations of their own, or to pronounce on the merits and defects of those executed by others, it is of essential importance that they should be able to separate what is pleasing from what obstructs the agreeable effect. Independently of experience, however, the most exquisite sensibility, seconded by the most acute intellect, cannot lead to a single conclusion concerning the particular circumstances from which the pleasure or uneasiness arises. In proportion, indeed, to the degree of the observer's sensibility, he will be delighted with the former, and offended with the latter; but till he is able to draw the line distinctly between them, his sensibility will afford no lights of which he can avail himself in future, either as an artist or as a judge. It is in this *distinguishing* or *discriminating* perception, that the power denoted by the word Taste seems to me chiefly to consist.

The fact is perfectly analogous in that *bodily sense* from which this mental power derives it name. A dealer in wines is able, in any of the common articles of his trade, to detect the least ingredient which does not properly enter into the composition; and, in pronouncing it to be good or bad, can fix at once on the specific qualities which please or offend. It is not on the sensibility of his organ that this power depends. *Some* degree of sensibility is undoubtedly necessary to enable him to receive any sensation at all; but the degree of his distinguishing power is by no means proportioned to the degree of his sensibility. At the same time, it is manifestly this distinguishing power alone, which renders his judgments in wine of any use to himself in his purchases, or of any value to those whose gratification is the object of his art.

...

Another circumstance, remarkably characteristical of intellectual Taste, is the *instantaneousness* with which its decisions appear, in most instances, to be formed. In this respect, likewise, it resembles the external sense after which it is named; and, indeed, the analogy between the two powers is, in various points, so complete, as sufficiently to account for an application of the same expressions to both; and even to justify those writers who have attempted to illustrate the theory of the former, by an examination of the more obvious and familiar perceptions of the latter.

...

The metaphorical use of the word Taste in the languages of modern Europe is perfectly analogous to various other expressions transferred to the Mind from the external senses. Such, for example, is the word Sagacity, borrowed from the sense of smelling; the words Foresight, Intuition, and many others, borrowed from the sense of seeing; Acuteness and Penetration, borrowed from touch. The use made by the French of the word *tact*, is a circumstance still more directly in point; indeed so much so, that the definition given of it by some of their best authors may be applied very nearly to Taste in its figurative acceptation. "The word *tact*", says Roubaud, "is now, in general, employed to express a decision of the mind, prompt, subtle, and just; a decision which seems to anticipate the slow processes of reflection and reasoning, and to proceed from a sort of instinctive suggestion, conducting us instantaneously and unerringly to the truth".

The chief difference in the meaning of these two words seems to me to consist in this, that Taste presupposes a certain degree of original susceptibility, and a certain degree of relish, stronger or weaker, for the beauties of nature; whereas the word *tact* is appropriated to things in which the power of judging is wholly acquired; as, in distinguishing the hands of different masters in painting, and in the other decisions concerning the merits of artists which fall under the province of the *connoisseur*. It is applied also to a quick perception of those delicate shades in character and manners, which are objects of study to the man of the world. In this last sense, the English proverbial expression of *feeling one's way*, seems to suppose such a power as the French denote by the word *tact*; and has probably been suggested by some similar association.

> The spider's touch, how exquisitely fine,
> Feels at each thread, and lives along the line.

The two circumstances which I have chiefly enlarged upon, in the foregoing observations on the principle of Taste, are: First, its power of analytical discrimination or discernment in the examination of its appropriate objects; and Second, the promptitude with which its decisions are commonly pronounced. The process by which these characteristical qualities of taste are gradually formed, may be easily conceived from some remarks which I have stated in the *Philosophy of the Human Mind*, when treating "of the influence of casual associations on our speculative conclusions".[2]

"As the connexions among physical events", I have there observed, "are discovered by experience alone, it is evident that, when we see a phenomenon preceded by a number of circumstances, it is impossible for us to determine, by any reasoning *a priori*, which of these circum-

[2] [All quotations are from *Elements*, 1, V, pt. ii, 1-2.]

stances are to be regarded as the *constant*, and which as the *accidental* antecedents of the effect. If, in the course of our experience, the same combination of circumstances be always exhibited to us without any alteration, and be invariably followed by the same result, we must for ever remain ignorant, whether this result be connected with the whole combination, or with one or more of the circumstances combined; and, therefore, if we are anxious, upon any occasion, to produce a similar effect, the only rule that we can follow, with perfect security, is to imitate, in every particular circumstance, the combination which we have seen. It is only where we have an opportunity of separating such circumstances from each other; of combining them variously together, and of observing the effects which result from these different experiments, that we can ascertain, with precision, the general laws of nature, and strip physical causes of their accidental and unessential concomitants".

This view of the process by which the general laws of the material world are investigated, I have endeavoured to illustrate, in the same Section of that Work, by comparing it with the natural progress of the healing art, from the superstitious ceremonies employed among savage tribes, to that simplicity of practice which distinguishes an enlightened and philosophical physician.

In the Section which immediately follows, I have observed, that the substance of the foregoing quotation is strictly applicable to the process, by which the principle of Taste is formed in the mind of an individual". That certain objects are fitted to give pleasure, and others disgust, to the mind, we know from experience alone; and it is impossible for us, by any reasoning *a priori*, to explain how the pleasure or the pain is produced. In the works of Nature, we find, in many instances, the elements of Beauty involved among circumstances, which are either indifferent, or which obstruct the general effect; and it is only by a train of experiments that we can separate these circumstances from the rest, and ascertain with what particular qualities the pleasing effect is connected. Accordingly, the inexperienced artist, when he copies Nature, will copy her servilely, that he may be certain of securing the pleasing effect; and the beauties of his performances will be encumbered with a number of superfluous or of disagreeable concomitants. Experience and observation alone can enable him to make this discrimination; to exhibit the principles of beauty pure and unadulterated, and to form a creation of his own more faultless than ever fell under the examination of his senses".

"This analogy", I have added, "between the natural progress of taste, and the natural progress of physical knowledge, proceeds on the supposition, that as, in the material world, there are general facts, beyond which philosophy is unable to proceed; so, in the constitution of man, there is an inexplicable adaptation of the mind to the objects with which his faculties are conversant; in consequence of which, these objects are fitted to produce agreeable or disagreeable emotions. In both cases, reasoning may be employed with propriety to refer particular phenomena to general principles; but in both cases, we must at last arrive at principles of which no account can be given, but that such is the will of our Maker".

Notwithstanding, however, the strong analogy between the two cases, there are some important circumstances in which they differ from each other. One of these was already hinted at when I remarked, in a former part of this discussion, that as, in our experimental researches concerning the laws of Matter, the ultimate appeal is always made to our external senses, so in our experimental researches concerning the principles of Beauty, the ultimate appeal is always made to our own pleasant or unpleasant emotions. In conducting these last experiments, we cannot, it is evident, avail ourselves of anything analogous to the instrumental aids which the mechanical arts have furnished to our bodily organs; and are somewhat in the same situation in which the chemist would be placed, if he had nothing to appeal to in his estimates of Heat, but the test of his own sensations. The only expedient we can have recourse to for supplying this defect is to repeat our experiments, under every possible variation of circumstances by which the state and temper of our minds are likely to be affected; and to compare the general result with the experience of others, whose peculiar habits and associations are the most different from our own.

On the other hand, it is important to observe, that if the circumstance just remarked lays us under some inconvenience in our researches concerning the principles of Beauty, we possess, in conducting these, the singular advantage of always carrying about with us the materials of our experiments. In the infancy of Taste, indeed, the first step is to compare object with object; one scene with another scene; one picture with another picture; one poem with another poem; and, at all times, such comparisons are pleasing and instructive. But when the mind has once acquired a certain familiarity with the beauties of Nature and of Art, much may be effected, in the way of experiment, by the power of Imagination alone. Instead of waiting to compare the scene now before me with another scene of the same kind, or of actually trying the effects resulting from the various changes of which its parts are susceptible, I can multiply and vary my ideal trials at will, and can anticipate from my own feelings, in these different cases, the improvement or the injury that would result from carrying them into execution. The fact is still more striking, when the original combination is furnished by Imagination herself, and when she compounds and decompounds it, as fancy or curiosity may happen to dictate. In this last case, the materials of our experiments, the instruments employed in our analysis or synthesis, and the laboratory in which the whole process is carried on, are all alike intellectual. They all exist in the observer's mind; and are all supplied, either immediately by the principles of his nature, or by these principles cultivated and assisted by superinduced habits.

The foregoing comparison is not the less just, that experimental researches concerning the principles of Beauty are seldom or never instituted with the same scientific formality as in chemistry or physics; or, that the mind is, in most cases, wholly unconscious that such experiments have ever been made. When the curiosity is once fairly engaged by this particular class of objects, a series of intellectual experiments is from that moment begun, without any guidance from the rules of philosophizing. Nor is this a singular fact in human nature; for it is by a process perfectly similar, (as I remarked in a former Essay,)[3] that the use of language is at first acquired. It is by hearing the same word used, on a variety of different occasions, and by constant attempts to investigate some common meaning which shall tally with them all, that a child comes at last to seize, with precision, the idea which the word is generally employed to convey; and it is in the same manner that a person of mature understanding is forced to proceed, in decyphering the signification of particular phrases, when he studies, without the help of a dictionary, a language of which he possesses but a slight and inaccurate knowledge. There is here carried on, in the mind of the child, a process of *natural induction*, on the same general principles which are recommended in Bacon's philosophy: and such exactly do I conceive the process to be, by which the power of Taste acquires, in sensibly, in the course of a long and varied experience, a perception of the general principles of Beauty.

The account which has now been given of the habits of observation and comparison, by which Taste acquires its powers of *discrimination* or *discernment*, explains, at the same time, the *promptitude* with which its judgments are commonly pronounced. As the experiments subservient to its formation are carried on entirely in the mind itself, they present, every moment, a ready field for the gratification of curiosity; and in those individuals whose thoughts are strongly turned to the pursuit, they furnish matter of habitual employment to the intellectual faculties. These experiments are, at the same time, executed with an ease and celerity unknown in our operations on Matter; insomuch, that the experiment and its result seem both to be comprehended in the same instant of time. The process, accordingly, vanishes completely from our recollection; nor do we attempt to retrace it to ourselves in *thought*, far less to express it to others *in words*, any more than we are disposed, in our common estimates of distance, to analyze the acquired perceptions of vision.

In the experimental proceedings of Taste, another circumstance conspires to prevent such an analysis; I mean the tendency of the pleasurable effect to engross, or at least to distract, the attention. I took notice, in the work last quoted, of "the peculiar difficulty of arresting and detecting our fleeting ideas, in cases where they lead to any interesting conclusion, or excite any pleasant emotion"; and I mentioned, as the obvious

[3] [See selection 19]

reason of this difficulty, that "the mind, when once it has enjoyed the pleasure, has little inclination to retrace the steps by which it arrived at it". I have added, in the same place, that "this last circumstance is one great cause of the difficulty attending philosophical criticism".

In order to illustrate the full import of this remark, it is necessary for me to observe, that when any dispute occurs in which Taste is concerned, the only possible way of bringing the parties to an agreement, is by appealing to an induction similar to that by which the judging powers of Taste are insensibly formed; or by appealing to certain acknowledged principles which critics have already investigated by such an induction. Indeed, it is in this way alone that any general conclusions, in matters of this sort, can be ascertained. The difference which has been so much insisted on by some writers, between philosophical criticism, and that which they have been pleased to call experimental or tentative, turns entirely on the greater or less generality of the principles to which the appeal is made. Where the tentative critic contents himself with an accumulation of parallel passages and of critical authorities, the philosopher appeals to the acknowledged sources of pleasure in the constitution of human nature. But these sources were at first investigated by experiment and induction, no less than the rules which are deduced from an examination of the beauties of Homer and of Virgil; or, to speak more correctly, it is the former alone that are ascertained by induction, properly so called; while the others often amount to little more than the statements of an empirical and unenlightened experience.

A dispute somewhat analogous to this might be conceived to arise about the comparative distances of two different objects from a particular spot, (about the distances, I shall suppose, of two large and spreading Oaks;) each party insisting confidently on the evidence of his senses, in support of his own judgment. How is it possible to bring them to an agreement, but by appealing to those very circumstances, or signs, upon which all our perceptions of distance proceed, even when we are the least aware of any exercise of thought? If the one party should observe, for instance, to his companion, that the minute parts of the tree, which the latter affirms to be the most remote, that its smaller ramifications, its foliage, and the texture of its bark, are seen much more distinctly than the corresponding parts of the other; he could not fail in immediately convincing him of the inaccuracy of his estimate. In like manner, the philosophical principles of criticism, when obtained by an extensive and cautious induction, may be fairly appealed to in questions of Taste; although Taste itself, considered as a power of the mind, must, in every individual, be the result of his own personal experience; no less than the acquired powers of perception by which his eye estimates the distances and magnitudes of objects.

...

I intend to resume, on some future occasion, the subject of this Chapter, and to illustrate that progress of Taste from rudeness to refinement, which accompanies the advancement of social civilisation. In this respect, its history will be found to be somewhat analogous to that of human Reason; the taste of each successive age being formed on the study of more perfect models than that of the age before it; and leaving, in its turn, to after times a more elevated ground-work, on which they may raise their own superstructure.

This traditionary Taste (imbibed in early life, partly from the received rules of critics, and partly from the study of approved models of excellence) is all that the bulk of men aspire to, and perhaps all that they are qualified to acquire. But it is the province of a *leading mind* to outstrip its contemporaries, by instituting new experiments for its own improvement; and, in proportion as the observation and experience of the race are enlarged, the means are facilitated of accomplishing such combinations with success, by the multiplication of those selected materials out of which they are to be formed.

In individuals of this description, Taste includes Genius as one of its elements; as Genius, in anyone of the fine arts, necessarily implies a certain portion of Taste. In both cases, precepts and models, although of inestimable value, leave much to be done by an inventive imagination.

In the mind of a man who feels and judges for himself, a large proportion of the rules which guide his decisions exist only in his own understanding. Many of them he probably never thought of clothing with language even to himself; and some of them would certainly, if he should attempt to embody them in words, elude all his efforts to convey their import to others.

...

Eight

Politics and History

SELECTION 21

Science of Politics

The foregoing remarks, on the dangers to be apprehended from a rash application of general principles,[1] hold equally with respect to most of the practical arts. Among these, however, there is one of far superior dignity to the rest; which, partly on account of its importance, and partly on account of some peculiarities in its nature, seems to be entitled to a more particular consideration. The art I allude to is that of Legislation; an art which differs from all others in some very essential respects, and to which the reasonings in the last Section must be applied with many restrictions.

Before proceeding farther, it is necessary for me to premise, that it is chiefly in compliance with common language and common prejudices that I am sometimes led, in the following observations, to contrast theory with experience. In the proper sense of the word Theory, it is so far from standing in opposition to Experience, that it implies a knowledge of principles, of which the most extensive experience alone could put us in possession. Prior to the time of Lord Bacon, indeed, an acquaintance with facts was not considered as essential to the formation of theories; and from these ages, has descended to us, an indiscriminate prejudice against general principles, even in those cases in which they have been fairly obtained in the way of induction.

But not to dispute about words: there are plainly two sets of political reasoners; one of which consider the actual institutions of mankind as the only safe foundation for our conclusions, and think every plan of legislation chimerical, which is not copied from one which has already been realized; while the other apprehend that, in many cases, we may reason safely *a priori* from the known principles of human nature combined with the particular circumstances of the times. The former are commonly understood as contending for experience in opposition to theory; the latter are accused of trusting to theory unsupported by experience; but it ought to be remembered, that the political theorist, if he proceeds

[1] [On general principles see selection 12, pt. III.]

cautiously and philosophically, founds his conclusions ultimately on experience, no less than the political empiric; as the astronomer, who predicts an eclipse from his knowledge of the principles of the science, rests his expectation of the event on facts which have been previously ascertained by observation, no less than if he inferred it without any reasoning, from his knowledge of a cycle.

There is, indeed, a certain degree of practical skill which habits of business alone can give, and without which the most enlightened politician must always appear to disadvantage when he attempts to carry his plans into execution. And as this skill is often (in consequence of the ambiguity of language) denoted by the word Experience, while it is seldom possessed by those men who have most carefully studied the theory of legislation, it has been very generally concluded that politics is merely a matter of routine, in which philosophy is rather an obstacle to success. The statesman who has been formed among official details, is compared to the practical engineer, the speculative legislator, to the theoretical mechanician who has passed his life among books and diagrams. In order to ascertain how far this opinion is just, it may be of use to compare the art of legislation with those practical applications of mechanical principles, by which the opposers of political theories have so often endeavoured to illustrate their reasonings.

I. In the first place, then, it may be remarked, that the errors to which we are liable, in the use of general mechanical principles, are owing, in most instances, to the effect which habits of abstraction are apt to have in withdrawing the attention from those applications of our knowledge, by which alone we can learn to correct the imperfections of theory. Such errors, therefore, are in a peculiar degree incident to men who have been led by natural taste, or by early habits, to prefer the speculations of the closet to the bustle of active life, and to the fatigue of minute and circumstantial observation.

In politics, too, one species of principles is often misapplied from an inattention to circumstances; those which are deduced from a few examples of particular governments, and which are occasionally quoted as universal political axioms, which every wise legislator ought to assume as the ground-work of his reasonings. But this abuse of general principles should by no means be ascribed, like the absurdities of the speculative mechanician, to over-refinement and the love of theory; for it arises from weaknesses which philosophy alone can remedy, an unenlightened veneration for maxims which are supposed to have the sanction of time in their favour, and a passive acquiescence in received opinions.

There is another class of principles from which political conclusions have sometimes been deduced, and which, notwithstanding the common prejudice against them, are a much surer foundation for our reasonings: I allude, at present, to those principles which we obtain from an examination of the human constitution, and of the general laws which regulate the course of human affairs; principles which are certainly the result of a much more extensive induction than any of the inferences that can be drawn from the history of actual establishments.

In applying, indeed, such principles to practice, it is necessary (as well as in mechanics) to pay attention to the peculiarities of the case; but it is by no means necessary to pay the same scrupulous attention to minute circumstances, which is essential in the mechanical arts, or in the management of private business. There is even a danger of dwelling too much on details, and of rendering the mind incapable of those abstract and comprehensive views of human affairs, which can alone furnish the statesman with fixed and certain maxims for the regulation of his conduct. …

II. The difficulties which, in the mechanical arts, limit the application of general principles, remain invariably the same from age to age; and whatever observations we have made on them in the course of our past experience, lay a sure foundation for future practical skill, and supply, in so far as they reach, the defects of our theories. In the art of government, however, the practical difficulties which occur are of a very different nature. They do not present to the statesman the same steady subject of examination which the effects of friction do to the engineer. They arise chiefly from the passions and opinions of men, which are in a state of perpetual change; and therefore, the address which is necessary to overcome them, depends less on the accuracy of our observations with respect to the past, than on the sagacity of our conjectures with respect to the future. In the present age, more particularly, when the rapid communication, and the universal diffusion of knowledge by means of the press, render the situation of political societies essentially different from what it ever was formerly, and secure infallibly, against every accident, the progress of human reason; we may venture to predict, that they are to be the most successful statesmen who, paying all due regard to past experience, search for the rules of their conduct chiefly in the peculiar circumstances of their own times, and in an enlightened anticipation of the future history of mankind.

III. In the mechanical arts, if at any time we are at a loss about the certainty of a particular fact, we have it always in our power to bring it to the test of experiment. But it is very seldom that we can obtain in this way any useful conclusion in politics; not only because it is difficult to find two cases in which the combinations of circumstances are precisely the same, but because our acquaintance with the political experience of mankind is much more imperfect than is commonly imagined. By far the greater part of what is called matter of fact in politics, is nothing else than theory; and very frequently, in this science, when we think we are opposing experience to speculation, we are only opposing one theory to another.

…

IV. The art of government differs from the mechanical arts in this, that in the former it is much more difficult to refer effects to their causes than in the latter; and, of consequence, it rarely happens, even when we have an opportunity of seeing a political experiment made, that we can draw from it any certain inference with respect to the justness of the principles by which it was suggested. In those complicated machines, to which the structure of civil society has been frequently compared, as all the different parts of which they are composed are subjected to physical laws, the errors of the artist must necessarily become apparent in the last result; but in the political system, as well as in the animal body where the general constitution is sound and healthy, there is a sort of *vis medicatrix* which is sufficient for the cure of partial disorders, and in the one case, as well as in the other, the errors of human art are frequently corrected and concealed by the wisdom of nature. Among the many false estimates which we daily make of human ability, there is perhaps none more groundless than the exaggerated conceptions we are apt to form of that species of political wisdom, which is supposed to be the fruit of long experience and of professional habits. ... The truth is, (however paradoxical the remark may appear at first view,) that the speculative errors of statesmen are frequently less sensible in their effects, and, of consequence, more likely to escape without detection than those of individuals who occupy inferior stations in society. The effects of misconduct in private life are easily traced to their proper source, and therefore the world is seldom far wrong in the judgments which it forms of the prudence or of the imprudence of private characters. But in considering the affairs of a great nation, it is so difficult to trace events to their proper causes, and to distinguish the effects of political wisdom, from those which are the natural result of the situation of the people, that it is scarcely possible, excepting in the case of a very long administration, to appreciate the talents of a statesman from the success or the failure of his measures. In every society, too, which, in consequence of the general spirit of its government, enjoys the blessings of tranquillity and liberty, a great part of the political order which we are apt to ascribe to legislative sagacity, is the natural result of the selfish pursuits of individuals; nay, in every such society (as I already hinted) the natural tendency to improvement is so strong, as to over come many powerful obstacles which the imperfection of human institutions opposes to its progress.

From these remarks it seems to follow, that although in the mechanical arts the errors of theory may frequently be corrected by repeated trials, without having recourse to general principles, yet, in the machine of government, there is so great a variety of powers at work beside the influence of the statesman, that it is vain to expect the art of legislation should be carried to its greatest possible perfection by experience alone.

...

... [I]t is of importance to add that, in every government, the stability and the influence of established authority must depend on the coincidence between its measures and the tide of public opinion; and that, in modern Europe, in consequence of the invention of printing, and the liberty of the press, public opinion has acquired an ascendant in human affairs, which it never possessed in those states of antiquity from which most of our political examples are drawn. The danger, indeed, of sudden and rash innovations cannot be too strongly inculcated; and the views of those men who are forward to promote them, cannot be reprobated with too great severity. But it is possible also to fall into the opposite extreme, and to bring upon society the very evils we are anxious to prevent, by an obstinate opposition to those gradual and necessary reformations which the genius of the times demands. The violent revolutions which, at different periods, have convulsed modern Europe, have arisen, not from a spirit of innovation in sovereigns and statesmen; but from their bigoted attachment to antiquated forms, and to principles borrowed from less enlightened ages. It is this reverence for abuses which have been sanctioned by time, accompanied with an inattention to the progress of public opinion, which has, in most instances, blinded the rulers of mankind, till government has lost all its efficiency, and till the rage of innovation has become too general and too violent to be satisfied with change, which, if proposed at an earlier period, would have united in the support of established institutions, every friend to order and to the prosperity of his country.

...

The general conclusion to which these observations lead, is sufficiently obvious; that the perfection of political wisdom does not consist in an indiscriminate zeal against reformers, but in a gradual and prudent accommodation of established institutions to the varying opinions, manners, and circumstances of mankind. In the actual application, however, of this principle many difficulties occur, which it requires a very rare combination of talents to surmount; more particularly in the present age, when the press has to so wonderful a degree emancipated human reason from the tyranny of ancient prejudices, and has roused a spirit of free discussion, unexampled in the history of former times.

...

In order to lay a solid foundation for the science of politics, the first step ought to be, to ascertain that form of society which is perfectly agreeable to nature and to justice, and what are the principles of legislation necessary for maintaining it. Nor is the inquiry so difficult as might at first be apprehended, for it might be easily shown, that the greater part of the political disorders which exist among mankind, do not arise from a want of foresight in politicians, which has rendered their laws too general, but from their having trusted too little to the operation of those simple institutions which nature and justice recommend; and, of consequence, that as society advances to its perfection, the number of laws may be expected to diminish instead of increasing, and the science of legislation to be gradually simplified.

The Economical system[2] which, about thirty years ago, employed the speculations of some ingenious men in France, seems to me to have been the first attempt to ascertain this ideal perfection of the social order; and the light which, since that period, has been thrown on the subject in different parts of Europe, is a proof of what the human mind is able to accomplish in such inquiries, when it has once received a proper direction. To all the various tenets of these writers, I would by no means be understood to subscribe, nor do I consider their system as so perfect in every different part, as some of its more sanguine admirers have represented it to be. A few of the most important principles of political economy, they have undoubtedly established with demonstrative evidence; but what the world is chiefly indebted to them for, is the commencement which they have given to a new branch of science, and the plan of investigation which they have exhibited to their successors. ...

...

To delineate that state of political society to which governments may be expected to approach nearer and nearer as the triumphs of philosophy extend, was, I apprehend, the leading object of the earliest and most enlightened patrons of the economical system. It is a state of society which they by no means intended to recommend to particular communities, as the most eligible they could adopt at present; but as an ideal order of things, to which they have a tendency of themselves to approach, and to which it ought to be the aim of the legislator to facilitate their progress. In the language of mathematicians, it forms a *limit* to the progressive improvement of the political order; and, in the meantime, it exhibits a standard of comparison by which the excellence of particular institutions may be estimated.

...

According to this view of the subject, the speculation concerning the perfect order of society, is to be regarded merely as a description of the ultimate objects at which the statesman ought to aim. The tranquillity of his administration, and the immediate success of his measures, depend on his good sense and his practical skill. And his theoretical principles only enable him to direct his measures steadily and wisely to promote the improvement and happiness of mankind, and prevent him from being

---

[2] [Stewart refers to the French Physiocratic school. He usually had in view François Quesnay (1694–1774); Anne-Robert-Jacques Turgot (1727–81); Paul-Pierre Mercier de la Rivière (1719–1801); Pierre Samuel Dupont de Nemours (1739–1817).]

ever led astray from these important objects, by more limited views of temporary expedience.

SELECTION 22

Political Economy

The phrase *Political Economy* is to be understood in the most extensive sense of these words. By most of our English writers, as well as by those in the other countries of Europe, this phrase has been hitherto restricted to inquiries concerning *Wealth and Population*; or to what have sometimes been called *the resources of a State*. It is in this limited sense it is used by the disciples of *Quesnai* in France, and also by Sir James Steuart, Mr. Smith, and a long list of respectable authors in this Island, both before and after the publication of Quesnai's works. Without, however, presuming to censure in the slightest degree the propriety of their language, I think that the same title may be extended with much advantage to all those speculations which have for their object the happiness and improvement of Political Society, or, in other words, which have for their object the great and ultimate *ends* from which Political regulations derive all their value; and to which *Wealth and Population* themselves are to be regarded as only subordinate and instrumental. Such are the speculations which aim at ascertaining those fundamental Principles of Policy, which Lord Bacon has so significantly and so happily described, as "*Leges Legum, ex quibus informatio peti possit, quid in singulis Legibus bene aut perperam positum aut constitutum sit*".[3] In this employment of the phrase *Political Economy*, I may perhaps be accused of a deviation from established practice; but the language does not afford me another expression less exceptionable, for denoting this particular department of Political Science; and the use which Dr. Johnson and other classical authorities have made of the word *Economy*, to denote "disposition and regulation in general", justifies me at least in some measure, for extending its ordinary acceptation when applied to the internal policy of nations.

...

To begin, then, with that science, which, in the judgment of the most enlightened politicians, is the most essential of all to human happiness, I mean the *Science of Agriculture*; how various and important are the subjects which belong exclusively to its province! The general principles of vegetation; the chemical analysis of soils; the theory of manures; the principles which regulate the rotation of crops, and which modify the rotation, according to the diversities of soil and climate; the implements

[3] ["Laws of laws, whereby we may derive information as to the good or ill, set down and determined in every law". *De Augmentis Scientiarum*, VIII, iii.]

of agriculture, both mechanical and animal; and a thousand other topics of a similar description. To none of these articles does the *Political Economist* profess to direct his attention; but he speculates on a subject, without a knowledge of which, on the part of the Legislator, that of the other, how generally soever it may be diffused, is of no value. He speculates on the *motives which stimulate human industry*; and according as he finds these favoured or not in the classes of the people on whose exertions agriculture depends, he predicts the agricultural progress or decline of a nation. He considers with this view the state of landed property, and the laws which regulate its alienation or transmission; the state of the actual occupiers of the ground; the security they possess for reaping, unmolested, the reward of their labours; and the encouragement they enjoy in comparison of that held out in the other walks of lucrative enterprise. Nor does he confine his views to the plenty or scarcity of the immediately succeeding seasons, but endeavours to investigate the means of securing permanent abundance and prosperity to his fellow-citizens. In this respect, too, the principles on which he proceeds differ essentially not only from those of the practical agriculturist, but from those which regulate the views of all the other orders of men who think merely of their individual interests. The exertions of the farmer, it may be reasonably presumed, will be proportioned to the recompense he expects; spirited and vigorous after a few years of high prices, and languid when over-stocked markets have for a length of time disappointed his just expectations. The manufacturer, on the other hand, and the various orders of annuitants and stipendiary labourers, exult when the farmer repines, and repine when the farmer exults. In the midst of this conflict of contending interests and prejudices, it is the business of the Political Economist to watch over the *concerns of all*, and to point out to the Legislator the danger of listening exclusively to claims founded in local or in partial advantages, to remind him that the pressure of a temporary scarcity brings along with it in time its own remedy, while an undue depression of prices may sacrifice to a passing abundance years of future prosperity; above all, to recommend to him such a policy, as by securing in ordinary years a regular *surplus*, may restrain the fluctuation of prices within as narrow limits as possible; the only effectual method of consulting at once the real and permanent interests of proprietors, cultivators, and consumers.

What has now been said with respect to agriculture, may be extended to the various other employments of human industry, all of which furnish, in a greater or less degree, interesting subjects of scientific examination. This is exemplified very remarkably in *Manufactures*, in which the chemists and mechanists of the present age have found so ample a field of observation and of study; and to the improvement of which they have so largely contributed by their discoveries and inventions. To the *Philosopher* also, manufactures present a most interesting spectacle, and that whether he takes the trouble or not to enter into the detail of their various processes. What are the circumstances which attract manufacturers to one part of a country in preference to another? In what respects is it in the power of the Legislator to encourage them by roads, canals, harbours, and other public works? What are the effects of that division of labour, which takes place in a manufacturing country, on the intellectual and moral powers of the lower orders? What are the political effects of those mechanical contrivances by which labour is abridged? *These*, and many other questions of a similar nature, depend for their solution, not on that knowledge which is to be acquired in workshops, but on an acquaintance with the nature and condition of man. Such questions, I conceive, belong properly to *that science*, of which I am now endeavouring to describe the objects.

While the Political Economist thus investigates the sources of Agricultural and Manufacturing wealth, he is naturally led to consider these two great divisions of manual industry in their *mutual relations;* to inquire in what manner they act and re-act on each other; and how far it is in the power of the statesman to combine their joint influence for increasing the happiness and improvement of the community. Where the freedom of industry is unjustly restrained by laws borrowed from less enlightened ages, and more especially where that species of industry on which man depends for his subsistence is depressed below its proper level, it is his *duty* to remonstrate against so fatal a perversion of Political Institutions. In doing so, he does not arrogate to himself any superiority of practical knowledge over those whose professional labours are the subject of his discussions; but he thinks himself entitled to be heard, while his conclusions rest, not on the details of any particular art, but on the principles of human nature, and on the physical condition of the human race.

According to the idea of Political Economy which I have adopted, this science is not confined to any particular description of Laws, or to any particular department of the general science of Legislation. Among the means, for example, of advancing *national wealth*, what are so efficacious as the laws which give security to the right of property, and check an inordinate inequality in its distribution? To secure these ends, is one great aim both of civil and criminal jurisprudence; and therefore, even those regulations which appear, on a superficial view, to be altogether foreign to the subject of *national resources*, may yet involve in the consequences, the most effectual provisions by which national resources are to be secured and augmented.

The science of *Political Economy*, considered in its more extensive signification, as comprehending every regulation which affects the sum of national improvement and enjoyment, must necessarily embrace discussions of a still more miscellaneous nature. Among its various objects, however, one of the most important is the solution of that problem which Mr. Burke has pronounced to be one of the finest in legislation: "*to ascertain what the State ought to take upon itself to direct by the public wisdom, and what it ought to leave, with as little interference as possible, to individual discretion"*. The mischievous consequences that may result from the tendency of mistaken notions on this point, to produce an undue multiplication of the objects of law, must be evident to every person who has the slightest acquaintance with Mr. Smith's political disquisitions. In point of fact, it is the very problem stated by Mr. Burke, which renders it so difficult to define with precision the object of *Political Economy*. Its general aim is to enlighten those who are destined for the functions of government, and to enlighten public opinion with respect to their conduct; but unless it be previously ascertained how far the legitimate province of the Statesman extends, it is impossible to draw the line distinctly between those subjects which belong properly to the science of Legislation, and those of which the regulation ought to be entrusted to the selfish passions and motives inseparable from human nature.

I have dwelt the longer on this subject, as I was anxious to point out its intimate connexion with the *Philosophy of the Human Mind*. The only infallible rules of political wisdom are founded ultimately on a knowledge of the prevailing springs of human action, and he who loses himself in the details of the social mechanism, while he overlooks those moral powers which give motion to the whole, though he may accumulate a mass of information highly useful in the pursuits of private life, must remain in total ignorance of those primary causes on which depend the prosperity and safety of nations.

...

In most of the Systematical Treatises published by political writers, the attention of the student is directed, in the *first instance*, to an examination and comparison of the different Forms of Government, and is *afterwards* led to some of those subjects which I have comprehended under the title of *Political Economy*. On a superficial view, this arrangement is apt to appear the most natural; for it is to the establishment of Government we are indebted for the existence of the Social Order; and without the executive power of Government, *Law* would be merely a *dead letter*. In this instance, however, I am inclined to think, as in many others, the most obvious arrangement is not the most natural; and that it would be better to *invert* the arrangement commonly followed, by beginning, first with the Principles of *Political Economy*, and afterwards proceeding to the Theory of Government. My reasons for thinking so are various, but the following are some of the most important.

It is on the particular system of Political Economy which is established in any country, that the happiness of the people *immediately* depends; and it is from the *remote* tendency that wise forms of Government have to produce wise systems of Political Economy, that the utility of the former in a great measure arises. The one, indeed, leads *naturally* to the other; but it does not lead to it *necessarily*; for it is extremely possible that inexpedient laws may, in consequence of ignorance and prejudice, be sanctioned for ages by a Government excellent in its constitution, and just in its administration; while the evils threatened by a Government fundamentally bad, may, to a great degree, be corrected by an enlightened system of internal policy.

An idea very similar to this is stated by Mr. Hume, (though in a manner somewhat too paradoxical,) in one of his Essays. "We are, therefore, to look upon all the vast apparatus of our Government as having *ultimately* no other object or purpose but the distribution of *Justice*, or the *support of the twelve Judges*. Kings and parliaments, fleets and armies, officers of the court and revenue, ambassadors, ministers and privy councillors, are all subordinate in their *end*, to *this* part of administration. Even the clergy, as their duty leads them to inculcate morality, may justly be thought, so far as regards this world, to have no other useful object of their institution".

In farther illustration of this fundamental principle, it may be remarked, that there are two very different points of view in which *Laws* may be considered; *first*, with respect to their *origin*; and, *second*, with respect to their *tendency*. If they are equitable in *both* respects, that is, if they arise from a just constitution of Government, and if they are favourable to general happiness, they possess every *possible* recommendation; but if they are to want the one recommendation or the other, the former (it ought always to be recollected) is of trifling moment in comparison of the latter. Unfortunately, however, for the world, the contrary idea has very generally prevailed; and has led men to direct their efforts much more to improve the Theory of Government, than to ascertain the just principles of *Political Economy*. What has contributed much to produce this effect is, that every change in an established form of administration, presents an immediate field of action to the ambitions and the turbulent; whereas improvements in Political Economy open only those distant prospects of general utility, which, however they may interest the calm benevolence of speculative men, are not likely to engage the passions of the multitude, or to attract the attention of those who aspire to be their leaders.

... *Happiness* is, in truth, the only object of legislation which is of *intrinsic* value; and what is called *Political Liberty*, is only one of the means of obtaining this end. With the advantage of good laws, a people, although not possessed of political power, may yet enjoy a great degree of happiness; and, on the contrary, where laws are unjust and inexpedient, the political power of the people, so far from furnishing any compensation for their misery, is likely to oppose an insurmountable obstacle to improvement, by employing the despotism of numbers in support of principles of which the multitude are incompetent to judge.

On the other hand, it is no less evident, that the only effectual and permanent bulwark against the encroachments of tyranny is to be found in the political privileges which the Constitution secures to the governed. This, indeed, is demonstrated by the history of all those arbitrary establishments in which the condition of the subjects is decided by the personal character of the Sovereign; and hence the jealousy with which, under better constitutions, every encroachment on these privileges has been watched by the enlightened friends of freedom. The want of them, however, does not, like that of *civil liberty*, necessarily affect the happiness, nor impair the natural rights of individuals; for their value is founded entirely on considerations of political expediency; and, therefore, the *measure* of them, which a wise man would desire for himself and his fellow-citizens, is determined, not by the degree in which every individual consents, directly or indirectly, to the laws by which he is governed; but by the share of power which it is necessary for the people to possess, in order to place their civil rights beyond the danger of violation. In so far as this object is attained under any establishment, the civil liberty of the people rests on a solid foundation; and their political power accomplishes completely the only purpose from which its value is derived. Nor must it be forgotten, how often it has happened in the history of mankind, that a people, by losing sight of the *end*, in the blind pursuit of the *means*, have forfeited both the one and the other.

These considerations, added to what was formerly stated, appear fully sufficient to justify my general position, that of the two branches of Political Science, (the Theory of Government and Political Economy,) the latter is that which is most immediately connected with human happiness and improvement; and which is therefore entitled, *in the first instance*, to the attention of the student. But this is not all. Some knowledge of Political Economy is indispensably necessary to enable us to appreciate the different Forms of Government, and to compare them together, in respect of their fitness to accomplish the great ends to which they ought to be subservient: whereas Political Economy may be studied without any reference to constitutional forms; not only because the *tendency* of laws may be investigated abstractedly from all consideration of their *origin*, but because there are *many* principles of Political Economy which may be sanctioned by governments very different in their constitutions; and *some* so essentially connected with the happiness of society that no Government can violate them, without counteracting the very purposes for which Government is established.

In contrasting, as I have now done, the study of Political Economy with that of the Theory of Government, I think it necessary for me once more to repeat, that I do not mean to deny their very intimate connexion with each other. I have already said that it is only under equitable constitutions that we can have any reasonable prospect of seeing wise systems of policy steadily pursued; and it is no less true, on the other hand, that every improvement which takes place in the internal policy of a State, by meliorating the condition and the morals of the great mass of the people, has a tendency to prepare society for undergoing, without any shock or convulsion, those gradual alterations which time produces on all human institutions.

***

They who have turned their attention, during the last century, to inquiries connected with population, national wealth, and other collateral subjects, may be divided into two classes; to the one of which we may, for the sake of distinction, give the title of *political arithmeticians*, or *statistical collectors*; to the other, that of *political economists*, or *political philosophers*. The former are generally supposed to have the evidence of *experience* in their favour, and seldom fail to arrogate to themselves exclusively the merit of treading closely in the footsteps of *Bacon*. In comparison with *them*, the latter are considered as little better than visionaries, or, at least, as entitled to no credit whatever, when their conclusions are at variance with the details of *statistics*.

In opposition to this prevailing prejudice, it may, with confidence, be asserted, that, in so far as either of these branches of knowledge has any real value, it must rest on a basis of well ascertained facts; and that the difference between them consists only in the different nature of the facts with which they are respectively conversant. The facts accumulated by the statistical collector are merely *particular results*, which other men have seldom an opportunity of verifying or of disproving; and which, to those who consider them in an insulated state, can never afford any important information. The facts which the political philosopher professes to investigate are exposed to the examination of all mankind; and while they enable him, like the general laws of physics, to ascertain numberless particulars by *synthetic reasoning*, they furnish the means of estimating the credibility of evidence resting on the testimony of individual observers.

It is acknowledged by Mr. Smith, with respect to himself, that he had "no great faith in political arithmetic"; and I agree with him so far as to think, that little, if any, regard is due to a *particular phenomenon*, when stated as an objection to a conclusion resting on the *general laws* which regulate the course of human affairs. Even admitting the phenomenon in question to have been accurately observed, and faithfully described, it is yet possible that we may be imperfectly acquainted with that combination of circumstances whereby the effect is modified; and that, if these circumstances were fully before us, this apparent exception would turn out an additional illustration of the very truth which it was brought to invalidate.

If these observations be just, instead of appealing to political arithmetic as a check on the conclusions of political economy, it would often be more reasonable to have recourse to political economy as a check on the extravagancies of political arithmetic. Nor will this assertion appear paradoxical to those who consider, that the object of the political arithmetician is too frequently to record apparent exceptions to rules sanctioned by the general experience of mankind; and, consequently, that in cases where there is an obvious or a demonstrative incompatibility between the alleged exception and the general principle, the fair logical inference is not against the truth of the latter, but against the possibility of the former.

It has long been an established opinion among the most judicious and enlightened philosophers that, *as the desire of bettering our condition appears equally from a careful review of the motives which habitually influence our own conduct, and from a general survey of the History of our species, to be the master spring of human industry*, the labour of slaves never can be so productive as that of freemen. Not many years have elapsed since it was customary to stigmatize this reasoning as visionary and metaphysical; and to oppose to it that species of evidence to which we were often reminded that all theories must bend; the evidence of experimental calculations, furnished by intelligent and credible observers on the other side of the Atlantic. An accurate examination of the fact has shown how wide of the truth these calculations were, but, independently of any such detection of their fallacy, might it not have been justly affirmed that the argument from *experience* was decidedly against their credibility (the facts appealed to resting solely upon the good sense and good faith of individual witnesses) while the opposite argument, drawn from the principle of the human frame, was supported by the united voice of all nations and ages?

If we examine the leading principles which run through Mr. Smith's *Inquiry into the Nature and Causes of the Wealth of Nations*, we shall find that all of them are general *facts* or general *results*, analogous to that which has been just mentioned. Of this kind, for instance, are the following propositions, from which a very large proportion of his characteristical doctrines follow, as necessary and almost manifest corollaries: That what we call the Political Order, is much less the effect of human contrivance than is commonly imagined; That every man is a better judge of his own interest than any legislator can be for him, and that this regard to private interest (or, in other words, this desire of bettering our condition) may be safely trusted to as a principle of action universal among men in its operation, a principle stronger, indeed, in some than in others, but constant in its habitual influence upon all; That, where the rights of individuals are completely protected by the magistrate, there is a strong tendency in human affairs, arising from what we are apt to consider as the selfish passions of our nature, to a progressive and rapid improvement in the state of society; That this tendency to improvement in human affairs is often so very powerful, as to correct the inconveniencies threatened by the errors of the statesman; And that, therefore, the reasonable presumption is in favour of every measure which is calculated to afford to its farther development, a scope still freer than what it at present enjoys; or, which amounts very nearly to the same thing, in favour of as great a liberty in the employment of industry, of capital, and of talents, as is consistent with the security of property, and of the other rights of our fellow-citizens. The premises, it is perfectly obvious, from which these conclusions are deduced, are neither hypothetical assumptions, nor metaphysical abstractions. They are practical maxims of good sense, approved by the experience of men in all ages of the world; and of which, if we wish for any additional confirmations, we have only to retire within our own bosoms, or to open our eyes on what is passing around us.

From these considerations it would appear, that in politics, as well as in many of the other sciences, the loudest advocates for experience are the least entitled to appeal to its authority in favour of their dogmas; and that the charge of a presumptuous confidence in human wisdom and foresight, which they are perpetually urging against political philosophers, may, with far greater justice, be retorted on themselves. An additional illustration of this is presented by the strikingly contrasted effects of *statistical* and of *philosophical* studies on the intellectual habits in general; the former invariably encouraging a predilection for restraints and checks, and all the other technical combinations of an antiquated and scholastic policy; the latter, by inspiring, on the one hand, a distrust of the human powers, when they attempt to embrace in detail, interests at once so complicated and so momentous; and, on the other, a religious attention to the designs of Nature, as displayed in the general laws which regulate her economy; leading, no less irresistibly, to a gradual and progressive simplification of the political mechanism. It is, indeed, the never failing result of all sound philosophy, to humble, more and more, the pride of science before that Wisdom which is infinite and divine; whereas, the farther back we carry our researches into those ages, the institutions of which have been credulously regarded as monuments of the superiority of unsophisticated good sense, over the false refinements of modern arrogance, we are the more struck with the numberless insults offered to the most obvious suggestions of nature and of reason. We may remark this, not only in the moral depravity of rude tribes, but in the universal disposition which they discover to disfigure and distort the bodies of their infants; in one case, new-modelling the form of the eyelids; in a second, lengthening the ears; in a third, checking the growth of the feet; in a fourth, by mechanical pressures applied to the head, attacking the seat of thought and intelligence. To allow the human form to attain, in perfection, its fair proportions, is one of the latest improvements of civilized Society; and the case is perfectly analogous in those sciences which have for their object to assist nature in the cure of diseases; in the development and improvement of the intellectual faculties; in the correction of bad morals; and in the regulations of *political economy*.

SELECTION 23

Progress

The slight Historical Sketch which I have now attempted to trace,[4] seems fully to authorize this general inference; that from the Revival of Letters to the present times, the progress of mankind in knowledge, in mental illumination, and in enlarged sentiments of humanity towards each other, has proceeded not only with a steady course, but at a rate continually accelerating. When considered, indeed, *partially*, with a reference to local or to temporary circumstances, human reason has repeatedly exhibited the appearance of a pause, if not of a retrogradation; but when its advances are measured upon a scale ranging over longer periods of time, and marking the extent as well as the rapidity of its conquests over the surface of our globe, it may be confidently asserted, that the circle of Science and of Civilisation has been constantly widening since that era.

...

Before, however, I enter upon this argument, some notice is due to an objection, not unfrequently urged by the disciples of Machiavel and of Hobbes, against the utility of such prospective speculations concerning the history of the world. Of what consequence (it has been asked) to the happiness of the existing generation to be told, that a thousand, or even a hundred years hence, human affairs will exhibit a more pleasing and encouraging aspect than at present? How poor a consolation under the actual pressure of irremediable evils! To persons of either of these descriptions I despair of being able to return a satisfactory answer to this question; for we have no common principles from which to argue. But to those who are not systematically steeled against all moral feelings, or who have not completely divested themselves of all concern for an unborn posterity, some of the following may not be unacceptable.

And here I would observe, in the first place, that if it be grateful to contemplate the order and beauty of the Material Universe, it is so, in an infinitely greater degree, to perceive, amidst the apparent irregularities of the moral world, order beginning to emerge from seeming confusion. In tracing the History of Astronomy, how delightful to see the Cycles and Epicycles of Ptolemy, which drew from Alphonsus his impious censure on the wisdom of the Creator, give way to the perfect and sublime simplicity of the Copernican system! A similar remark may be applied to the discoveries since made by Newton and his followers; discoveries which fully justify what a late eminent writer has said of the argument from final causes for the existence of God, "That it gathers strength with the progress of Human Reason, and is more convincing to-day than it was a thousand years ago".

[4] [Stewart means his *Dissertation*. This is the third and last part of it.]

Is nothing analogous to this to be discovered in the History of Man? Has *no* change taken place in the aspect of human affairs since the revival of letters; since the invention of printing; since the discovery of the New World; and since the Reformation of Luther? Has not the happiness of our species kept pace, in every country where despotism has not dried up or poisoned the springs of human improvement, with the diffusion of knowledge, and with the triumphs of reason and morality over the superstition and profligacy of the dark ages? What else is wanting, at this moment, to the repose and prosperity of Europe, but the extension to the oppressed and benighted nations around us, of the same intellectual and moral liberty which are enjoyed in this island? Is it possible, in the nature of things, that this extension should not, sooner or later, be effected? Nay, is it possible, (*now* when all the regions of the globe are united together by commercial relations,) that it should not gradually reach to the most remote and obscure hordes of barbarians? The prospect may be distant, but nothing *can* prevent it from being one day realized, but some physical convulsion which shall renovate or destroy the surface of our planet.

...

I have already hinted, that the Epicurean idea which ascribes entirely to chance the management of human affairs, is altogether irreconcilable with the belief of a progressive system of order and happiness. The aim of the policy, accordingly, which is dictated by the lessons of this school, is to leave as little as possible to the operation of natural causes; and to guard with the utmost solicitude against whatever may disturb the artificial mechanism of society, or weaken the authority of those prejudices by which the multitude may more easily be held in subjection. The obvious tendency of these principles is to damp every generous and patriotic exertion, and to unite the timid and the illiberal in an interested league against the progressive emancipation of the human mind. A firm conviction, on the contrary, that the general laws of the moral, as well as of the material world, are wisely and beneficently ordered for the welfare of our species, inspires the pleasing and animating persuasion, that by studying these laws, and accommodating to them our political institutions, we may not only be led to conclusions which no reach of human sagacity could have attained, unassisted by the steady guidance of this polar light, but may reasonably enjoy the satisfaction of considering ourselves, (according to the sublime expression of the philosophical emperor,) as *fellow-workers with God* in forwarding the gracious purposes of his government. It represents to us the order of society as much more the result of Divine than of human wisdom; the imperfections of this order as the effects of our own ignorance and blindness; and the dissemination of truth and knowledge among all ranks of men as the only solid foundation for the certain though slow amelioration of the race. Such views, when under the control of a sound and comprehensive judgment, cherish all the native benevolence of the mind, and call forth into exercise every quality both of the head and the heart, by which the welfare of society may be promoted.

I have been led into this train of thinking, by a controversy which has been frequently agitated, during the last fifty years, with respect to the probable issue of the present state of human affairs. The greater part of writers, resting their conclusions chiefly on the *past* history of the world, have taken for granted, that nations, as well as individuals, contain within themselves the seeds of their decay and dissolution; -that there are limits prescribed by nature to the attainments of mankind, which it is impossible for them to pass; and that the splendid exertions of the two preceding centuries in arts, in commerce, and in arms, portend an approaching night of barbarism and misery. The events which we ourselves have witnessed since the period of the American Revolution, have been frequently urged as proofs, that the reign of Science and of Civilisation is already drawing to a close.

In opposition to this very prevalent belief, a few, and but a few, philosophers have ventured to suggest, that the experience of the past does not authorize any such gloomy forebodings; that the condition of mankind at present differs, in many essential respects, from what it even was in any former age and that, abstracting entirely from the extravagant doctrine of some of our contemporaries about the indefinite *perfectibility* of the race,[5] the thick cloud which at present hangs over the civilized world, affords no solid argument for despairing of its future destiny.

...

***

... [I]t may be remarked in general, that in the course of these latter ages, a variety of events have happened in the history of the world, which render the condition of the human race essentially different from what it ever was among the nations of antiquity, and which, of consequence, render all our reasonings concerning their future fortunes, in so far as they are founded merely on their past experience, unphilosophical and inconclusive. The alterations which have taken place in the art of war, in consequence of the invention of firearms, and of the modern science of fortification, have given to civilized nations a security against the irruptions of barbarians, which they never before possessed. The more extended, and the more constant intercourse, which the improvements in commerce and in the art of navigation have opened, among the distant quarters of the globe, cannot fail to operate in undermining local and national prejudices, and in imparting to the whole species the intellectual acquisitions of each particular community. The accumulated experience of ages has already taught the rulers of mankind, that the

[5] [Stewart probably has in mind Jean Antoine Caritat Condorcet and some author of the Associationist school.]

most fruitful and the most permanent sources of revenue, are to be derived not from conquered and tributary provinces, but from the internal prosperity and wealth of their own subjects; and the same experience now begins to teach nations, that the increase of their own wealth, so far from depending on the poverty and depression of their neighbours, is intimately connected with their industry and opulence; and consequently, that those commercial jealousies, which have hitherto been so fertile a source of animosity among different states, are founded entirely on ignorance and prejudice. Among all the circumstances, however, which distinguish the present state of mankind from that of ancient nations, the invention of printing is by far the most important; and, indeed, this single event, independently of every other, is sufficient to change the whole course of human affairs.

The influence which printing is likely to have on the future history of the world, has not, I think, been hitherto examined by philosophers, with the attention which the importance of the subject deserves. One reason for this may, probably, have been, that as the invention has never been made but once, it has been considered rather as the effect of a fortunate accident, than as the result of those general causes on which the progress of society seems to depend. But it may be reasonably questioned how far this idea be just; for, although it should be allowed that the invention of printing was accidental with respect to the individual who made it, it may, with truth, be considered as the natural result of a state of the world, when a number of great and contiguous nations are all engaged in the study of literature, in the pursuit of science, and in the practice of the arts; insomuch, that I do not think it extravagant to affirm, that if this invention had not been made by the particular person to whom it is ascribed, the same art, or some analogous art, answering a similar purpose, would have infallibly been invented by some other person, and at no very distant period. The art of printing, therefore, is entitled to be considered as a step in the natural history of man, no less than the art of writing; and they who are sceptical about the future progress of the race, merely in consequence of its past history, reason as unphilosophically as the member of a savage tribe, who, deriving his own acquaintance with former times from oral tradition only, should affect to call in question the efficacy of written records, in accelerating the progress of knowledge and of civilisation.

What will be the particular effects of this invention, (which has been, hitherto, much checked in its operation, by the restraints on the liberty of the press in the greater part of Europe,) it is beyond the reach of human sagacity to conjecture; but, in general, we may venture to predict with confidence, that in every country it will gradually operate to widen the circle of science and civilisation; to distribute more equally among all the members of the community, the advantages of the political union; and to enlarge the basis of equitable governments, by increasing the number of those who understand their value, and are interested to defend them.

The science of legislation, too, with all the other branches of knowledge which are connected with human improvement, may be expected to advance with rapidity; and, in proportion as the opinions and institutions of men approach to truth and to justice, they will be secured against those revolutions to which human affairs have always been hitherto subject.

The revolutions incident to the democratical states of antiquity, furnish no solid objection to the foregoing observations; for none of these states enjoyed the advantages which modern times derive from the diffusion, and from the rapid circulation of knowledge. In these states, most of the revolutions which happened arose from the struggles of demagogues, who employed the passions of the multitude in subserviency to their own interest and ambition; and to all of them, the ingenious and striking remark of Hobbes will be found applicable; that "Democracy is nothing but an aristocracy of orators, interrupted sometimes by the temporary monarchy of a single orator". While this continued to be the case, democratical constitutions were, undoubtedly, the most unfavourable of any to the tranquillity of mankind; and the only way to preserve the order of society was, by skilfully balancing against each other, the prejudices and the separate interests of different orders of citizens. That such balances, however, will every day become, less necessary for checking the turbulence of the democratical spirit in free governments, appears probable from this, -that among the various advantages to be expected from the liberty of the press, one of the greatest is, the effect which it must necessarily have in diminishing the influence of popular eloquence, both by curing men of those prejudices upon which it operates, and by subjecting it to the irresistible control of enlightened opinions. In the republican states of antiquity, the eloquence of demagogues was indeed a dangerous engine of faction, while it aspired to govern nations by its unlimited sway in directing popular councils. But now when the effusions of the orator are, by means of the press, subjected to the immediate tribunal of an inquisitive age, the eloquence of legislative assemblies is forced to borrow its tone from the spirit of the times; and if it retain its ascendant in human affairs, it can only be by lending its aid to the prevailing cause, and to the permanent interests of truth and of freedom.

Of the progress which may yet be made in the different branches of moral and political philosophy, we may form some idea from what has already happened in physics, since the time that Lord Bacon united, in one useful direction, the labours of those who cultivate that science. At the period when he wrote, physics was certainly in a more hopeless state than that of moral and political philosophy in the present age. A perpetual succession of chimerical theories had till then amused the world; and the prevailing opinion was, that the case would continue to be the same forever. Why then should we despair of the competency of the human faculties to establish solid and permanent systems upon other subjects, which are of still more serious importance? Physics, it is true, is free from many difficulties which obstruct our progress in moral and political inquiries; but perhaps this advantage may be more than counterbalanced by the tendency they have to engage a more universal and a more earnest attention, in consequence of their coming home more immediately to our "business and our bosoms". When these sciences too, begin to be prosecuted on a regular and systematical plan, their improvement will go on with an accelerated velocity; not only as the number of speculative minds will be every day increased by the diffusion of knowledge, but as an acquaintance with the just rules of inquiry will more and more place important discoveries within the reach of ordinary understandings. ...

Nor must we omit to mention the value which the art of printing communicates to the most limited exertions of literary industry, by treasuring them up as materials for the future examination of more enlightened inquirers. In this respect the press bestows upon the sciences an advantage somewhat analogous to that which the mechanical arts derive from the division of labour. As in these arts the exertions of an uninformed multitude are united by the comprehensive skill of the artist, in the accomplishment of effects astonishing by their magnitude, and by the complicated ingenuity they display; so in the sciences the observations and conjectures of obscure individuals on those subjects which are level to their capacities, and which fall under their own immediate notice, accumulate for a course of years, till at last some philosopher arises, who combines these scattered materials, and exhibits in his system, not merely the force of a single mind, but the intellectual power of the age in which he lives.

It is upon these last considerations, much more than on the efforts of original genius, that I would rest my hopes of the progress of the race. What genius alone could accomplish in science, the world has already seen; and I am ready to subscribe to the opinion of those who think that the splendour of its past exertions is not likely to be obscured by the fame of future philosophers. But the experiment yet remains to be tried, what lights may be thrown on the most important of all subjects, by the free discussions of inquisitive nations, unfettered by prejudice, and stimulated in their inquiries by every motive that can awaken whatever is either generous or selfish in human nature. How trifling are the effects which the bodily strength of an individual is able to produce, (however great may be his natural endowments,) when compared with those which have been accomplished by the conspiring force of an ordinary multitude? It was not the single arm of a Theseus, or a Hercules, but the hands of such men as ourselves, that in ancient Egypt raised those monuments of architecture which remain from age to age, to attest the wonders of combined and of persevering industry; and while they humble the importance of the individual, to exalt the dignity and to animate the labours of the species.

These views with respect to the probable improvement of the world, are so conducive to the comfort of those who entertain them, that even although they were founded in delusion, a wise man would be disposed to cherish them. What should have induced some respectable writers to controvert them with so great an asperity of expression, it is not easy to conjecture; for whatever may be thought of their truth, their practical tendency is surely favourable to human happiness; nor can that temper of mind which disposes a man to give them a welcome reception, be candidly suspected of designs hostile to the interests of humanity. One thing is certain, that the greatest of all obstacles to the improvement of the world, is that prevailing belief of its improbability, which damps the exertions of so many individuals; and that in proportion as the contrary opinion becomes general, it realizes the event which it leads us to anticipate. Surely if any thing can have a tendency to call forth in the public service the exertions of individuals, it must be an idea of the magnitude of that work in which they are conspiring, and a belief of the permanence of those benefits which they confer on mankind by every attempt to inform and to enlighten them. As in ancient Rome, therefore, it was regarded as the mark of a good citizen never to despair of the fortunes of the republic, so the good citizen of the world, whatever may be the political aspect of his own times, will never despair of the fortunes of the human race, but will act upon the conviction, that prejudice, slavery, and corruption, must gradually give way to truth, liberty, and virtue; and that in the moral world, as well as in the material, the farther our observations extend, and the longer they are continued, the more we shall perceive of order and of benevolent design in the universe.

Nor is this change in the condition of Man, in consequence of the progress of reason, by any means contrary to the general analogy of his natural history. In the infancy of the individual, his existence is preserved by instincts, which disappear afterwards when they are no longer necessary. In the savage state of our species, there are instincts which seem to form a part of the human constitution, and of which no traces remain in those periods of society in which their use is superseded by a more enlarged experience. Why, then, should we deny the probability of something similar to this, in the history of mankind considered in their political capacity? I have already had occasion to observe, that the governments which the world has hitherto seen, have seldom or never taken their rise from deep-laid schemes of human policy. In every state of society which has yet existed, the multitude has, in general, acted from the immediate impulse of passion, or from the pressure of their wants and necessities; and, therefore, what we commonly call the political order, is, at least in a great measure, the result of the passions and wants of man, combined with the circumstances of his situation; or, in other words, it is chiefly the result of the wisdom of nature. So beautifully, indeed, do these passions and circumstances act in subserviency to her designs, and so invariably have they been found, in the history of past ages, to conduct him in time to certain beneficial arrangements, that we can hardly bring ourselves to believe, that the end was not foreseen by those who were engaged in the pursuit. Even in those rude periods of society, when, like the lower animals, he follows blindly his instinctive principles of action, he is led by an invisible hand, and contributes his share to the execution of a plan, of the nature and advantages of which he has no conception. The operations of the bee, when it begins, for the first time, to form its cell, convey to us a striking image of the efforts of unenlightened Man, in conducting the operations of an infant government.

A great variety of prejudices might be mentioned, which are found to prevail universally among our species in certain periods of society, and which seem to be essentially necessary for maintaining its order, in ages when men are unable to comprehend the purposes for which governments are instituted. As society advances, these prejudices gradually lose their influence on the higher classes, and would probably soon disappear altogether, if it were not found expedient to prolong their existence, as a source of authority over the multitude. In an age, however, of universal and of unrestrained discussion, it is impossible that they can long maintain their empire; nor ought we to regret their decline, if the important ends to which they have been subservient in the past experience of mankind, are found to be accomplished by the growing light of philosophy. On this supposition, a history of human prejudices, as far as they have supplied the place of more enlarged political views, may, at some future period, furnish to the philosopher a subject of speculation, no less pleasing and instructive than that beneficent wisdom of nature which guides the operations of the lower animals, and which, even in our own species, takes upon itself the care of the individual in the infancy of human reason.

I have only to observe farther, that, in proportion as these prospects, with respect to the progress of reason, the diffusion of knowledge, and the consequent improvement of mankind, shall be realized, the political history of the world will be regulated by steady and uniform causes, and the philosopher will be enabled to form probable conjectures with respect to the future course of human affairs.

It is justly remarked by Mr. Hume, that "what depends on a few persons, is, in a great measure, to be ascribed to chance, or secret and unknown causes: what arises from a great number, may often be accounted for by determinate and known causes". "To judge by this rule", he continues, "the domestic and the gradual revolutions of a state must be a more proper object of reasoning and observation, than the foreign and the violent, which are commonly produced by single persons, and are more influenced by whim, folly, or caprice, than by general passions and interests". ...

From these principles, it would seem to be a necessary consequence, that, in proportion as the circumstances shall operate which I have been endeavouring to illustrate, the whole system of human affairs, including both the domestic order of society in particular states, and the relations which exist among different communities, in consequence of war and negotiation, will be subjected to the influence of causes which are "known and determinate". Those domestic affairs, which, according to Mr. Hume, are already proper subjects of reasoning and observation, in consequence of their dependence on general interests and passions, will become so more and more daily, as prejudices shall decline, and knowledge shall be diffused among the lower orders: while the relations among different states which have depended hitherto, in a great measure, on the "whim, folly, and caprice" of single persons, will be gradually more and more regulated by the general interests of the individuals who compose them, and by the popular opinions of more enlightened times.

SELECTION 24

Conjectural History

When, in such a period of society as that in which we live, we compare our intellectual acquirements, our opinions, manners, and institutions, with those which prevail among rude tribes, it cannot fail to occur to us as an interesting question, by what gradual steps the transition has been made from the first simple efforts of uncultivated nature, to a state of things so wonderfully artificial and complicated. Whence has arisen that systematical beauty which we admire in the structure of a cultivated language, that analogy which runs through the mixture of languages spoken by the most remote and unconnected nations, and those peculiarities by which they are all distinguished from each other? Whence the origin of the different sciences and of the different arts, and by what chain has the mind been led from their first rudiments to their last and most refined improvements? Whence the astonishing fabric of the political union, the fundamental principles which are common to all governments, and the different forms which civilized society has assumed in different ages of the world? On most of these subjects very little information is to be expected from history, for long before that stage of society when men begin to think of recording their transactions, many of the most important steps of their progress have been made. A few insulated facts may perhaps be collected from the casual observations of travellers, who have viewed the arrangements of rude nations; but nothing, it is evident, can be obtained in this way, which approaches to a regular and connected detail of human improvement.

In this want of direct evidence, we are under a necessity of supplying the place of fact by conjecture; and when we are unable to ascertain how men have actually conducted themselves upon particular occasions, of considering in what manner they are likely to have proceeded, from the principles of their nature, and the circumstances of their external situation. In such inquiries, the detached facts which travels and voyages afford us, may frequently serve as landmarks to our speculations; and sometimes our conclusions *a priori*, may tend to confirm the credibility of facts, which, on a superficial view, appeared to be doubtful or incredible.

Nor are such theoretical views of human affairs subservient merely to the gratification of curiosity. In examining the history of mankind, as well as in examining the phenomena of the material world, when we cannot trace the process by which an event *has been* produced, it is often of importance to be able to show how it *may have been* produced by natural causes. Thus, in the instance which has suggested these remarks, although it is impossible to determine with certainty what the steps were by which any particular language was formed, yet if we can show, from the known principles of human nature, how all its various parts might gradually have arisen, the mind is not only to a certain degree satisfied, but a check is given to that indolent philosophy, which refers to a miracle, whatever appearances, both in the natural and moral worlds, it is unable to explain.

To this species of philosophical investigation, which has no appropriated name in our language, I shall take the liberty of giving the title of *Theoretical* or *Conjectural History*, an expression which coincides pretty nearly in its meaning with that of *Natural History*, as employed by Mr. Hume, and with what some French writers have called *Histoire Raisonnée*.

The mathematical sciences, both pure and mixed, afford, in many of their branches, very favourable subjects for theoretical history; and a very competent judge, the late M. D'Alembert, has recommended this arrangement of their elementary principles, which is founded on the natural succession of inventions and discoveries, as the best adapted for interesting the curiosity and exercising the genius of students. The same author points out as a model a passage in Montucla's *History of Mathematics*, where an attempt is made to exhibit the gradual progress of philosophical speculation, from the first conclusions suggested by a general survey of the heavens, to the doctrines of Copernicus. It is somewhat remarkable, that a theoretical history of this very science, (in which we have, perhaps, a better opportunity than in any other instance whatever, of comparing the natural advances of the mind with the actual succession of hypothetical systems,) was one of Mr. Smith's earliest compositions, and is one of the very small number of his manuscripts which he did not destroy before his death.

I already hinted, that inquiries perfectly analogous to these may be applied to the modes of government, and to the municipal institutions which have obtained among different nations. It is but lately, however, that these important subjects have been considered in this point of view;

the greater part of politicians before the time of Montesquieu having contented themselves with an historical statement of facts, and with a vague reference of laws to the wisdom of particular legislators, or to accidental circumstances, which it is now impossible to ascertain. Montesquieu, on the contrary, considered laws as originating chiefly from the circumstances of society, and attempted to account, from the changes in the condition of mankind, which take place in the different stages of their progress, for the corresponding alterations which their institutions undergo. It is thus, that in his occasional elucidations of the Roman jurisprudence, instead of bewildering himself among the erudition of scholiasts and of antiquaries, we frequently find him borrowing his lights from the most remote and unconnected quarters of the globe, and combining the casual observations of illiterate travellers and navigators, into a philosophical commentary on the history of law and of manners.

The advances made in this line of inquiry since Montesquieu's time have been great. Lord Kames, in his *Historical Law Tracts*, has given some excellent specimens of it, particularly in his *Essays on the History of Property and of Criminal Law*, and many ingenious speculations of the same kind occur in the works of Mr. Millar.

In Mr. Smith's writings, whatever be the nature of his subject, he seldom misses an opportunity of indulging his curiosity, in tracing from the principles of human nature, or from the circumstances of society, the origin of the opinions and the institutions which he describes. I formerly mentioned a fragment concerning the *History of Astronomy* which he has left for publication, and I have heard him say more than once, that he had projected, in the earlier part of his life, a history of the other sciences on the same plan. In his *Wealth of Nations*, various disquisitions are introduced which have a like object in view, particularly the theoretical delineation he has given of the natural progress of opulence in a country, and his investigation of the causes which have inverted this order in the different countries of modern Europe. His lectures on jurisprudence seem, from the account of them formerly given, to have abounded in such inquiries.

...

I shall only observe farther on this head, that when different theoretical histories are proposed by different writers, of the progress of the human mind in anyone line of exertion, these theories are not always to be understood as standing in opposition to each other. If the progress delineated in all of them be plausible, it is possible at least, that they may all have been realized, for human affairs never exhibit, in any two instances, a perfect uniformity. But whether they have been realized or no, is often a question of little consequence. In most cases, it is of more importance to ascertain the progress that is most simple, than the progress that is most agreeable to fact; for, paradoxical as the proposition may appear, it is certainly true, that the real progress is not always the most natural. It may have been determined by particular accidents, which are not likely again to occur, and which cannot be considered as forming any part of that general provision which nature has made for the improvement of the race.

Bibliography

Stewart's works are collected in *The Collected Works of Dugald Stewart*, ed. by W. Hamilton, Edinburgh, Th. Constable, 1854-60 and subsequent editions (T&T Clark, 1877, Gregg Int. Publ., 1971, Thoemmes Press, 1994\1997) except *A Short Statement of some Important Facts Relative to the Late Election of a Mathematical Professor in the University of Edinburgh*, Edinburgh, 1805.

Works content is as follows:

Vol. I – *Dissertation: Exhibiting the Progress of Metaphysical, Ethical and Political Philosophy since the Revival of Letters in Europe*, (pt. I: 1815; pt. II: 1821; pt. III: 1854)

Vol. II – *Outlines of Moral Philosophy* (1793), pt. I; *Elements of the Philosophy of the Human Mind*, vol. 1 (1792)

Vol. III – *Elements of the Philosophy of the Human Mind*, Vol. 2 (1814)

Vol. IV – *Elements of the Philosophy of the Human Mind*, Vol. 3 (1827); *Some account of James Mitchell a Boy born Deaf and Blind* , (1812)

Vol. V – *Philosophical Essays* (1810)

Vol. VI – *Outlines of Moral Philosophy* (1793), pt. II; *The Philosophy of the Active and Moral Powers of Man*, B. I-II (Vol. 1, 1828)

Vol. VII – *The Philosophy of the Active and Moral Powers of Man*, B. III-IV (Vol. 2, 1828)

Vol. VIII – *Outlines of Moral Philosophy* (1793), pt. III; *Lectures on Political Economy*, B. I-II (Vol. 1, 1856)

Vol. IX – *Lectures on Political Economy*, B. II (cont.) III-IV (Vol. 2, 1856)

Vol. X – *Memoir of Dugald Stewart; Accounts of the Life and Writings of Adam Smith* (1793), *William Robertson* (1796), *Thomas Reid* (1803)

Vol. XI – *Index*

Further Reading

Aarsleff, Hans, *The Study of Language in England, 1780-1860*, Princeton: Princeton University Press, 1967.

Bergheaud, Patrice, 'Language, Ethics and Ideology: Dugald Stewart's "Common Sense" Critique of Empiricist Historical and Genetic Linguistics', in H. Aarsleff (ed.), *Studies in the History of Language Sciences*, XXXVIII, 1987, pp. 399-413.

Brown, Michael P., 'Creating a Canon: Dugald Stewart's construction of the Scottish Enlightenment', in *History of Universities*, XVI (1), 2000, pp. 135-54.

Corsi, Pietro, 'The Heritage of Dugald Stewart: Oxford Philosophy and the Method of Political Economy', in *Nuncius – Annali di storia della scienza*, II, 1987, pp. 87-144.

Davie, George E., *The Scotch Metaphysics: A Century of Enlightenment in Scotland* (1953), London: Routledge, 2001.

Fontana, Biancamaria, *Rethinking the Politics of Commercial Society: the "Edinburgh Review", 1802-1832*, Cambridge. Cambridge University Press, 1985.

Friday, Jonathan, 'Dugald Stewart on Reid, Kant and the Refutation of Idealism', in *British Journal for the History of Philosophy*, 13 (2), 2005, pp. 263-86.

Grave, Selwyn A., *The Scottish Philosophy of Common Sense*, Oxford: Clarendon, 1960.

Haakonssen, Knud, *Natural Law and Moral Philosophy. From Grotius to the Scottish Enlightenment*, Cambridge: Cambridge University Press, 1996

Levi Mortera, Emanuele, 'Dugald Stewart's Theory of Language and Philosophy of Mind', in *Journal of Scottish Philosophy*, 1 (1), 2003, pp. 35-56.

___________________ , 'Reid, Stewart and the Association of Ideas', *Journal of Scottish Philosophy*, 3 (2), 2005, pp. 157-70.

Macintyre, Gordon, *Dugald Stewart. The Pride and Ornament of Scotland*, Brighton-Portland: Sussex Academic Press, 2003.

Madden, Edward H., 'Stewart's Enrichment of the Commonsense Tradition', in *History of Philosophy Quarterly*, 3, 1986, pp. 45-63.

McCosh, James, *The Scottish Philosophy: Biographical, Expository, Critical from Hutcheson to Hamilton*, (London, 1875), Hildesheim: Olms, 1966.

Milgate, Murray, Stimson, Shannon C., 'The Figure of Smith: Dugald Stewart and the Propagation of Smithian Economics', in *European Journal of the History of Economic Thought*, 3 (2), 1996, pp. 225-53.

Olson, Richard, *Scottish Philosophy and British Physics:1750-1880. A Study in the Victorian English Style*, Princeton: Princeton University Press, 1975.

Phillipson, Nicholas T., 'The Pursuit of Virtue in Scottish University Education: Dugald Stewart and Scottish Moral Philosophy in the Enlightenment', in N. Phillipson (ed.), *Universities, Society and the Future*, Edinburgh: Edinburgh University Press, 1983, pp. 82-101.

Rashid, Salim, 'Dugald Stewart, «Baconian» Methodology and Political Economy', in *Journal of the History of Ideas*, 46, 1985, pp. 245-57.

____________, 'Political Economy as Moral Philosophy: Dugald Stewart of Edinburgh', in *Australian Economic Papers*, 1987, pp. 145-56.

Robinson, Daniel N., 'Thomas Reid's Critique of Dugald Stewart', in *Journal of the History of Philosophy*, 27 (3), 1989, pp. 405-22.

Segerstedt, Torgny T., *The Problem of Knowledge in Scottish Philosophy*, Lund, 1935.

Shinohara, Hisashi, 'Dugald Stewart at the Final Stage of the Scottish Enlightenment: Natural Jurisprudence, Political Economy and the Science of Politics', in T. Sakamoto and I. Tanaka (eds.), *The Rise of Political Economy in the Scottish Enlightenment*, London: Routledge, 2003, pp. 179-93.

Tannoch-Bland, Jennifer M., 'Dugald Stewart on Intellectual Character', in *British Journal For the History of Science*, 30 (3), 1997, pp. 307-20.

Veitch, John, 'Memoir of Dugald Stewart', in *The Collected Works of Dugald Stewart*, ed. W. Hamilton, Edinburgh, 1854-60, 11 vols., vol. X, pp. i-clxxvii.

Winch, Donald, 'The System of the North: Dugald Stewart and his Pupils', in D. Winch, S. Collini, J. Burrow (eds.), *That Noble Science of Politics: A Study in Nineteenth Century Intellectual History*, Cambridge: Cambridge University Press, 1983, pp. 23-61.

Wood, Paul B., 'The Hagiography of Common Sense: Dugald Stewart's "Account of the Life and Writings of Thomas Reid"', in A.J. Holland (ed.), *Philosophy, its History and Historiography*, Dordrecht: Reidel, 1985, pp. 305-22.

____________, 'Dugald Stewart and the Invention of "the Scottish Enlightenment"', in P.B.

Wood (ed.), *The Scottish Enlightenment. Essays in Reinterpretation*, Rochester: Rochester University Press, 2000, pp. 1-35.

Textual Notes

Selections 1, 5, 6, 11, 12, 13, 21 and 23 (second part) are from *Elements of the Philosophy of the Human Mind*, vol. 1 (1792), *Works*, vol. II. Selection 1: Introduction, pt. I, "Of the Nature and Object of the Philosophy of the Human Mind," pp. 45-56; selection 5: chap. I, §4, pp. 113-119; selection 6: chap. I, §2, pp. 96-108; selection 11: chap. II, "Of Attention," pp. 120-43; selection 12: chap. IV, "Of Abstraction," §1, pp. 159-65; §2, pp. 165-82; §§ 5-6, pp. 198-211]; selection 13: chap. V, "Of the Association of Ideas," Pt. I: "Of the Influence of Association in Regulating the Succession of Our Thoughts," pp. 252-69; Pt. II: "Of the Influence of Association on the Intellectual and Active Powers," pp. 305-41; selections 21 and 23 (second part): as selection 12, §8, pp. 219-40 and pp. 242-50.

Selections 2, 3, 4, 7 (first part) and 22 (second part) are from *Elements of the Philosophy of the Human Mind*, vol. 2 (1814), *Works*, vol. III. Selection 2: chap. IV, "Of the method of Inquiry Pointed Out in the Experimental or Inductive Logic," §1, pp. 230-52; selection 3: as selection 2, §4, pp. 299-315; selection 4: chap. I, "Of the Fundamental Laws of Human Belief; Or the Primary Elements of Human Reason", §1, pp. 24-39; selection 7 (first part): as selection 4, §2, pp. 40-50; selection 22 (second part): as selections 2 and 3, §5, pp. 331-35.

Selections 8, 9, 19 and 20 are from *Philosophical Essays* (1810), *Works*, vol. V. Selection 8: Pt. I, Essay I "On Locke's Account of the Sources of Human Knowledge, and Its Influence on the Doctrines of some of His Successors," chaps. I-II, pp. 55-62; selection 9: Pt. I, Essay II, "Of the Idealism of Berkeley," chaps. I-II, pp. 87-92, 101-106, 113-119; selection 19: Pt. I, Essay V, "On the Tendency of some Late Philological Speculations," chaps. I-III, pp. 149-76; selection 20: pt. II, Essay III, "On Taste," chap. II, pp. 339-56.

Selections 10, 14, 15 and 16 are from *The Philosophy of the Active and Moral Powers of Man*, (1828), *Works*, vols. VI-VII. Selection 10 (*Works*, vol. VII): Book III: "Of the Duties Which Respect the Deity - Of the Existence of the Deity," chap. II, §§ 1-2, pp. 12-51; selection 14 (*Works*, vol. VI): "Introduction", pp. 121-25; selection 15: as selection 14, Book II, "Of our Rational or Governing Principles of Actions", chap. V, §1, pp. 280-99; selection 16: as selection 14, Book II, "Appendix", §1, pp. 343-52.

Selections 17 and 18 are from *Elements of the Philosophy of the Human Mind*, vol. 3 (1827), *Works*, vol. IV. Selection 17: chap. I, "Of Language," §§ 1-2, pp. 5-21; selection 17: chap. II, "Of the Principle or Law of Sympathetic Imitation," §2, pp. 132-40.

Selection 7 (second part) is from *Account of the Life and Writings of Thomas Reid* (1803), §2, *Works*, vol. X, pp. 303-307.

Selection 22 (first part), is from *Lectures on Political Economy* (1856), *Works*, vol. VIII, Introduction, chap. I, pp. 9-25.

Selection 23 (first part) is from *Dissertation: exhibiting the Progress of Metaphysical, Ethical and Political Philosophy since the Revival of Letters in Europe*, pt. III, (1854), *Works*, vol. I, pp. 487-92.

Selection 24 is from *Account of the Life and Writings of Adam Smith* (1793), §3, *Works*, vol. X, pp. 33-37.

Index